C000257092

The All

Its Landscape and Culture

*David Crouch
and Colin Ward*

THE ALLOTMENT

This edition published in 1997
and reprinted in 1999, 2001, 2003 and 2007
by Five Leaves Publications,
PO Box 8786, Nottingham, NG1 9AW.

Original edition published by Faber and Faber in 1988
First paperback edition published by Mushroom Bookshop in 1994

Cover illustration by Kaoru Miyake

Printed in Great Britain by Antony Rowe

ISBN 978 0 907123 91 0

Contents

JOHN MAYDEW, *or* THE ALLOTMENT

Ranges
   of clinker heaps
      go orange now:
through cooler air
   an acrid drift
      seeps upwards
from the valley mills;
   the spoiled and staled
      distances invade
these closer comities
   of vegetable shade,
      glass-houses, rows
and trellises of redly
   flowering beans.
      This
is a paradise
   where you may smell
      the cinders
of quotidian hell beneath you;
   here grow
      their green reprieves
for those
   who labour, linger in
      their watch-chained waistcoats
rolled-back sleeves—
   the ineradicable
      peasant in the dispossessed
and half-tamed Englishman.
   By day, he makes
      a burrow of necessity
from which
   at evening, he emerges
      here.

A thoughtful yet unthinking man,
    John Maydew,
        memory stagnates
in you and breeds
    a bitterness; it grew
        and rooted in your silence
from the day
    you came
        unwitting out of war
in all the pride
    of ribbons and a scar
        to forty years
of mean amends . . .
    He squats
        within his shadow
and a toad
    that takes
        into a slack and twitching jaw
the worms he proffers it,
    looks up at him
        through eyes that are
as dimly faithless
    as the going years;
        For, once returned
he found that he
    must choose between
        an England, profitlessly green
and this—
    a seamed and lunar grey
        where slag in lavafolds
unrolls beneath him.
    The valley gazes up
        through kindling eyes
as, unregarded at his back
    its hollows deepen
        with the black, extending shadows
and the sounds of day

explore its coming cavities,
the night's
refreshed recesses.
Tomorrow
he must feed its will,
his interrupted pastoral
take heart into
those close
and gritty certainties that lie
a glowing ruse
all washed in hesitations now.
He eyes the toad
beating
in the assuagement
of his truce.

— Charles Tomlinson, *A Peopled Landscape*,
Oxford, 1963

INTRODUCTION

The Plot

Since writing the first edition of The Allotment a decade ago, tens of thousands of allotment plots have been lost to the powerful forces of development. There has also been an enormous growth in popularity of allotments amongst new groups of enthusiasts and on television. In the same period garden sizes in the average new house have decreased — housing densities are higher, yet gardening remains the most participated way of people spending their leisure time. The story of the allotment remains that of one of our long term relationships with the land. It is also a story of the change in the city and the country. It is also an alternative to the supermarket, the car park and barren fields.

The BBC film The Plot, one of the television films which drew on this book, achieved nearly two million viewers. I think that is some measure of the interest, the popular interest, that allotments have come to hold. The familiar imagery of the photograph taken fifty years ago, a site misty and damp and covered in straggly Brussels sprouts is only an image of the past, a memory perhaps. The picture and story of allotments is very different today, though the plot still follows the weather. But that memory still rouses, and maybe detracts. It rouses because it holds a spirit of energy, effort and of enterprise. In the nineties we can add hope, struggle, hard work and friendship, family gathering in. And let us add love and care, both of these for growing — for growing something for the family, for looking after the ground, in solitude or with others. Allotments stimulate metaphors about the way we live now: about storing produce; about looking after the earth; about friendships; about fighting to keep the biggest vandals — rogue local councils — off the land; about creativity, self reliance and mutual help; about growing for the future, by direct intervention in the land yourself...

There is a lot of drudgery in this — staking plants, watering the spinach, making the fencing good, clearing up after vandals. These simple activities do matter. We tried in The Plot to represent in small things something of the "bigger world" of which allotments speak. We used five metaphors on which to hang what allotments are about: the compost heap, the home freezer, the shed, the shovel and the seed. This makes up a ready iconography of the allotment, but more than that. It makes a simple, everyday iconography of the way we make sense of the world around us — by moving around the place, and by getting to know it with others. Not by gazing in amazement at the wonders there, but by making a knowledge of the world, almost incidentally. It seems to be that in these small things, at the end of a millenium, we are rediscovering ways of being and making them our own in our own ways. To have a plot is to work with simple objects, but their significance in the lives of the plotters is often very big. In this first part of the Introduction we make a note of some of the things people on that programme said.

The Compost Heap

The Compost Heap makes the allotment top of many environmentalist's lists. In Spain, just outside Bilbao, on the train that treks up to Guernica, you pass hundreds of acres of land whose owners have largely given up. It is laid bare and waste, loosely developed. In little interces and often abutting the line, there are richly coloured patterns of things growing. Unsurprisingly, these are allotments. Compost heaps mean, of course, recycling, growing, looking after the world, saving up. The heap is fun, with amazing riches of often sweetly stinking material. It brings a chance for exercise, and juicier, more colourful, sweeter smelling things growing next year. More than that, using these plots is about tenderness, love and care, for the plants, the ground.

We know about the world less from what we find out is happening the other side of it than what is happening around where we are — on the street, in the garden, across the estate, in the park, and the bits of the country we get to know. "We come here for the peace and quiet..." "It's like being in the countryside, in the city... to come here on a nice summer's day, you feel you are in the country." (Carl and Patricia Tipping, plotholders in Handsworth).

The plot is a sustainable place. "If you give somebody anything, they say — where did you get it from — I say I grew it myself. You feel proud in yourself that you grows it, you know... If you got it out the shop, some of it don't have any taste, everybody knows that... On the allotment you plant something and it will take nine months to come to... In the farm, it may be three weeks and its ready. So it can't be any good." (Lynton Carby, Handsworth)

Such apparently homespun, and perhaps exaggerated, wisdom understands more than agricultural policy that "sets aside" rather than changes the structure to produce more sustainable cultivation and avoids wasted surplus. "It doesn't require pounds of aviation fuel to get the food home." (Martin Stott, Oxford). You know what it's grown with, "fresh air and sunshine." (Deirdre Rendell)

The Home Freezer

A couple of neighbour-allotment plotters filmed in The Plot talked about how they couldn't agree on how long they've known each other. They discuss what their friendship means.

"We disagree as to how long we've been doing it. He says it's ten years since we've been neighbours, but I don't think so."

"Well it should be and it must be, because I retired at sixty five... I came and found her here. We learn things from each other. You are very social and you are very kind. You make me feel good, you don't come and call at me... things in your garden, you always hand me... little fruits... which I have appreciated ever so much..."

"And I've learnt a lot from him, I've learnt some ways of planting, I've learnt real skills about planting... I've learnt Jamaican ways of growing and cooking... always said that you can tell an Afro-Caribbean allotment, or an Asian allotment, or an English allotment. And I've also learnt about patience and goodness and religion, too, it all links in." (Alen Harrison, John Newell, Birmingham)

Love and care then, human relationships through working the land. With something to spare, something to share. But also, something to recycle, something to store. Having a plot means you have something to give, always a part of allotment life. This is a market where you can give and take, with pleasure.

"Rather than go on the state I grow all my own food as long as I possibly can. That's the sort of thing, self help." "...freezer full of vegetables to last the winter." (Deirdre Rendell, Dick Verlaine, Northampton)

The Shed

"It was always a refuge from rain, and a refuge from reality, too, because you could go in your shed and dream you were quite somewhere else; you were in your little island of the allotment, with this shed place where you pretended you lived." This is Charles Tomlinson, on The Plot, talking about childhood memories. But the capacity to play is not only childlike; "I think that was how the gardeners often felt, say, after a hard days work, a slight battle with the missis, and come up here and find a bit of peace. So gardening and feeling you had a bit of property, even a humble structure like the shed, gave you something against which to rebound from the world and its wounds."

Allotment holding can mean hard work; arthritis feeling worse; getting work done; but it is about much more, about using imagination, letting go. There is a thing, too, about ownership that we usually understand in a legal, or financial way. Of course, that limits the realm of what we feel, we know, to be ours, and land like this is a prime example, like the park, the piece of country, a stake in the ground. Yet of course "ownership" as security does matter, too. When others seek to remove the basic right of land, people resist.

The Shovel

As our data, considered later in this Introduction, shows, all over the country developers, of course, are on the lookout for sites. Local councils, almost always the owners of allotments, can apply their market dogma ignorant that life can have deeper meanings. Some use the crude deception that allotment holders are the enemy of the poor who need homes. The reality is that they are fighting against the real enemy which ignores them both,

"Five times they moved us on, in the town... I have said I'd chain myself to the gates, I feel very strongly about it... We fought it before and we'll fight it again... they'll have to do it over my dead body." (Nora Gregory, a grandmother from Northampton)

Even leisure has to fit into today's marketplace. It is said that big business increases our choice, but if it decides that one recreation has no value, it can do away with it. Instead, the way we ourselves make sense of places and activities for leisure has the power to make little use of market consumption, instead being aware of the deeper meanings and sources of those meanings from our own lives, relationships, actions, efforts, dreams. This, then, is the real popular culture, which we make ourselves, in and through what we do in everyday practice and in the imagination that alights.

The shovel is significant in other ways. Digging is, peculiarly, a way of making knowledge of the intimate geography of our life. The rhythm of movement, as we turn, bend, balance, brings us, without trying, to an awareness of space, of things round us changing their shape, their position, their mark on our vision, around our bodies in movement. This makes a way to get to know the make up of the geography around us. Movement, rather than gazing, is the way we cover ground, streets, fields, places. We don't see the "picture" in the view — the grand avenue and the landed estate — but move around it, within it, across it. And people around us become focused not as in a Lowry painting, but as lives around us, also moving, coping, enjoying. What we see is very important, but this is part of a wider knowledge of place around us, as our body moves, feels in a multiplicity of ways, and this is something very real in the allotment. This is why efforts to assert an "allotment aesthetic" have failed, being ignorant of the ways people know places.

We can begin to fit these elements together. The Allotment is a metaphor itself, about working the land, holding onto the ground, being close to the earth, about caring, about contesting space we cultivate, sharing space with other people, and about ways of making movement through which we construct our knowledge of the world around us. In these metaphors, and in the everyday actions and practices we make, we make our own geography. There is one last metaphor to unpick.

The Seed

"My son has a plot on the allotment. I have a lot of energy and I like to put a lot of my energy into my plot... there's a lot of digging, a lot of physical work, a lot of satisfaction too... yes I think young people ought to be involved. It's very healthy, you keep very fit by the work which is involved." (Clare Hammond, a young mother from Durham)

It is often Councils that seem to hold the future of what allotments may — or may not — be. Instead, we argue that it is young people who hold the future of what allotments may mean with a youthful interest in values, politics, and action. Plotholding is one of the most direct means through which we can exercise sustainability ourselves; and use land in cooperation rather than competition. It offers, then, a crucible of new values about land.

However, we argue more than this. The social base that made up allotment holding has been dispersed over recent decades through economic changes, such as the virtual closure of the mining industry. Middle class people are living inside the cities again, often in new housing with more garage than space...[1] These and other such changes have led to an increasing diversity of plotholders — more women, younger people, from more diverse occupations, often seeking allotments to make up for tiny gardens. This wider culture brings with it enormous potential for a new focus of values which could successfully contest the narrow mindedness that has appropriated too many plots.

From the old guard of allotment holders has gradually emerged a diverse group, and the allotment world will only benefit from being more and more inclusive, and open. Allotment holding is not going to benefit from being a specialist interest that marginalises itself, but by being part of a very large movement it will be able to gain the support of huge numbers of people; to be part of a growing future rather than a dwindling past. That wider culture revolves around participation in networks of the "green", environmental, conservation, cooperative and LETS economy culture. This wider popular culture embraces huge numbers of people whose values intertwine, and offers real scope for lobbying, contesting developments, making politics.

In 1995 and 1996 two particular publications have demonstrated the increased width of this movement. One is about food, the other about city parks — Food Growing in Cities[2]; and Parklife[3] (a neat play on the Blur album). Food Growing in Cities is the report from the working party of the same name, much informed by The Allotment, which argues the case for extending the chance to grow food, in cities. This is supported by its values in providing opportunity to decide the kind of food to eat, learning how to nurture the land, sustain communities, improve environments, altogether a huge endorsement of what allotments continue to be about. That report includes many examples of how people have come together to make land available for cultivation, including some vacant land and neglected land on housing estates. The report includes many examples such as enabling people fed up with living on run down estates to take over land to cultivate.

Parklife examines what has happened to city parks, and how these have become alienated from the very people they were intended, 100 years ago, to serve. This has been the result of neglect of public space during the 1980s. The report shows how important parks are to children and to people of all ages in being with friends, being alone, enjoying the outdoors, playing. Once again, the evidence of what leisure people spend their money on, and the "success" of leisure companies belies the way people make enjoyment and what really makes an impact on their lives, just as in the case of allotment holding.

The new campaigning group This Land is Our Land has taken up the contest outside the cities to confront the waste of farmland in its ownership and control. No longer is the issue of countryside only about footpaths, but about what is done with the land, how it is looked after and who owns it. The half-hearted attempt at managing the environment with set aside at least demonstrates the real choices of making land available to more people cultivating better, rather than simply mixing overintensive cultivation with space left to grant-aided trees, which die in dry summers. Civic and Conservation Societies, Friends of the Earth, LETS schemes, and the environmental campaigning group Common Ground are further points where allotments connect. A government report, The Health of the Nation, published in the early 1990s, focuses a further dimension of the case for allotments because it demonstrates the health value of gardening. If people have no land to work, this is not available to them.

Many councils respect plotholders and the value people find in allotments, because they understand. There are, however, many that do not. In all these cases, it is absolutely necessary that plotholders are alert to what is happening around them, alert to the possible loss of plots. However, the defence of sites from development is not the moment when activity should start, but be the last resort. The experience of places as far apart as Newham, London, Durham, Northampton, East Sussex, Devon, and Brailes in South Warwickshire has demonstrated that the real time to secure a site from development is every week, every year. An active local group of plotholders, working with other local societies as noted just above, keeping their members involved in looking after the site, making the site good, keeping in regular touch with the landowner — these are the means of security in a world where power does not always understand the way people make their lives and values.

The article "Don't diss my cress, man", in a Weekend Telegraph in 1996 showed how 60 people in a local neighbourhood in down-town Detroit took back the derelict sites — from an uncaring market and from crack dealers. They dug allotment plots and shifted plotting back into therapy and making community. Compost was the key weapon, because the crack dealers disliked the smell! A coalition of groups got together, the city council was persuaded to provide the seeds, and many of the 8,000 derelict sites in the city have been cultivated.

***

However, allotments are being lost, in a way which defies the whole direction and popular weight of argument that has been happening. So it is important to know both to understand the wider context of change, and how to be alert, to be ready to question the way this is happening, often using assumptions about vacancies; about values turned into efficiency criteria. Sites can be developed because a council demonstrates they are full of vacant plots. The claim that vacant plots has anything to do with allotment popularity is a myth. Vacancies have more to do with rumours/proposals of development, lack of site promotion and poor maintenance. It also can be about the failure of some allotment societies in keeping members alert, or plotholders keeping active on their site and giving an impression of vacancy. Allotments societies can publicise their sites too. One of the best ways to get holders alert to what is likely to happen on their site is to be involved in managing the land. Where the plotholders are active, there is a good chance that a landlord will find great difficulty in disposing of the site. That can be made even more difficult if there is a wider network of local support. Crucially, allotment holders need to be involved with the kind of groups noted earlier, perhaps organising joint events, so their wider value and popular support is clear. That happened in the case of the Margery Lane Allotments in Durham, where 11,000 people signed the plotholders' petition.

The Trends: the evidence
Allotments are part of the life of one in sixty-five families in Britain today. There are now two sources of data which have been produced with the National Society of Allotment and Leisure Gardeners Limited (NSALG) and the Department of the Environment (DOE). In addition to the Survey of National Society members made in 1993 by the NSALG and Professor Peter Saunders (Towards Allotments 2000) we now have the Survey of Allotment Land in England[4] (with Wales to follow) undertaken jointly by the Society and this author, at Anglia University. Taken together these Surveys provide very important intelligence on what is happening in the allotment world.

There are fewer allotments left than this author thought ten years ago — there had been no available evidence then for ten years, now for twenty. There are more vacant plots now than in the late 1970s, but fewer than in the early 1970s. There are smaller waiting lists now than in the mid seventies; but these are twice the size they were in the early seventies. Allotment popularity changes.

Year	acreage	total plots	vacant	waiting list	% statutory*
1970	58,242	532,964	111,126	5,870	49%
1977	49,873	497,793	20,572	121,027	n/a
1978	49,105	479,301	23,178	n/a	54%
1996	25,393	295,630	43,740	10,000	74.4%

*(*Statutory sites have legal protection)*

The figures from 1970–78 included England and Wales, those for 1996 are for England alone.

There are 300,000 allotments in England. 15% of these are vacant — about 44,000 plots; and about ten thousand people are on local Council allotment waiting lists at the present time. Levels of availability, vacancy and evident demand vary across the country. One valuable measure is the number of families who have allotments compared with total families. In England as a whole, one in 65 households has a plot. Extremes are Durham where one in 33 households have plots, and in Cheshire, where the figure is one in a hundred. The information on Wales will be published later, but there are approximately 50,000 plots there.

The loss between 1970 and 1978, and 1978 and 1996 shows a very steep rise in the loss of allotment plots. The greatest number of plots are owned by local Councils — Parishes, Town and Village Councils, Districts, Boroughs, Counties. In addition to the Church, there are still local Charitable Trusts, private landowners especially farmers, who own sites, and some are owned by the plotholders themselves. Cottingley Bridge Allotments Ltd, near Bradford, for example, held its 75th anniversary in 1994.

The breakdown of allotment ownership shows that Councils own 85% (Statutory 71%, Temporary 14%) and a further 11% in the hands of private owners.

We know that there is a large growth of interest in allotment holding. Those two million people who watched The Plot, was the highest viewing figure of a "community programme" over twenty years. The Members Survey (1993) shows a widening of the population interested in plotholding (15% plotholders being women, the age of holders overall evenly spread between 35–50, 50–65, over 65).

The reasons for fewer on waiting lists is the same as the increase in vacant plots, and has little to do with a decline in popularity. Evidence is needed on the awareness people at large have of allotments; that there are some in their area; that they are themselves eligible to have one; that Councils can — and should — enable take-up by promoting these sites, and clearing them ready for cultivation. Seeing vacant plots around yours, covered in weeds and weed seeds, is a disincentive to keep going. Hearing that a Council wants/intends to develop a site is an even greater disincentive, and Councils can increase vacancies in order to demonstrate that there is an actual decline in popularity, thus justifying a sale they sought in the first place. Finally, some sites are very hard to cultivate, others far from home. However, when local activists alert people to plots being available vacancies are turned into cultivated plots. An example of this is in Nottingham where a local campaign to publicise allotments on the old Hungerhill allotment site has brought in many new tenants.

One ironically good sign is that it is the temporary sites, ie those without protection or without the need to gain permission to develop from the DOE, which are the sites in the main that have been developed over recent years. This is obviously bad news for those whose sites were developed. These can be developed with little democratic accountability. Some temporary sites have been made "permanent" by local Councils. In future, it will be the statutory sites, which need DOE permission to sell (*dispose of*), that will need to be fought by the plotholders, who have to be properly informed and the Council must go through a process of seeking permission- including gathering evidence of vacancy and waiting list. Councils can still be quiet in making people aware of this process, and it is up to plotholders to watch out for what their council is doing. Even better than this is for plotholders to be regularly participating on liaison groups with the Council, and preferably committees whose decisions matter. Our Survey shows that only one quarter of local councils have policies on allotment provision — although all have to provide plots if more than five people demand them to do so — a little known piece of law (see Allotment Law and Lore in the main text).

Nearly a third of Councils delegate some management of the sites to the plotholders — a chance to encourage people to take part, but not to be exploited. Fewer than 10% of sites have toilets; nearly a fifth have a communal hut where plotholders can shelter, buy seeds, sometimes beer, and get together in the cold and in the heat. Only one quarter of councils promote their allotments to anyone who may want one, so many shroud their availability and then wonder why plots are vacant.

Half of councils do give incentives like clearing plots for new gardeners. One fifth have special rates, especially for retired or unemployed people. This means that, respectively, half and four fifths of local councils do not do this — there is room for lobbying, and improvement. Plotholders themselves can help make allotments more attractive, accessible and familiar to people in the surrounding area. The Hungerhill campaign, mentioned above, included an exhibition touring local libraries — many of the new tenants came from the St Anns area, right beside the allotments. Potential tenants often need to be told that plots are available and how to apply!

146 allotment sites do have special facilities for disabled people, helped by raised beds — but that is only 2% of the total. Nearly one half of sites in England have waste cleared; the rest do not, and the service varies in frequency in those that do. Most sites do have water, and over half have fencing — important against vandalism. However, the quality of fencing and the distance from the water tap can vary — further points for local lobbying and improvement. Obviously rents that you pay for a plot vary in relation to the facilities you have. Rents do vary enormously, not always in direct relation to facilities provided, and sometimes more in relation to the attitudes of local councillors towards providing the plots in the first place. It is the plotholders' right to find out what position their own local council takes on these different facets, or work through the National Society.

Many, many Councils provide excellent allotments, Councils are not solely to be associated with the negative side of allotment holding. Two thirds of Councils have some kind of consultation with their plotholders — but one third has none whatever. Only 10% have Customer Care policies. Those that do can be very good; there is much room for extending this across the country. The Church of England also owns sites, often in wonderful positions inside cities, surrounded by high-value land and giving Church Commissioners hopes of sale. As the Durham case showed, the proposal to sell a site, even if it is owned by the Church, can be taxing and frightening for plotholders.

Greening: New Values, a new case.

In the pressure for local councils having to be efficient in only monetary terms, there are real concerns for anyone who values allotments. New cases need to be made, about the importance of allotments, for example, in providing a chance/choice for people to make identity, promote self respect and for making community, recovering people from crime or for providing lessons in sustainability first-hand. Their value across these themes is huge either in school or throughout life. Allotments are extremely cheap in any version of holistic accounting. In addition, there is the role they play in conservation; in making good environments, green lungs, wedges, spaces and neighbourhoods.

It is ironic, but not nostalgic, to listen to Edward Owen Greening, Editor of One and All Gardening, in 1909. Greening wrote:

> *"Travelling through rural England, Scotland, Ireland and Wales, one would almost fancy at times the people had left the land altogether, so few are seen for miles and miles. Hundreds of acres of good land can be bought in Great Britain at less than it would cost to enclose and bring Colonial land into cultivation."*[5]

He goes on to talk of land being "laid waste". This echoes, or prefigures, where we are now. The categories of the issues remain similar, but we put them in very different values.

Land is not "laid waste" in the same sense, but effectively is so by parts of contemporary agriculture and horticulture (where also people are paid little). It may not make good value to compare the value today of allotments with opening up "the Colonies", but transport and aviation fuel to speed Africa's "French" beans over in the winter so that we can eat beans, sugar peas and underdeveloped sweet corn at the whim of the day, is today's fair and worrying comparison.

Owen Greening urged people to get together in Co-operatives to buy, rent, hold, and sublet allotment lands. Ingenuity must be around that would make this a feasible proposition today. Local Councils and other agencies may be able to work with plotholders in piecing together land, funding and energy in order to produce secure allotment sites. We may need to think of new ways to do it, and new legislation. Greening talked about making gardening use of city sites otherwise vacant — pointing to the example, then, of the Vacant Lands Association — exactly what George Monbiot's organisation This Land is Ours is doing; not in returning to a time gone by, but in still trying to resolve a problem that is still with us, with mainstream politics apparently looking the other way. Land has not stopped being wasted. We remember the Cottingley Bridge Allotment Limited, mentioned above. There the plotholder-owners have voted repeatedly not to sell up to developers and Government bodies, for supermarkets and roads. Both ironic use of land in view of allotments growing food near home.

We would however turn away from Greening's emphasis of why we need plots — "Men who saunter about street corners... the ever open door of the bright public house..."! Not only did he ignore the desire of women for plots, but now, we argue the value of plots to empower, to enable; to provide a choice that frees from the marketplace and responds to the deeper meanings that life has. But Deirdre Rendell from Northampton put it another way: "Surely it is better to grow food for your family than to `click` a little ball around a piece of green." She was comparing the value of allotment holding with the time and resources spent on golf, not "idleness" (then maybe, ...)!

Greening, so well named, was able to write of "the number of applicants exceeding the area". Where local councils, now the main site owners, promote their plots and shift the dated aura of allotments, what is latent demand is realised, and people come forward. In areas of new housing in villages, people are seeking to have allotments set out, using corners of fields whose fecundity is a shadow of what allotments could be, as we showed on the Anglia TV programme Cabbage Patch Wars in 1996. Bristol City Council showed that through vigourous advertising, plots can be fully used. The tenacity of holders in Northampton, Durham, Newham and many other places shows the value people link with their sites. Greening's elegy is resuscitated, with language and meaning that resonates with where our popular culture is today, for the twenty-first century, in Food Growing in Cities, mentioned above.

Amongst these ideas there is a base for much-needed new legislation that does not threaten allotments, but provides them with a sustainable basis and future in the new century, as the cultural value and political activity is as hot as it was a century ago. As noted above, this may mean new, perhaps imaginative means. At time of writing, the people of Newcastle are locked into a battle between allotments and a new football ground. The arguments are complex, and counterposes the desire of Newcastle United to have a more roomy ground for their currently swelling support (and keep a stadium in the city) to the great value that these plots have for the holders. There is no other available land in easy reach for either. The land is a millenium-old slice of the Town Moor, owned by the Freemen of the City, who agreed in principle late in 1996 to let it go. Perhaps this is the moment for a new kind of celebration, to take popular culture into the twenty-first century. As allotments are today's living heritage more than any great house of yesterday's wealthy, it is time for the National Trust to buy an allotment site. To make this Newcastle's Town Moor site would be an ideal way to mark the Millenium. Alternatively, Newcastle Football Club could give it its security, and negotiate more difficult land elsewhere.

At the end of The Plot Billy Bragg sang William Blake's Jerusalem as we panned across the Margery Lane allotments, near Durham Cathedral, perhaps a poignant conclusion to a story about the church seeking to sell land. We then filmed from a helicopter over the multicultural allotment holders and their well-kept plots on the large site in Handsworth, just west of the centre of Birmingham; a patchwork of cultures, a fitting note on a positive future for Britain. In today's climate, allotments are rarely misty and damp, and so the other trappings of old plots give way to a whole range of new enthusiasms in plotholding. Making space to look after, to show friendship and care — and other values not understood by the contemporary market place, allotment holding gives us a means to get out of our own home and join others in making good our future environment. This is what geography, a popular geography, is all about.

David Crouch,
Kelvedon, April 1997

1. Social Trends (HMSO), annually
2. Food Growing in Cities (National Food Alliance), London, 1996
3. Parklife: The Popular Culture of City Parks by David Crouch (Demos-Comedia), London and Stroud, 1995
4. Survey of Allotment Land in England is published by the National Society of Allotment and Leisure Gardeners Limited and Anglia University, 1997. A summary leaflet may be obtained from the NSALG Office, O'Dell House, Hunter's Road, Corby, Northants. The survey provides the Society with an up to date data base on allotments. The author thanks the NSALG for granting permission to use the data presented here.
5. This quote was kindly pointed out to me by my friend, the Quaker (and grower of 100 varieties of apples) John Tann.

Acknowledgements

We gratefully acknowledge the help of the Leverhulme Trust in awarding us a joint research fellowship to enable us to explore the allotment world. Inside that world people have given generously of their most precious possession: their time. We are indebted to many past and present office-holders and staff of the National Society of Allotment and Leisure Gardeners, and to innumerable plot-holders who have paused to talk to us.

Among the people to whom we owe a particular debt are Elizabeth Galloway, who was research officer to the late Professor Harry Thorpe's Committee of Inquiry into Allotments and to the one-time Allotments Research Unit at Birmingham University; Tom Hume of the London Association of Recreational Gardeners; Clive Birch, secretary of the Birmingham and District Allotments Council; Abe Hall of the Capel St Mary Allotments Association; and Ted Harwood of the Waltham Forest Allotments Federation.

Our thanks are due to Sheila Allen and her husband, Keith Armstrong, Chris Bacon, D. G. Baxter, Sheila Beskine, Harry Bone and his wife, Arnie Broughton, Peter Brown, Clive Canham, John Carey, Mr Chappel, Cecil Clark, Ian Clark, Nigel Cooper, Geoffrey Crossick, Colin Crouch, Griffiths Cunningham, Stephen Daniels, Jon Gower Davies, Joanna Davis, Kristina Elmstrom, Irene Evans, Alan Fairleigh, Ray Garner, Bill Gladwell, Mrs J. Grundon, Peter Hammond, Mr Hornsby, Michael Hyde, Fred Inglis, Harry James, Mal Jones, Ron King, Sirrka-Liisa Konttinen, Gwynneth Leach and Emma Lindsay, Richard Mabey, Ron MacParlen, Terry Melville, Alan Newins, Ray Pahl, Mr Read, John Rees, Phyllis Reichel, Terry Rendall, Peter Riley, Anthony Rolfe, Dr Schwitzer, Walter Scott and his friends, Hilary Scuffham, Amartya Sen, Mrs Sitch, Shane Smith, Larry Somers, Lady Strawson, Helen Taylor, Tommy

Taylor, Dave Thomas, Cedric Thompson, Charles Thompson, Alan Todd, Alan Tomlinson, Norio Tsuge, John Wall senior and junior, Barbara Whitter, Douglas Wood, Patrick Wright, Carol Youngson and many others.

David Crouch would like to add especial thanks to the late Ken Hatton for his introduction to the humanity of the allotment. We are much obliged to Charles Tomlinson for permission to reproduce his poem 'John Maydew, *or* The Allotment', to Paul Thompson for permission to use the transcribed interviews in the Family Life and Work Experience Before 1918 project in the Department of Sociology, University of Essex, and to Mr A. Buxton of Wroxham, Norfolk, for his kind permission and co-operation in allowing us to use his painting by Harry Allen on the jacket of this book.

We are grateful to all these people, but none of them should be blamed for any of our conclusions.

1
The allotment image

'My mental pictures revolved around "the small man" and his allotment, vegetable garden or smallholding. I was thinking of his improvisations; of his tool shed, his greenhouse of window frames or fertilizer bags, of his bird scarers or scarecrows, of his weather vanes, bean supports and cloches. I thought of his marvellous ingenuity and of the way he puts his private stamp upon a shared community of skill and tradition amounting to folk art; of how his well-grown produce can appear like a kind of trophy on his table . . .'

Nigel Henderson, foreword to *Fruit & Veg*,
Eastern Arts Association, 1980

Allotment gardens are a familiar and ubiquitous feature of the British landscape, and have been for almost two hundred years. They are to be seen on the fringe of towns and villages, small and large, scattered among the suburban houses around every city, and even on sites in the city itself, either through hallowed tradition at the Town Moor in Newcastle or through recent efforts to reclaim derelict land close to the heart of the city at Moss Side in Manchester.

Land designated for use as allotments was usually simply land which did not find a more profitable use. It was seldom chosen for its horticultural potential, though of course the labour of the cultivators and their manuring of the soil have improved it over the years. For the sites were usually just the spaces left over, behind the houses or factories, limited in access from roads, or in the floodplains of rivers, or enclosed by the sweeping curves of railway lines.

The railway traveller has always had the best view of the patchwork quilt of allotment landscapes. This is partly because the one-time railway companies were second only to local authorities as providers of allotment sites. Like other public utilities and services – the gas, electricity, canal and

1

coal-mining companies – they had large holdings of land not required for their own operating purposes, divided into allotments in the first place for their own employees, but secondarily for rent by members of the public. Within the fenced area of the railway tracks themselves, long narrow strips of vegetable garden could be seen between the platform end and the signal box.

Even though the number of railway allotments has declined sharply in the last thirty years, the train still provides a grandstand view of the allotment gardening scene. The traveller glides out of the central station, and, apart from the spectacle of industrial dereliction, the first thing to intrigue the eye is the rear view of the streets of nineteenth-century terrace housing backing on to the tracks: the private world concealed from the road. The voyeur of this intimate private townscape is being prepared for the horticultural landscape of the allotment, as different from the empty countryside of commercial agriculture as the course-grained texture of the rebuilt city is from the fine-grained backyards of the citizens.

Watching from the train we see how the houses become newer, the density lower and the gardens larger. Parks, playing fields and recreation grounds appear among them, cemeteries, hospitals, car-breakers' yards, and, of course, allotments. Like the urban backyards, the panorama of allotments is best appreciated from the train, for often they are invisible from the road, approached only through a narrow driveway in a gap between the houses.

Our modern train traveller, on the route between Coventry and Birmingham, or from Birmingham to Kings Norton, can actually look down on the deeply hedged and intimate secret gardens that have been urban allotments continuously for a century and a half. On newer wide-open sites on a summer Sunday families can be seen picnicking on their plot, with rows of cars, their boots and hatchbacks open to reveal forks, spades and bags of compost, but the traveller will still perceive the allotment image through the lenses of photographers of fifty years ago: a grainy wintry landscape of straggling rows of sprouts and cabbages, little home-made huts and broken fences, smouldering bonfires – and the solitary figure of a cloth-capped unemployed worker, his shabby collar turned up against the wind, pushing his bicycle home with a bunch of carrots over the handlebars.

These mental images are about three things. They concern our perception of the *landscape* of the allotment: what it looks like. They are also about what goes on in allotments, who the people are who are doing it, and its importance in their lives. And finally they are about the *idea* of allotment gardening: the meaning it has for us in late-twentieth century Britain. In each case, these images of how in the broadest sense we 'see' allotments are tied up with the attitudes of mind that arise when we think about, or glimpse from the train, or recollect from the lives of parents and relations, or actually visit, allotments – or, as plot-holders, work our own patch of earth and incorporate it into the routine of life.

Images of allotment landscapes are partly to do with what the site itself looks like – the overall layout and atmosphere, each and every individual plot and shed. Beyond this there is the matter of where they are, the surroundings of the site. What the site looks like includes the ingredients of the makeshift or uniform sheds, the hedges and fences, and the arrangement and care bestowed upon the plants. Yet it also draws upon the way in which we place values, consciously or not, upon different kinds of appearance in the landscape. 'Who can endure a cabbage bed in October?' asked Jane Austen.

Our valuation depends also upon our interpretation of the way people use these places – our concept of how *they* value them. Then there is the matter of whether the landscape comes across to us as purposefully designed and whether that seems to us to be good or bad. Do we applaud or deplore the municipal improvers' efforts to tidy up the site? Where they are located will also have a crucial influence on our image of the allotment, both in individual cases and in an imaginary abstraction. The site in Gas Lane, along the inner-city railway sidings or in the spaces left over by the new motorway roundabout, has often been reckoned as a visible sign of failure in the competition for urban space, taken as an underlining of the *awkwardness* of the allotment: not desirable or exciting in the consumer city, not part of the mainstream of modern life, not pleasant in its associations with frugality and improvisation.

Yet there is another complication here, because this location very often presents the way in which the allotment was valued at some time in the past by powerful people – by a landlord, a colliery owner or gas undertaking, or a local authority using up space left over after other, more significant purposes, or earmarking a site for an eventual extension to the cemetery. But there are other locations too, in suburbs and villages, and even separate from the village. Different notions creep in, of a distinction between urban and suburban and rural allotments. Beyond this there is a point where the allotment merges with the smallholding, and thereon into the open landscape of agriculture. As children we all learnt in history lessons about the open fields and about the strip system of cultivation. Did the landscape of arable farming once look like one vast allotment site? Beryl Bainbridge was struck by this thought in 1985, close to the centre of Liverpool: 'The allotment is on a ridge of land not far from the houses. If it was possible to look from a height on this southern aspect of the Mersey and by some miracle to peel back time so that years passed in a space of seconds, demolishing in minutes that grand expansion of the nineteenth century, leaving nothing but a waste of common ground rising from a deserted foreshore towards a plateau of cultivated plots, one might see in that rural landscape some resemblance to the present.'[1]

If we have a variety of images of the physical environment of the allotment, then the view of the culture of the allotment – the social world of the plot-holders themselves – offers a more unified picture, even a caricature. It is built around the fellow with the carrots over his handlebars, or if that suggests too much agility, trudging home along the towpath with a bulging shopping bag in each gnarled hand. This is an abstract man, it being 'necessarily' a man's role or enjoyment. He is elderly, fairly poor, relying on a remnant of subsistence survival, a dying anachronism. The culture is seen as odd, a bit funny or eccentric, the last of the summer wine, prize leeks, pigeons, and a messy use of materials that has not caught up with the DIY superstores. There is an image not only of the individual in his particular social circumstances and grasp of life skills, but of his role in the household, in the community and in society at large, pastimes enjoyed, awareness of what is going on around him, a place of work (or more likely a presentation clock on the mantelpiece or a redundancy payment when the works closed down).

These images come together in an allotment *idea*. The word 'allotment' is curiously abstract: a legalistic term meaning simply 'a portion', but it is shorthand for a number of images of people, places and activities. It is loaded with assumptions, attitudes and experiences that bring us back into our own culture, whether or not we are plot-holders. The word occupies an obscure corner in contemporary culture, but an absorbingly interesting one. It may imply something out of the way, passing out of ordinary experience, overcome by the real concerns of the late-twentieth century. But it is also tinged with nostalgia for the world we think we have lost, an image of humility from the days when our grandparents would urge us to: 'Use it up and wear it out/Make do or do without'. Yet it also implies the idea of something 'worthwhile' to occupy the weekend, a concern with the quality of the food we eat, an attractive alternative culture.

How selective the images and caricatures of landscape and culture are, can be appreciated by considering the different presentations of the allotment image. These approaches include those of the media, dominant purveyors of images in the twentieth century, by local councils fulfilling or evading their statutory responsibilities to allotment-holders, by the academics and professionals of land and landscape, by writers, poets and artists, and finally by the allotment-holders themselves. *EastEnders*, a contemporary TV soap-opera with a reputation for presenting working-class life as it really is, features a character who removes himself from his home anxieties to meet his peers down on the allotment. There is a painting by Eric Holt depicting busy but slightly dotty activity among rotund and slightly odd growers. A Finnish photographer in Newcastle records allotment people by their seed trays, proudly holding their cabbages and their pigeons, a powerful celebration of attachment. Dave Thomas and several others pursue the same themes.[2] The treasured reclusiveness of the allotment is communicated with great feeling in the poems of Peter Walton and Charles Tomlinson.[3]

Local authorities vary enormously in their attitudes towards the allotments in their care. Some work carefully with the secretaries of local societies, upgrading sites and carefully maintaining waiting lists, while others see their allotments as a messy and wasteful use of valuable sites. The image of the allotment expressed by an Inspector of Local Planning in response to inquiries from central government was that the site was important since 'the openness it offers is generally valued by local residents'.[4] But the dominant and typical professional view, shared by administrators and landscape academics, was epitomized in a government report. In the 1960s the pressure on urban land, as well as its market price, steadily increased, and the Wilson government of 1964 appointed Fred Willey to the short-lived Ministry of Land and Natural Resources. One of his first decisions was to commission a Departmental Committee of Inquiry into Allotments 'to review general policy on allotments in the light of present-day conditions in

England and Wales and to recommend what legislative and other changes, if any, are needed'. It was chaired by the late Harry Thorpe, professor of geography at the University of Birmingham, and it reported in 1969 to a different minister in a different department. As this long out-of-print report, with its 460 pages and 927 well-considered paragraphs, was a landmark in the history of allotments, we will refer to it henceforth as the 'Thorpe report'.[5] The committee took its task more seriously than the government did, and produced forty-four major recommendations, none of which have been acted upon by any subsequent government. They were based on two propositions. The first was that the existing legislation was vague, obsolete and incomprehensible, and in urgent need of revision by one new Act. The second was that the very word 'allotment' had a 'stigma of charity' about it and needed to be replaced by the concept of the 'leisure garden', with sites improved and upgraded as a recreational facility for the whole family, like the examples that the committee had admired in other European countries.

New and simple legislation has not been introduced. The result is chaos when a local authority interprets the law one way and is faced by plot-holders anxious to invoke it *their* way, but all too often lacking the expertise to defend their interests. Nor has central government responded to the committee's espousal of the leisure-garden concept, even though several local authorities, both before and after the report was published, embarked on programmes for changing the 'allotment image', a theme to which Thorpe devoted a whole chapter. He later recalled that at that time the term 'allotment' conjured up for many people:

. . . a rather sordid picture of a monotonous grid of rectangular plots, devoted mainly to vegetables and bush fruits, and tended by an older stratum of society, particularly men over forty, including many old-age pensioners. Prominent over many sites were assemblages of ramshackle huts, redolent of 'do it

yourself', from the corrugated iron roofs of which sag-
ging down-spouting carried rainwater into a motley
collection of receptacles, long since rejected elsewhere,
but again pressed into service here and ranging from
antiquated baths to old zinc tanks and rusting oil
drums. One in every five of the plots lay uncultivated,
with weeds flourishing waist-high in summer, almost
reaching the tops of abandoned bean-poles from which
tattered pennants of polythene still fluttered noisily to
scare birds from non-existent crops.[6]

Indeed, by the time of Thorpe's inquiry, allotments had
become labelled as neglected eyesores. The vocabulary
needed to be revised. The new image of the leisure garden
metamorphosed out of the shabby, tatty leftovers from
poverty and necessity, and epitomized both a different landscape *and* a changed culture. The image-changers had in
common the assumption that there is something aesthetically inferior about vegetable gardening. 'To most
people,' says the Thorpe report, 'a prize onion or leek never
looks quite as attractive as a prize chrysanthemum or dah-
lia'.[7] But would this appraisal make sense to the panel of
judges in a horticultural show? Would it be useful to tell a
farmer that a field of barley is less attractive than a field of
lupins? When the committee actually found flowers, 'these
have invariably been planted like vegetables, in serried
rows with no conscious attempt to arrange them to make an
attractive *garden*'.[8] No doubt they were being grown for
cutting, but in any case the committee forgot that for centuries the aesthetics of gardening demanded that flowers
should be grown that way. Thus in the seventeenth century
Andrew Marvell's poem 'The Garden' began with the lines:
'See how the flowers, as at parade,/Under their colours stand
display'd:/Each regiment in order grows,/That of the tulip,
pink and rose.'

The same predilection for the romantic or picturesque
concept of gardening, as opposed to the classical or formal,

dominates efforts to change the allotment image. Designs
for new sites are praised for their 'informality' and their
'complete departure from the old-fashioned rectilinear
style'. The Thorpe committee explained that: 'Although
there is nothing intrinsically wrong with rectilinearity,
there is no reason why a leisure garden *must* be oblong in
shape; the extreme formality which is so characteristic of
the allotment garden site and which shows a complete lack
of imagination in design must be avoided at all costs.'[9] Not
only this, but: 'Each site should be subjected to a programme
of landscaping and improvement *under the guidance of a
landscape architect* [Thorpe's italics] with the dual object of
making the appearance of the site from beyond its perimeter
as pleasing as possible, while increasing the attractiveness
of the interior of the site for the benefit of the plot-holders,
both existing and prospective.'[10]

To Thorpe's committee it was self-evident that the aesthetics of the English flower garden, themselves the product
of a Victorian and Edwardian concept of landscape design,
could be imported into the utilitarian layout of vegetable
growing. The diverse conceptions of painters, poets, council
officers, geographers and landscape architects, demonstrate
the interplay of the three forms of 'image': the landscape,
the culture, and an abstract idea of the allotment. They can
each be stressed to argue a particular case. Indeed, some
local authorities, eager to profit from the disposal of allotment sites for redevelopment, have resorted to the caricature
in order to press home their case. However, people whose
mental picture of the allotment world has been absorbed
from popular mythology have often been surprised.

In the 1970s a team of film-makers discovered an allotment site of a thousand plots in the London Borough of
Newham, 'surrounded by the economics of the city – a trunk
road, a sewage plant, gas works, and cranes from the docks'.
They saw it as 'a piece of land protected by history and
structured by the whims and traditions of the people working there'. It was, they thought, an 'old school' kind of

9

allotment, the sort usually described as an eyesore. Then they got to know the plot-holders and their perception was changed. Their surprise that the users of this vast hidden site were as varied a section of citizens as the inhabitants of a street illustrates the strength and persistence of our mental stereotype of the plot and the plot-holder.[11] A historian of the First World War observes that 'the allotments of 1917 and 1918 played their part in the universal blurring of class lines – the gardening proletariat was well on the high road to middle-class respectability'.[12] But it was in the Second World War, when food production was once again perceived as a social duty, that a propagandist for the national effort explained that: 'Forty years ago, on the outskirts of any provincial town, you would find a patch a ground, distinctly marked by little black wooden huts for the keeping of tools, and known locally as the allotments. It was divided by narrow grass strips into plots, each of which was tended by one man – one had the idea that these gardeners were mostly railway porters, policemen and postmen and other people who worked out of doors and consequently never felt "at home" within four walls. It was generally regarded as rather a quaint hobby, quite different from the absolutely normal one of growing flowers.'[13]

As well as insisting that the guidance of a landscape architect was needed on every site, Thorpe's committee recommended that 'no tenant should be permitted to erect any form of structure on his leisure garden without the prior approval of the planning authority, and such approval must cover design, materials, size, colour and location'.[14] These recommendations have a curiously old-fashioned ring today. They seem to belong to a period when there was a faith in the design professions and their wisdom, a faith since eroded by experience. Now, the allotment and its makeshift sheds are seen as one of the last bastions of individualism against the onslaughts of the professional designer, and against municipal tidiness and imposed order.

The Dutch architect John Habraken sees this urge to tidy

and restore order to the environment as a sign of the decline of building as a popular social and personal activity. 'One has only to look at the backs of the poorer housing districts of some forty years ago. The quantity of extensions, balconies, pigeon lofts, sheds, conservatories and roof houses come, in their chaotic character, as a relief to the observer who would rather see people than stones.'[15] And the town-planner Sir Colin Buchanan draws the same conclusion from the train-window view: 'There you will see in profusion the sheds and the shacks, the pigeon lofts and the makeshift greenhouses, the lean-to shelters and the children's huts – all by some blessed oversight escaped from planning control, all standing as reminders of needs which contemporary housing policies have failed to meet.'[16]

The allotment garden shed is seen by another architect, Ray Garner, as 'probably Britain's most prolific and vigorous' remaining example of the self-builder's art, precisely because it has evaded the criteria of imposed controls on design. 'The shed-builder has no such constraints; there are no precise rules to be followed; his components need not be assembled in such an exacting way. The limitations are to do with lack of craftsmanship and "proper" materials. The freedom is the abrogation of responsibility to the manners of craftsmanship and aesthetics. Anything "will do". This separation from a mechanical system and rules, together with a need to innovate, is the force which clears the way for creativity and subconscious expression.'[17]

And within the allotment movement there are many who would deny Thorpe's assumptions about the 'charitable' background of the allotment and the 'stigma' associated with it. They see it instead as yet another example of those expressions of working-class self-help and mutual aid, like the friendly societies, the trade unions and the co-operative movement, which were a response to the impact of the industrial revolution in nineteenth-century Britain. Thus a plot-holder writes that:

Too many people have a wrong impression about allotments. The movement is not wholly dependent for its
well-being upon the encouragement given to it by
government and local authorities ... Allotments had
their origin in self-help (not charity), and even now the
concept of self-help remains fundamental .. Throughout its entire history the motive force behind the allotment movement has always been self-help. This is
exemplified by the labourers displaced from the
countryside during the periodic downturns in the trade
cycle that punctuated Victorian times, who, being
forced to seek work in the towns (often working fifty-
five hours per week in the dreariest of employments),
eagerly canvassed alternatives to factory work, and
were only too keen to turn to spade husbandry whenever the opportunity arose ... It is surprising that so
many found the strength and determination and genuine love of gardening needed to tend their allotments,
yet here are signs of a deep working-class sentiment
and attitude.[18]

But there is a whole further series of images. One is of a
quiet calm. Allotment gardeners often talk of the peaceful-
ness of the site as something they value, and we have felt it
on numerous visits up and down the country. However, this
calm associated with the satisfaction of work done is accompanied by another, almost balancing image. This is one of
hard work, a perpetual grind of effort in all weathers that
adds a sterner face to the romance of the plot. But there is
also recollected pleasure. Many people have recalled to us
the happiest of their childhood days as those spent on the
allotment with their fathers. And in spite of the traditionally male image of the plot, there are innumerable reminiscences of the allotment as a day out for *all* the family.
Respondents to a questionnaire from the Thorpe committee
talked of the 'therapeutic value' that they, as outsiders,
associated with allotment gardening. And this blends with

the other images of creativity, hard work, calm and pleasure. With the spread of ideas implying that we ourselves, rather than the medical services, are responsible for our own health, the allotment has increasingly become associated with healthy living. It is, and always was, a provider of exercise and of fresh food. Vegetable eating is popularly and professionally linked with the avoidance of disease. More and more people believe in the virtues of organic husbandry and realize that you can't *know* that your food is grown in the approved way unless you have grown it yourself.

Allotment activity takes place in the open air. The very existence of the urban vegetable garden signifies the 'greening' of the city. The site, unlike that of commercial horticulture, is a wild-life refuge, as the joint meetings of Allotment Associations and naturalist bodies testify. The allotment garden is a visual relief, an open amenity, as a government inspector once observed. The promotion of allotment gardening by campaigning environmental bodies has extended this image to one of the reclamation of vacant, derelict and neglected places in towns.

Thorpe was sure that the allotment movement had lost its appeal to the young and would surely die out when the then current generation of elderly plot-holders had pulled its last bunch of carrots. But a decade after his report appeared, a study by Friends of the Earth showed that: 'Nearly all towns and cities in Great Britain were experiencing a boom in the interest shown in allotments. In England and Wales the local-authority waiting lists had gone up by a staggering 1600 per cent.'[19]

The new influx of aspirants into a movement thought to be slowly dying had images of the allotment far from that of the shed-fanciers or that of the cherishers of working-class culture. They were not necessarily supporters of the leisure-garden ideal either. They were concerned with food production just like the traditional allotment gardeners. And they wondered why there could be sites a century old still lacking an adequate water supply. Veteran plot-holders watched sceptically. They knew the time, skill and regular effort needed for successful gardening, especially when every session on the plot required a special journey. Not all the new entrants have stayed the course. But plenty of them have. Yet the newest of allotment gardeners are very close to their predecessors in some respects. They seem to be attracted by something that the Thorpe report disowned: the appeal of simply working the land, without frills. To many people today this is part of the attraction of Pissarro's paintings, or Millet's or Van Gogh's: a peasant stolidly walking up the hill, evidence of cultivation at a human scale in squares or strips and other prosaic shapes, people who understand and have a stake in the land. There are ordinary simple buildings, unfussy and workmanlike. The tilled landscape betrays a relationship between man and nature. The woman on the path is not accidental, but forms the pivot of the whole image, explaining why all the ephemeral aspects are there: the crops, the shapes of the plots, and why all these communicated meaning – then as now. The allotment is in the tradition of this image.

It is possible to buy a packet of frozen food and cook it instantly without knowing where or how or by whom it was produced. And this is less expensive than seeding, nurturing and harvesting the food yourself. Why, then, does the allotment garden continue to flourish? The answer must lie in its image, in the role of communal effort, in the feelings growers have in feeding a family through their own efforts. Our image of the allotment turns out to be, not a matter of the way we glimpse its landscape from the train, but a reflection of our image of the world as a whole and the social relationships we make in our small patch of it.

2
Cultural landscapes and freedom

'Sometimes a landscape seems to be less a setting for the life of
its inhabitants than a curtain behind which their struggles,
achievements and accidents take place. For those who, with
the inhabitants, are behind the curtain, the landmarks are no
longer geographic but also biographical and personal.'

John Berger
A Fortunate Man,
Writers and Readers, 1976

Soon after Pissarro painted so many peasants there was a
fervent debate on whether only the urban proletariat
deserved painting.[1] The allotment in history has been both
peasant and proletarian. However, like Pissarro's work the
allotment is not quaint and is not a representation of 'nature
unspoilt'. It is, today, an essentially urban phenomenon (at
least, there are simply many more allotments in town and
city than in county areas) and for the best part of this
century it was the urban proletariat that used it, that made
the allotment its own landscape. Landscape is not usually a
proletarian product, and as such the allotment breaks the
rules: it fails to comply with the accepted image.

The landscape does not readily reveal the nature of those
struggles that Berger speaks of, or betray the human relationships that produce it, although these relationships form
a critical part of the way that we enjoy or endure different
places. When we observe, the meaning that we perceive in
the landscape is the result of a filter of our own attitudes and
culture. This is as true of the allotment landscape as of any
other material representaion of our culture; but whose culture does the allotment represent? The image is part of the
predominant feeling about landscape, land, place and culture. 'Land' is an emotive word, a challenging idea. It has

15

long been the focus of political debate, at least since Wat Tyler, as well as of more recent intellectual concern.[2] 'Landscape' is a more comfortable word, something for enjoyment's sake, although people defend what they define as landscape with great fervour.[3] 'Culture' is popularly regarded as something *they* provide for *us*, and is increasingly regarded as a commodity.[4] The country and the city have been taken as separate identities; one a break from the other, one feeding parasitically on the other. These are the popular stereotypes, and have been assumed and fed by much scholarly research.[5] Meanwhile, advertising and, more specifically, the marketing of 'place' by developers, estate agents and tour operators have followed the arts in extending these stereotypes to a very wide market.[6]

For over half a million households the allotment is part of their everyday life. It is a recreation, and used to be important in the survival of thousands of poor families. Today, it may offer a way in which we can realize individual potential and endowments that find no room or recognition in our culture, in the outside world. It may be part of the choice we make to do something that is no longer 'with the grain' of our mainstream culture, as we select activities that correspond with our values, and with what may have become familiar parts of our local culture and of our family life. It is partly a matter of the way we choose to use places, buildings and land. In these choices we derive identity, from our surroundings, from the people and the place.[7] The word 'culture' is intended here to pull together the details of everyday activity with which everyone is familiar in their own idiosyncratic way, with the broader context of society and economy in which daily events take place in a longer trajectory of time. We need constantly to make sense of the world around us, and find meaning through what we do. It is often through codes and symbols that we derive our idea of things and places, and uses for things. People individually create their own symbols of their lives, consciously or not, according to the meaning that materials, events, landscapes and places have for them, and thereby create their own history.[8]

This is part of the security, continuity and identity that is so successfully presented in the media and especially in advertising; identity achieved through buying a product. The purities and certainties are found in 'nostalgia', whereby 'real communities', status and 'nature' are located.[9] These form part of our national culture, which provides a setting within which there are given expectations and associations. We become familiar with these in the way we choose to use leisure time, value places and relate to each other.[10] In turn, these influences in wider society constrain.

There is, however, an important balance between the constraints of the dominant culture and the everyday accessibility of feelings, customs and enjoyments. The shared circumstances of individual sub-cultures result in the distinctive appropriation of familiar things and places with their own symbols, images and meanings.[12] People relate collectively through places and things of their shared culture, and emerging from that activity, they share the way that landscape is created. This is not done in a vacuum, but draws selectively from the wider world and the constraints it imposes. It is in the context of these meanings and relationships that this book assesses the role of the allotment in contemporary Britain, a contemporary sub-culture that has a peculiar relationship with place and landscape, and the way in which people find meaning in their surroundings and in their everyday lives; how the surroundings that they create are an expression, a representation of their own culture of shared conditions, activities and relationships, and the wider culture in which they appropriate that space; how they relate collectively through the unselfconscious landscape that they create; and how the landscape is part of their individual and collective identity.

A class context

The culture in which the allotment grew up and was sustained was one of working-class agitation for improved conditions and of self-help. It began at a time when land was a strong political concern, and developed during a period when working-class self-organization, in the form of friendly societies, the co-operative movement and the trade unions, had become of national importance.

In the new urban world of the nineteenth century, when the greater part of the then new industrial proletariat was removed from rural life by only one generation, people living and working in the city were as involved in 'the land question' as the newest rural immigrants, directly displaced from employment on the land, whether by innovatory farming methods, new patterns of ownership, or by the agricultural depression that began in the 1870s and continued, with a brief respite during the First World War, until 1939. The Chartists concerned themselves with access to land,[13] and so did the trade unions – both those representing agricultural labour and those whose membership was predominantly urban. Publications like Robert Blatchford's *Merrie England*,[14] serialized in the *Clarion* in 1892 and 1893, which sold nearly a million copies as a book in the next few years, and his *Land Nationalisation* of 1898, were 'eloquent witness of the deep and lasting impression which land-reform doctrines had exerted on the minds of the working people.'[15]

Apart from its importance for the nascent socialist movement, the land issue had become a central plank of the Liberal Party platform, attempting to cope with the grievances of Ireland and Wales. In England, 'It was universally held that farm labourers and other landless men should have a real opportunity to acquire some land as a smallholding, or *at least* an allotment. There is no doubt, however, that the problem was not a rural one, it had become universal. The special problem which was presented in those areas where the land was inadequate for the people's needs had been raised and understood ... Land reformers were beginning to see the land problem as one whose principal implications were for the urban areas...'[16] Commentators at the time sought 'solutions' under various guises, from emigration to the creation of towns where everybody would have a place to cultivate.[17] However, in both city and country, the problem was political, including questions over rights to ownership, access and cultivation.

But there is another reason for the significance of land in political debate. 'For as long as workers own a set of tools enabling them to produce for their own needs, or a plot of land to grow some vegetables, and keep a few chickens, the fact of proletarianism will be felt to be accidental and reversible. For ordinary experience will continue to suggest the possibility of independence: workers will continue to dream of setting themselves up on their own ... "real life" exists outside your life as a worker ... a temporary misfortune.'[18] In this, the political powers from the turn of the century realized their fortune. Practical everyday experience reinforces the dream. Although, adapting Kropotkin, self-interest usually provides the best catalyst to political organization and thereby collective action.

In both these movements and aspirations there is a series of things that people are looking for. There is a direct and immediate need for food; a need for living space for people in crowded accommodation and mud yards; for health, recreation, and less emotional strain. With this powerful combination, there was a stimulus to agitation and, later, action on many fronts connected with land. Movements for land-ownership reform took the form of squatting, of plot-buying to provide an escape in the country for people of negligible means,[19] of campaigns for the reform of land taxation and of mass trespasses of enclosed common land. This last case was a challenge to the predominant view of the countryside, in the control of Gentlemen and to be seen as Landscape. In the 1930s organizations like the Ramblers, the cycling clubs and the Youth Hostels Association, joined in the effort to promote the notion of entitlement to the accessibility of land by common people. The *Daily Herald* published these claims in an attack on the privileged control over land.[20] This had been preceded by the famous Mass Trespass, in 1932, of Kinder Scout in the Peak District, with access for millions of factory workers' recreation and escape. There have been similar claims for the retention, and in many cases reclamation, of small areas of common land. In 1986 The Ramblers' Association organized a mass rally at the 'Secret Forest' of Wychwood in Oxfordshire, 'long closed to the public by hostile landowners . . .',[21] as part of their Forbidden Britain campaign, which shows how live such issues remain.[22]

Meanwhile there were campaigns and, later, regulations on the setting of minimum standards for room inside and outside the home.[23] Throughout this century, and before, there has been a growing recognition of the importance of space in people's surroundings, especially for the poor, often thwarted by political decisions that restrict funding. This has shifted ground so that now people living in contemporary poverty are claiming rights to better space and to resist adverse change to their surroundings. Bureaucratic regulations have translated these claims for rights into entitlements.

The economic circumstance of the working class, and its constraint of wage labour, usually factory work, ensured that it maintained pressure to achieve some advance on the rights that had borne fruit through legislation. However, the way it exercised that influence, and enjoyed the rights that became available, have varied as this century has progressed, reflecting changes within working-class culture and in the way that others have become involved in the particular issue of land. Crucial influences included changes in the nature of work and the workplace; affluence and the availability of affluence; the availability of land ownership and access to land; and attitudes connected with leisure and participation in leisure. These influences have been underlain by three key aspects: the redefinition of male and female roles; patterns of social relationship and forms of mutual activity: and attitudes to what places look like. Clearly, the shifts that have occurred are not only within a class, but in the relationship between that class and others, and within other classes themselves. Notably, there has been the cultural event of gentrification of parts of towns, of villages, and of leisure activities as these become attractive to the middle class although once the preserve of the working class.[24]

However, these changes have been far from ubiquitous or universal. There have been significant local differences. Amazingly, during a century of increasing influence on the national level, in government, investment and media, the variation locally has not been reduced; rather, it has changed in form. The changes noted have occurred with great variety of impact on different places just as local experience varies. The involvement of individuals in these changes is felt in very personal ways.

Work, home and reciprocity

Allotments were an important part of the way that families survived unemployment and casual labour.[25] The dominance of wage labour, regulated employment, 'a job', that characterized mid-twentieth-century Britain still left room for home production as an income support – self-provisioning that provided at least some addition to the family budget through doing things, usually by making, growing, rearing or acting as middle trader – and probably still does. There is also the critical role that this 'getting by on one's own' contributed to increasing confidence and independence, and in the 1920s and 1930s it provided crucial extra income.[26]

In Raymond Williams' autobiographical novel *Border Country*, which is set in the days of the General Strike of

1926, the father spends much time and energy cultivating a number of strips of land he has managed to rent from neighbouring farms. These provide not only important savings at a time of strike, but also income from produce, including honey sold for the local market. He was a railway signalman. His father and another would self-provision by gleaning and hop-picking. *His* father in turn had rented glebeland for pigs and potatoes. It was a family familiar with this kind of work supplement. *His* father was a farm labourer. The significance of gardening as both work and attachment is emphasized in this passage, after the strike had been broken: 'Like Harry, with his gardens, Morgan found ... that the journeys with his van [to market] were his real work, this actual centre, while the work at the [signal] box was just done in the margin, for a wage.'[27] Harry had four pieces of ground, called gardens, and part of a field alongside them. The satisfaction and self-fulfillment that this kind of culture offered, and the social world that surrounded it, were a crucial part of his life. His example was typical of the way that self-provisioning activities held together a family's labours.

Ray Pahl has reviewed the changes between times of predominantly agricultural work and those of 'wage labour'. He regards wage labour as having grown, through the addition to the self-provisioning work of the family farm, over a period of 150 years to the mid-present century. In the middle years of the last century, families *needed* the allotment as a critical source of their diet. 'In Lancaster, three labourers' families had mothers who did not earn wages. In two of them the allotment was responsible for providing an important part of the family's diet, in the other the father and children were skilled in "living off the land", collecting a variety of foods both to eat and to sell.'[28] Gradually wage labour expanded as family farms diminished, and most households have become entirely dependent on it, save those supported by the state insurance of the dole.

The important exception in the decline of this 'customary'

work was women's work inside the home. This expanded as the home became a more complicated part of life, with more tasks to be undertaken requiring increasingly more time for the *presentation* of the home;[29] despite labour-saving devices the home became more sophisticated, not simply 'easier', i.e. the time that was previously expended on hygiene was now spent on presentation. Moreover women absorbed into the labour market returned at the end of the day to pick up the household work, whilst the man was permitted to 'recreate'. The work in which women had been traditionally involved *outside* the home – self-provisioning like rearing poultry, growing herbs and vegetables – either did not get done or was 'left to men who had allotments . . .' In some towns women continued to keep hens and geese well into the twentieth century, and in certain rural areas the pattern has barely changed.[30]

People living in villages and commuting to their jobs in towns could do their self-provisioning more easily; they had access to land. Railway workers in Swindon, too, before the First World War, are reported to have had close involvement in their alternative source of income. 'Very often the village resident will work for an hour in his garden or attend to his pigs and domestic animals before leaving for the railway shed. If the neighbouring farmer is busy, or happens to be a man short, he may help him milk his cows, or a do a little mowing with the scythe and still be fresh for his work in the factory . . . and never missed going to gather mushrooms in the early mornings during autumn.'[31]

Pahl suggests that, save in the main conurbations and large estates, such activities have continued to the present day. This is not only illuminating in view of the 'supplementary income' through self-provisioning, but is important in terms of the general awareness of people's popular relationships with the ground and agricultural work.[32] It is the survival of work outside wage labour. When produce is sold, it is part of the 'black economy', or work outside employment, 'on the side'. This is typical of what has traditionally taken place in industrial areas and at times of high unemployment for generations.

Whilst wage labour demarcated the division of labour within the household, the delineation of 'women's work' was established also in the bourgeois ideals of individualism, elitism and privacy, and it was the organization of wage labour that required the participation of the working class in this system, even though they did not share the privacy. These were presented and broadcast in 'worthy' texts, exquisitely stated in this Victorian poem, 'Home':

> An ear upon the latch
> A hand upon the latch
> A step that hastens its sweet rest to win;
> A world of care without
> A world of strife shut out,
> A world of love shut in.[33]

The home was ideally a shelter but, importantly, separate from the 'public world'. It represented the extreme privacy in which individualism could flourish. The man outside the home could experience power, have access to ideas and relationships, and of course finance. The woman at home did not have access to these and was thereby 'in her place'. The roles of the members of a household were defined by taste, sex and age. Wives did not leave the precincts of domestic terrain, except with approval.[34] These separations also manifested themselves in the different forms of leisure pursuits that men and women enjoyed, or were allowed to enjoy.

Provisioning in this way was not only for the family. It sometimes took the form of sharing and exchange with others. Economic conditions and the nature of social relations have often combined to determine that the only gift between families would be something home-made or home-produced. The circumstances also precipitated situations where exchange was not just a good way to relate to neighbours, but a necessity.

Groups sharing particular spare-time pursuits are frequently involved in the informal economy too. In the mid-1980s there was a reported case of the state attempting to withhold benefits from a number of unemployed anglers in Shropshire. Provisioning like this, and, even more, barter or sale with friends and neighbours, brought into question their entitlement to unemployment benefit – however much the proceeds were seen as 'pocket money', often to be ploughed back into the enthusiasm itself.[35]

As Titmuss observed in a very different, but comparable case, the 'right to give' is cherished. Such a basis for human relationships is enhanced where there is not an institutionalized separation of people – and such a separation is *not* possible in the field of things grown or made at home. However, it is not all altruism.[36] Giving and sharing are underpinned by a feeling of inclusion in the community, awareness of the importance, socially, culturally and economically, of one's involvement in the community, and a stake in a relationship that may be reciprocated. On this scale, having the right to give, to choose to give and to exchange freely, forms an important bond between people. It is especially welcome in communities that feel themselves ineligible for the benefits available to wider society, and excluded from relationships with that society. The conditions of the working class, particularly in poorer districts, have thus promoted the creation of mutual bonds, from which the community has derived a strength – not least political. There remains, however, the simple enjoyment gained from giving and reciprocating with home-produced things, and in avoiding contemporary material bases for transactions, with all the inherent commercialism.

Leisure, recreation and the family

Influenced by the shortening of the working week and reductions in poverty through this century, there has been a movement of time and effort from self-provisioning to recreation.

Just as, for many people, economic benefits and redistribution of resources have overcome severe financial hardships since the Second World War, so many allotment-holders have come to find the allotment an enduring pastime rather than a necessity to augment the family budget. Others have latterly turned to it for the recreational benefits. However, at the same time there have been such considerable changes in the nature of recreation that the pursuits of half a century ago have lost their appeal for many, or have been taken up by new population groups. The pattern has varied between the classes, age groups – even within the household itelf.

The meaning of leisure is a mixture of intrinsic satisfaction, emanating from the support and cohesion existing within the participatory group, community or sub-culture, and providing for the development of our own and our friends' identity. There is a connection between our individual enjoyment, the behaviour expected of us by our peers and the way we use that activity in our own life and in the way in which we relate to others.[37] A study of recreation in Bristol and Leicester found that in the 114 different types of activity where groups had been formed for collective enjoyment, more activity and productivity was engendered through the mutual support generated.[38] Each group developed its own sub-language, rules and activities as an expression of cohesion, and its own distinctiveness.

Co-operative involvement in the sharing of enthusiasms also plays an important role in the 'activist' political projects of organizations like Friends of the Earth. The activities of such groups frequently reflect both political concerns and an interest in, for example, wildlife, the landscape and growing things. Thus there is a link with shared enthusiasms of the working class, which sought access to, and the use of, the land.

The social and cultural milieu in which an activity takes

place is significant in helping to shape its nature and the particular form it takes. Connections that 'locate' leisure within a wider culture include the values, motivations, aspirations and needs of the individual, his family, gender and class, and the relationship these have with their workplace. Before the First World War, leisure was for most people fairly non-commercial and frequently something experienced informally, at home or locally. It revolved around drink, the music hall and religion. The pub and the chapel often 'expressed the poles of respectability and roughness within a popular cultural repertoire embracing the working class and the intermediate strata'.[39] The early efforts by factory owners to dictate distinct periods of 'work' and 'recreation' sought to order the use of what spare time there was, and thereby enhance work performance. Recreation was regarded as a healthy activity to promote work, and was often linked with temperance.[40]

Non-profit-making organizations, the church and the Co-op, were important social institutions in the early 1900s, and dominated provision of a variety of local recreations. These, and others such as rambling and cycling clubs, were prominent, especially amongst the working-class districts, until the Second World War. Many were distinctive in being all-round leisure organizations. They grew from the needs of the working people, and education (in the widest sense), self-improvement and the extension of rights were all part of their repertoire. The Rambling Societies were involved in claiming popular access to the uplands that were close to working-class industrial cities and towns. However, the growth of organizations like cycle clubs reflected the changing character of clubs away from the diverse activities of chapel and Co-op and towards an increasing specialization.[41]

As affluence spread during the middle years of the twentieth century and leisure become more specialized, it made commercialization more likely. There was also a change in taste, and earlier leisure pursuits became associated with less affluent times, especially those pursuits that smacked of the *need* for self-provisioning. People emerging from the period between 1914 and 1945 wanted new directions and diversions. Marketing promotion and new technologies introduced a wide range of accessible leisure pursuits. In the search for new clientele to increase their markets, leisure outlets changed their images, expanding their appeal by creating and adapting 'style'. The upmarket creations in pubs are a telling example.[42] Style linked leisure participation with status – in dress, facilities and special equipment – and added distance from the pastimes linked with more depressed days. With their relatively new affluence, youth was targeted for the new leisure.[43] Participation required financial and social identity in a particular culture.[44] An alternative current came partly as a reaction to the large scale of commercialization that had occurred, combined with feelings of a lack of 'local' involvement, and a despair at the way standards had been adjusted to broaden markets. Pubs changed their purpose and their cultural representation, and people began to campaign for a return to what the pub used to mean – including 'real' ale.[45]

The car made the centralization of recreation facilities increasingly feasible, and concentrated the market. The commercialization of leisure saw a reduction in the kind of local-level control that had typified its diversity in the first half of this century. As leisure became increasingly capital intensive, the number of centres diminished and there was a unification of the kind of facility available. Bigger firms began to run chains of similar leisure centres. Recreation had become a commodity, subject to cash transactions, and its provision thus ever more dependent on profitability potential. The leisure producers, increasingly the most dominant influence on our leisure, are, paradoxically, very separated themselves from the very culture they service. Market research grows ever more important.[46]

In the wake of the leisure producers come sponsored

television presentations of what were once family and locally based recreations. These are mirrored by increasing sophistication in the local-authority sector. The public concern for recreation is inherited from the provision of libraries and baths in the nineteenth century. In the 1970s this became incorporated into a wider concern of 'sport for all'. The importance of leisure reached the stage when the concern was not only to *maintain* parks and baths, but for councils to make them available to more people for recreational purposes, thereby increasing their choice of activity and also improving their health.[47]

With the development of leisure patterns very different, nationally, from those that dominated between the wars came another more recent change, the gentrification of leisure. Partly about the creation of style and the appropriation of somebody else's pastime, this was influenced by population movements into working-class areas of cities, towns and villages, and by an awareness of the attractions of working-class culture – a culture ignored in the market promotion of leisure – gained through specific sections of the media.[48]

The value of recreation as escape is of continuing significance. Sometimes it takes over the dominant experience of life, as happened to the father in Raymond Williams' account of the inter-war village in *Border Country*: 'He kept up his gardens and had now seven hives of bees ... within all this his work in the box was only part of his life ... Gradually in the winter evenings he moved back, through Will (his son) into the home.'[49] In some cases, recreation assumes the form of physical as well as mental separation – as when experienced on the football pitch, the golf course or the riverbank, or through natural-history clubs, or even railways in the attic; likewise with the allotment. In turn, each outdoor activity has an effect on the landscape, and often requires a particular location and land – witness the ground pattern of the golf course and the cleared banks of the popular fishing venue ... Ball games, likewise, need flat surfaces. The landscape wherein a particular activity takes place can play a significant role in the presentation and promotion of that activity, as for example in the case of the seaside hall for variety entertainment or scrambling slopes. There are 'spontaneous' recreations, too, without the restrictions of rules, like street football and the use of park pitches when the keeper is out of sight.[50] These places form the centre of exchange of the matrix of relationships and solidarity associated with recreation.[51]

Just as there is the spatial separation between home – locus of the female world – and workplace – the man's – so there is the separation based on recreation, caricatured in time and place by the woman 'looking after' the home, the children and the Sunday dinner, and the man able to escape to take refuge from *his* week to enjoy a pastime – undertaken in the male preserve. These preserves, be they river bank, football stand or pitch, or the allotment, become the ideal refuge, where the man is free to indulge his idiosyncracies in personal relations or individual creativity, away from the sounds and associations of home.

The extension of home ownership and the home-centring effect of television have led to some convergence, in effect at least, of the working and middle classes, just as building-society advertisements link proper care of one's family with the ownership of a home. By the middle of the last century, the latter had become part of the artisan's claim to respectability, and whilst its achievement *was* a result of increased real wages, it was also a retreat from the loss of control over work.[52] For many, this produced a reaffirmation of the gender division of roles and of recreation – the car as against the cooker, DIY against clothes-making – although in some households it brought the achievement of role-sharing closer.[53]

There is another separation in the sexual identity of cultural representation, in the things that men and women 'like to' cultivate. A gardening magazine in the 1840s gave a clear demarcation of sexual roles as a metaphor for marriage: '. . . the husband's apple and pear trees, twinned by the wife's clematis; his cabbage bed fringed with her pinks and pansies; the tool house wreathed with roses; his tougher labour adorned by her gayer fancy, all speaking loudly of their hearts and tastes'.[54] There is an assumption here that women prefer red flowers, although men could raise them, perhaps for cutting for the *wife*'s display at home. They (the men) could also raise plants in a nursery bed, maybe on the allotment, for transplanting at home. Men were, however, much more interested in serious utilitarian food growing. The women would find this too hard (despite the labour of cleaning clothes before washing machines), dirty (despite their experience in cleaning the lavatory) and lacking prettiness. A small number of men were allotted eccentricity in, say, sweet peas ('really for the wife'), but then only for the men's competitive masculinity on the show bench. Otherwise it was just a bit pansy. Women double-digging was surely butch? It is seen that the bohemian middle class has broken ground and roles have integrated. Today there are numerous families that together cultivate the same flower beds and rows of vegetables, or even who dare to reverse this, once, 'proper allocation' of roles.

The aspect of escape is part of the search for alternative meaning, that in turn can legitimize our involvement in mainstream contemporary life, dissociated as it frequently is from local social relations. The surroundings, the landscape, play a role in this, providing visual, symbolic associations, a backdrop against which a particular activity is acknowledged, but also there are rules to be observed. Municipal gardens traditionally offered very ordered space, well supervised and controlled;[55] the pioneering plotland landscapes of the early twentieth century provided a landscape of freedom; the working-class terraced grid-iron streets became the image of close inter-family contact in their very local, very open-air leisure pursuits; while Georgian squares remain known for the politeness and privacy of their neatly arranged enclosures.[56]

Fields, plots and people

The allotment landscape does not have the ingredients that are popularly associated with landscape. People may contend that allotments are just 'there'. And yet they are frequently the subject of successful entries to the Royal Academy Summer Exhibition. This interest in the landscape of the allotment is bound up with two aspects of our culture. One is the nostalgic yearning for a once more leafy city, town and village that the allotment evokes. In the village, especially, this feeling is underlined by memories of widespread agricultural labour in the fields. The other aspect concerns the allotment's association with a subculture, a local culture of working the land, of making a personal 'imprint' therein. Yet neither is consistent with the dominant contemporary views of landscape.

The image presented by the media – TV in particular – frequently supports that dominant view. It is the landscape of the TV documentary and the grand serial. It was caricatured in a BBC series with John Betjeman in the early 70s, the expansive and lush landscape giving of the contours themselves, punctuated and clothed only by vegetation, all viewed from a balloon. People were in the lensfield at a distance only, or they were crusty old 'country' characters.[57] This is an empty landscape; empty also of human relations. In these images, the still, old person cut out from human association is like a hermit housed at a distance in a landed estate, sufficiently out of sight, or unobtrusive by manner, permitted to be just in vision, no more than an image.

This is the official landscape presented by the National Trust and in Shell advertisements.[58] Whilst both are out to attract patrons, the subject they present is the land and sky alone, empty and untrammelled. Visitors are attracted on the basis that they will share this status, that this 'virgin' ground is for them alone; a kind of Adam and Eve before the crowd. It is illusory, being but a part of the distancing of the country and the city that has preoccupied our national way of seeing things for some time.[59] The country is presented and organized so to be experienced as 'leisure', as a view. The visitor is the subordinate partner consuming the landscape. The National Trust presents an image of the purposeful skilful adjustment of nature, a Georgic representation of the raw material of nature transformed by those possessed of ownership, leisure and status. There is a demarcation in our culture between what is wild and what is not. 'When the environment was mainly wild, beauty was seen in order imposed by the hands of man. When the wastes had gone, to be replaced by a chequer-board countryside of enclosed fields, beauty came to be seen as wilderness.'[60] However, this simple equation requires the acceptable presentation of the enclosing landlord, as depicted in paintings like Gainsborough's *Mr and Mrs Andrews*.[61]

In practice, what contemporary culture perceives as 'nature' is not the wilderness, but rather a highly synthetic image of the landscaped estate and other cultivated ground – and though the cultivation is rarely seen, when it is, it is indeed a curious spectacle. Furthermore, nature is associated with some kind of 'natural' superiority.[62] This is part of so many arguments against developments that introduce *people* into the landscape. From this standpoint the more 'natural' a landscape, the higher its status. This has lent weight to the critical contrasts made between town, city and country, even though there are obvious flaws in the conventional view of the city as unhealthy and the country as a reservoir of natural health – whether this be measured in terms of the disease-ridden 'rural hovels' of the past, or in the under-investment in health care in many rural parts of contemporary Britain, or by the spill-over from toxic sprays and the build-up of nitrates in rivers and streams.

Still wilderness pleases. But the concept of the landscape as the object of solitary contemplation is a product of the romantic revolution in taste which our ancestors would not have understood. Why should we cherish the human environment rather than humanity itself? The poet and critic Herbert Read described his own experience of the empty landscape in these words: 'I am not so much conscious of this or that clump of trees, but of space that reaches to infinity, of the earth eroded with rhythmical contours, of the immense overreaching sky, and perhaps if some bird's cry pierces these sensations, it would break the spell.'[63]

Samuel Palmer felt that landscape would improve by being 'received into the soul' before he could paint it. Read described an almost spiritual experience (although he professed atheism): 'If I penetrate further into the Yorkshire Dales there are no farms or churches, not even a dry stone wall, but unbroken folds of heather and bracken, a tender desolation of purple and russet tints, and nothing else but the silently moving clouds, and perhaps a trickle of bog water in a ferny mill.' He associates the pathos of the empty landscape with a self-expression of romantic mystics, and he quotes a passage from Kirkegaard, describing the scene across the bare fields to Gilbjerg in Denmark: '. . . it has always been one of my favourite places . . . my eye met not a single sail on the vast expanse of water . . . the few that are dear to me came forth from their graves . . . I felt so content in their midst, I rested in their embrace . . . I stood alone, and everything vanished from my eyes, and I turned back with heavy heart to mix in the busy world.'[64]

There is a feeling of artistic and spiritual contemplation in this, and certainly Herbert Read was no misanthrope. He acknowledged the classical view that a healthy landscape is a populated one. Yet there is another position which is concerned more with social relations and practical conflict. The frequent opposition that greets plans to build new homes in villages or at surburban edges is one way that people express their claim to what they see as *their* landscape. Barthes envisaged landscape as 'a kind of loan made by the owners of the terrain'. People feel that they *own* the landscape, even though the title deeds remain elsewhere. This view of appropriated landscape is at once an assertion of inalienable status and of misanthropy. It is a refusal to accept the involvement of ordinary people in the landscape. The point is simply but strongly expressed in the words of Emerson: 'You cannot freely admire a noble landscape if labourers are digging in the fields nearby.'[65] To which we must ask, 'why not?'

Our contemporary society is dominated by the feeling that landscape is to be *seen*, not worked. It is self-conscious position that goes with the presentation of landscape as a commodity, bought and sold and paid for. It is an object of monetary value, increasingly a consumer object.[66] Landscape has an acquired status, and so its character is seen to be important in land values, and we can share this by association. It is seen and valued within a prescribed cultural context of ownership, status and commodity. It was one of Herbert Read's heroes, fellow anarchist Peter Kropotkin, who had a practical vision of a peopled landscape. In a volume of centenary selections, Read singled out Kropotkin's lament at the sight of 'The Empty Fields': 'But how can that land be cultivated when there is nobody to cultivate it? "We have fields, men go by but never go in", an old labourer said to me; and so it is in reality. Man is conspicuous by his absence from those meadows; he rolls them with a heavy roller in the spring; he spreads manure every two or three years, then he disappears until the time has come to make hay.'[67] This comment was made in the 1890s on a stretch of land from Harrow to Central London, with nothing but meadowland east or west. Yet Kropotkin recorded that the city was supplied with food from Jersey, Belgium, France and Canada. He contrasted this with the gardeners of Paris, cultivating a similar stretch with 2000 human beings.[68]

The 'nature' that had been valued in seventeenth-century art was 'human nature'. 'Until late in the seventeenth century the only acceptable part of the natural world was that which was cultivated.'[69] Beyond that lay suspicion and fear. But John Clare was to demonstrate something of the human reality associated with the cultivation of land in the particular social conditions of his day: 'The poor labourer

35

natives of the place ... o'come by labour and bowed down by time ...'[70] He refused to disguise real relations and experiences with the picturesque and the nostalgic.

In a similar vein to Kropotkin, though from different political standpoints, both Defoe and Cobbett had earlier sought the safeguarding of land labour in the face of the enclosure of commons and wastes. Thus, resisting a proposal to enclose 150 acres of Horton Heath in Dorset, Cobbett wrote: 'The cottagers produced from their little bits, in food, for themselves, and in things to be sold at market, more than any neighbouring farm of 200 acres ... I learnt to hate a system that could induce them to tear up "wastes" and sweep away occupiers like those I have described! Wastes indeed! Give a dog an ill name. Was Horton Heath waste? Was it a waste when a hundred, perhaps, of healthy boys and girls were playing there on a Sunday, instead of creeping about covered with filth in the alleys of a town?'[71] The vision of these propagandists was of a peopled landscape of real human activity, not the eccentric form of the estate envisaged by landscape architects like William Kent, who wanted to see just a few superannuated labourers acting the part of hermits as a romantic curiosity, to place the larger expanse of the landlord's dominance in an even vaster contrast with a lone figure in his ruined hut. The peopled landscape was a vision of a relationship between the land, the people, and the ground they worked. It was not simply a 'romantic' notion like that epitomized in Vita Sackville-West's *The Land*, which was a celebration of people and land in the particular farming context of the landed estate.[72]

This turning away from the urban social world was typical of the Back to the Land movement of the late-nineteenth century,[73] which sought not only a house in the country but a working relationship with the land. There was then a wider movement clamouring for a house in the country with a *view*, and at a distance from the urban population. A century later, this dream has become reality for a growing number of the population – in part, at least.

Now, more people are enjoying *the view*, either living in the country or visiting it, yet many remain frustrated by their inability to get closer to the ground.

More recently John Seymour has argued for the potential of the peopled landscape in terms of Kropotkin's argument for a use of land in which people control both their own lives and the landscapes they create. He knows a man, he says, who farms 10,000 acres with three men and seasonal contractors, growing barley for the subsidy, and he reflects: 'Cut that land (exhausted as it is) up into a thousand plots of ten acres each, give each plot to a family trained to use it, and within ten years the production coming from it would be enormous ... The motorist wouldn't have the satisfaction of looking out over a vast, treeless, hedgeless prairie of indifferent barley – but he could get out of his car and wander through a seemingly huge area of diverse countryside, orchards, young tree plantations, a myriad of small plots of land growing a multiplicity of different crops, farm animals galore, and hundreds of happy and healthy children ...'[74]

John Berger expresses landscape as 'a curtain' behind which our everyday struggles and achievements take place. These are, he interprets, the relationships between people and landscape depicted in Millet's painting, *Winter with Crows*: 'It is nothing but sky, a distant copse, a vast deserted plain of inert earth on which have been left a wooden plough and a harrow ... to cultivate its soil is a continual struggle ... back breaking'.[75] Even without a person on it, the painting reflects a deep preoccupation with people, and about their relationships with the landscape depicted. Millet painted people digging, lifting potatoes, pruning, manuring. Van Gogh followed this with canvases showing people in massive celebrations. The energy of his paintings releases the artist's own sense of empathy (not sympathy) with his subjects. The paintings demonstrate the relationship between the people's own culture and the landscape they worked, which they helped to create, however happily or desparingly. It was theirs. 'One's native land is not nature alone, there must also be human hearts who search for and see the same things. And only then is the native land complete, only then does one feel at home.'[76]

This is the harshness of experienced reality or, as the salon commentators saw it, the portrayal of cretins and degenerates.[77] For Fred Inglis the paintings, like landscape, are 'social relations made manifest'.[78] The landscape used or produced in these different situations then becomes part of the 'sign fields' of our environment. Individual landscapes signify particular experiences, circumstances, and above all relationships. In this – the real landscape – the result is richly varied at the local level. The working class who claimed, and to a degree won, access to the uplands did not want only to *see*; they wanted liberation, and in activity connected with a place that was theirs by right they secured meaning. The success of the consumer landscape is to divest 'place' of all reality and, save presented voyeurism, of meaning.

The meaning *may* be the same for those involved with the landscape as for those who look on. But the degree to which this is possible depends on how the landscapes experienced relate back into our individual and everyday lives, to our cultural experiences and other points of reference.[79]

3
The cottager's plot

'Since gardening hath crept out of Holland to Sandwich in Kent and thence into this county (Surrey), where though they have given six pounds an acre and upward, they made their rent, lived comfortably and set many people on work.

'Oh, the incredible profit by digging of ground! For though it is confessed that the plough beats the spade out of distance for speed (almost as much as the press beats the pen) yet what the spade wants in the quantity of the ground it manureth, it recompenseth with the plenty of the fruit it yieldeth; that, which is set, multiplying a hundred fold more than what is sown.

'Tis incredible how many poor people in London live thereon, so that in some seasons, gardens feed more poor people than the field. It may be hoped that in process of time aniseed, cumin seeds, caraway seeds, (yea, rice itself) with other garden ware now brought from beyond the seas, may hereafter grow in our land, enough for its use, especially if some ingenious gentleman would encourage the industrious gardeners by letting ground on reasonable rates unto them.'

Thomas Fuller,
The Worthies of England, 1662

Thomas Fuller spent the Civil War and Commonwealth years compiling a gazetteer of the nation's counties, their benefactors, products and manufactures, local breeds of sheep, pigs and cattle, their cheeses and the useful timber in their forests and coppices, describing the earthly paradise they could have made of their well-provided island. His exact contemporary, Gerrard Winstanley, is more famous in this century than in his own as another searcher for the earthly paradise through his assertion of the right to dig. The Digger's invasion of 'common' land next to Campe Close at St George's Hill, Walton-on-Thames in Surrey began on 1 April 1649, and the Council of State was immediately

informed by a local landowner that people were sowing the
ground with parsnips, carrots and beans, with the intention
of restoring 'the ancient community of enjoying the fruits of
the earth'. The Council of State sent the letter on the same
day to Lord Fairfax, Lord General of the Armed Forces of
the Commonwealth, urging him to send some forces 'to
Cobham in Surrey and thereabouts, with orders to disperse
the people so met, and to prevent the like for the future, that
a malignant and disaffected party may not under colour of
such a ridiculous people have any opportunity to rendezvous
themselves in order to do a greater mischief'.[1]

They were driven out, their vegetables uprooted and their
huts burned. Within eighteen months at least nine other
Digger colonies were set up and evicted. The events of 1649
were a dramatization of a process which had been a continuous feature of British history: the enclosure of land by the
rich and powerful, and the encroachment on land by the
poor and hungry. Tradition and a sense of natural justice
gave the inhabitants of any place the right to till the soil, in
what became the common fields, the right to the products of
woods and forests, the right to pasture domesticated
animals and to hunt, trap or fish wild creatures. These
rights were safeguarded by elaborate local rules and conventions, designed to prevent exploitation of the self-
balancing subsistence economy by those who chose to
demand too much and consequently to deny the rights of
others.

This delicately poised system was vulnerable. Starvation
could result from bad weather, bad harvests or bad luck, or
disease and pestilence among animals or humans. It was
also at the mercy of military marauders, kings, princes,
earls, barons and counts, who produced no food or shelter
themselves, but chose to extort it from others at the point of
a sword, bludgeon, axe, arrow or cannon-ball. That is why
Winstanley held the view that the Norman Conquest had
deprived the people of their land and that with the defeat of
Charles I, as ultimate heir of William I, the people had won

back their right to the use of the land, by right of conquest.

Remarkably, even in the late twentieth century we have authorities on ecology arguing that 'the tragedy of the commons', throughout the world, is due, not to the seizure of the land by kings, princes, governments and commissars, but to the peasants themselves, through their habit of over-cropping, over-stocking and over-felling, from the common fields, common pastures and common woodlands of a communal economy.[2] The argument is that: 'On common land each individual will try to keep as many sheep or cattle as possible. The logic of the process leads remorselessly to over-stocking. The tragedy of the commons is that individuals can only thrive by pursuing their own interests (which means increasing the herd when possible) at the expense of the collective good (limiting the total herd). The same process applies whether the commons are considered to be open pasture or whales or fossil fuel. In practice the commons were virtually ended by the Enclosures.'[3]

We can see now that the real tragedy of the commons is that powerful people, whether lords of the manor or governments, step in and blame the victims for the disruption of the ancient economy. In the 1980s a team of specialists was appointed by the United Nations Environment Programme to report on the alleged downward spiral of the Himalaya region's forests, where it was claimed that the rate of timber use had overtaken the rate of new growth. What they actually found was that for centuries the Sherpas 'managed their common forest resources with the help of their social institution of forest guardian – a rotating office within each village the annual holder of which, after due (but fairly casual) consultation, laid down the permissible extraction rates for fuelwood and constructional timber and extracted traditional fines on those villagers who did not comply'. But in the 1950s the forests of Nepal were nationalized and controlled by regionally based officials. The old system worked quite well. The new centralized system that destroyed it does not work at all.[4]

ACCOUNT
OF A
COTTAGE AND GARDEN
NEAR TADCASTER.
WITH
OBSERVATIONS
UPON LABOURERS HAVING FREEHOLD COTTAGES
AND GARDENS,

AND UPON A PLAN FOR SUPPLYING COTTAGERS
WITH COWS.

PRINTED AT THE DESIRE OF THE SOCIETY
FOR BETTERING THE CONDITION, AND
INCREASING THE COMFORTS OF THE POOR

LONDON:

PRINTED FOR T. BECKET, BOOKSELLER, PALL-MALL

1797.

PRICE ONE SHILLING A DOZEN.

The enclosure of the common fields, common lands and wastes was accomplished in Britain with a similar assumption that poor people were not to be trusted with their own resources. It was a continuous process for centuries which culminated in the period of Parliamentary Enclosures between the years 1750 and 1850. This final campaign of the enclosing urge gave birth to the modern allotment movement.

With the sanction of the state the last vestiges of common rights to the use of land were eliminated, except for a handful of survivals, from more ancient forms of land use. Just because of its significance in our view of the past and of the right of access to land, the enclosure of the fields and wastes is one of the most fiercely debated aspects of our history among professional historians. Every single assumption that we were obliged to learn at school as historical fact has been challenged by recent historians. Was there an agricultural revolution, who made it and who benefitted from it? Certainly the reputations of various individuals has been diminished. Thus one recent historian remarks that: 'It has been shown that "Turnip" Townshend was a boy when turnips were first grown on his estate and Jethro Tull was something of a crank and not the first person to invent a seed drill. Coke of Holkham was a great publicist (especially of his own achievements) but some of the farming practices he encouraged (such as employment of the Norfolk four-course rotation in unsuitable conditions) may have been positively harmful. More generally it is acknowledged that the traditional picture of a sudden and rapid transformation in the eighteenth century is mistaken . . .'[5]

Faced with such a dismissal of the 'facts' of agrarian history we all learned, what can we assume about the fate, under enclosure, of the smallholder, the cottager and the squatter? These people were the greater part of the rural population, and the effect of enclosure upon them was the theme of the most famous of all the accounts of the history of the time, *The Village Labourer* by J.L. and Barbara

Hammond.[6] Their account of the fate of the labouring poor, along with the stories about Townshend, Tull and Coke, influenced school history for many decades. We all absorbed the notion that the loss of traditional rights by the poor was devastating, but other students urged us to believe that it was 'historically necessary' to produce the new urban working class through migration and to increase the productivity of agriculture, hampered by the archaic system of the common fields and by poor people's rights over the 'wastes' which in the days when 'vast stretches of the English countryside were "no-man's land" in the real sense of the word',[7] provided a livelihood for the rural poor.

A later school of historians, now known as the revisionists,[8] contradicted the Hammond interpretation, using words like 'mistaken', 'exaggerated', 'overdrawn', 'unrealistic', 'unhistorical', 'partial and tendentious', 'seriously astray', 'biased', and 'illiberal',[9] only to be followed by a further group of scholars, the counter-revisionists, who have re-established the older point of view.[10] It is also claimed (in the same way that new investigators belatedly recognize the virtues of Himalayan villagers' control of their forests) that the recent historical reappraisal of open-field agriculture has established 'that the open fields were far more open to innovative and flexible agriculture than once supposed', and that 'the account of them as seriously backward and by nature inhibitive of new techniques is most certainly incorrect'.[11]

The economic historians will go on arguing about the causes and effects of enclosure. What remain in the minds of ordinary readers are the often-quoted passages from contemporary observers. Arthur Young, the foremost agricultural authority of his day, and an advocate of enclosure, became increasingly aware of the hardship and injustice that resulted. When secretary to the Board of Agriculture he wrote that 'the fact is that by nineteen enclosure bills out of twenty the poor are injured, in some, grossly injured', and he went on to praise the way in which traditional rights – the

44

right to build a cottage, to pasture animals, to gather fuelwood and to cultivate a patch of land, all extinguished by
enclosure – had sustained the rural poor, who were left by
enclosure as a burden on the parish poor rate:

> Nothing can be clearer than the vast importance which
> all these poor people, scattered as they are through so
> many counties ... attach to the object of possessing
> land, though no more than to set a cottage on. Of this
> there can be no dispute; and as an object does exist, the
> prospect ... will induce industry, frugality, patience,
> and exertion without bounds ... When we sit by our
> firesides and ask how a poor labourer can afford to build
> a comfortable cottage, enclose some land, break up and
> cultivate a rough waste, acquire some live stock, and
> get many conveniences about him, we defy calculation;
> there must be some moving principle at work which
> figures will not count, for in such an inquiry we see
> nothing but impossibilities. But we forget a thousand
> animating principles of human feeling. Such effects
> could not possibly have been produced without a series
> of years of great industry and most economical savings
> – to become independent, to marry a girl and fix her in a
> spot they can call their own, instigates to a conduct not
> a trace of which would be seen without the motive ever
> in view. With this powerful impulse they will exert
> every nerve to earn, call into life and vigour every
> principle of industry, and exert all the powers of
> frugality to save. Nothing less can account for the spec-
> tacle, and such animating prospects will account for any
> thing.

Go to an alehouse kitchen of an old enclosed county,
and there you will see the origins of poverty and poor
rates. For whom are they to be sober? For whom are
they to save? (Such are their questions.) For the parish?
If I am diligent, shall I have leave to build a cottage? If I
am sober, shall I have land for a cow? If I am frugal,

shall I have half an acre of potatoes? You offer no motives; you have nothing but a parish officer and a workhouse! – Bring me another pot . . .[12]

Arthur Young thought that his pamphlet of 1801, 'An Inquiry into the Proprietry of Applying Wastes to the Better Maintenance and Support of the Poor', was ('though it never had the smallest effect except in exciting opposition and ridicule') the most important of his writings, and that if put into effect 'would have diffused more comfort among the poor than any proposition that ever was made'.[13] His appeal to his fellow landowners and rate-payers was based on the common knowledge that enclosure, while it may have increased the income of those who benefited, also increased the poor rate they were obliged to pay, since it operated as a machine guaranteed to extrude paupers.

In fact, the advocacy of allotments had been pursued in the columns of the *Gentleman's Magazine* from 1765 onwards, with what were known as 'cow and cot' schemes for resettling the displaced poor. At the very end of the period of early allotment propaganda studied by Griffiths Cunningham, an anonymous correspondent was claiming in that journal that 'granting small allotments in lieu of common rights was fraudulent as it was impossible to compensate for the loss of common rights'; but he was in favour of waste-land reclamation as large amounts of it were not used by anyone. Reclamation could proceed by the parcelling out of allotments for conversion to tillage 'without recourse to the method of inclosure, and extinction of ancient privileges belonging to the humble British peasant'.[14] This was by no means the usual opinion to be found in the *Gentleman's Magazine* and the *Annals of Agriculture* about the many proposals for cow-and-cot schemes and the occasional actual experiments. 'Clearly the articulate upper classes monopolize the historical record and we end up with a vision of well-meaning reformers and zealous improvers generously serving the needs of the labouring poor. The record, however, does show that the poor did act in the promotion of their rights, and riot and tumult must have played some role in forcing action for the benefit of the victims of development.'[15]

Early provision of land for the poor seldom led to anything resembling the allotment gardens that developed in the nineteenth century. Land had often been bequeathed for the benefit of the poor, but invariably it was the rent of the land, rather than the land itself, that was distributed by trustees or by the parish. In enclosures by mutual agreement before the period of parliamentary enclosure the land allotted to compensate tenants was attached to the cottage itself, or took the form of a 'cowgate', which was the right to use a common pasture. But it was not until the last decades of the eighteenth century that a few large landlords provided more than 'fuel allotments' for their labourers. The examples described in the *Gentleman's Magazine* demanded, as Thorpe put it, 'a rare combination of philanthropy and wealth'. Parliament rejected both a private member's Bill in 1790 and a General Inclosure Bill which in 1796 was intended to require all future Inclosure Acts to include the allotment of land to the poor.

It was the vast rise in poor relief that obliged Parliament to authorize the provision of land for the poor, just as it had authorized their deprivation.

An Act of 1782 enabled guardians of the poor to enclose up to ten acres of waste land near the poor house, for the purpose of cultivating it for the benefit of the poor, but there was no suggestion that the land was to be allotted to individuals. Similarly the General Inclosure Act of 1801 ... provided that small allotments of land made in Inclosure Awards might be grouped together and worked in common, in order to reduce the cost of fencing. The first Public Act to make specific reference to the provision of allotments for the poor came in 1819. An Act of that year empowered parish wardens 'for the promotion of industry among the poor' to let up to twenty acres of parish land to individuals at a reasonable rent and the limit was increased to fifty acres in 1831. A further Act of 1832 allowed the wardens of fuel allotments which had been provided under enclosure awards, and which had now been exhausted, to break them down into small units and to let them for individual cultivation at economic rents.[16]

The first Inclosure Act to stipulate that in the allocation of land, a portion should be set aside as allotments for the labouring poor, was the one passed in 1806 for the village of Great Somerford, Wiltshire, which made available five to eight acres out of the 970 acres enclosed. This provision for 'poor's' allotments was included in numerous subsequent Acts, but it was omitted from many more, and it was not until the mid-century with the General Inclosure Act of 1845 that this kind of provision finally became mandatory. The Act 'empowered the Inclosure Commissioners to specify as one of the conditions of enclosure the appropriation of such an allotment for the labouring poor as they thought necessary. It went on to permit the wardens of Inclosure Acts to set aside land as "field gardens" (limited to a quarter of an acre in extent) for the poor, and, more important, required them to account to the Commissioners for any failure to do so. Thus, the association of enclosure with allotment provision was at last ratified. This came, of course, far too late . . .'[17] Nor was it particularly effective, since an estimate made in 1869 concluded that of 614,800 acres enclosed since the Act of 1845, only 2223 had been assigned to the poor.[18]

Hostility to allotments

The countenance of Lord Marney bespoke the character of his mind; cynical, devoid of sentiment, arrogant, literal, hard . . . Lord Marney expressed his imperious

hope that no infant schools would ever be found in his
neighbourhood ... He eulogized the new poor law,
which he declared would be the salvation of the country,
provided it was 'carried out' in the spirit in which it was
developed in the Marney Union; but then he would add
that there was no district except their union in which it
was properly observed. He was tremendously fierce
against allotments, and analysed the system with
merciless sarcasm ...

Benjamin Disraeli,
Sybil; or The Two Nations, 1845

In 1844 Disraeli attended a dinner at the Oddfellows' Hall
at Bingley in Yorkshire 'for the purpose of celebrating the
successful Introduction of Field Gardens into the Parish, as
well as the formation of the Bingley Cricket Club', and made
a speech eulogizing the allotment movement. But many
landowners and farmers resented the idea of allotments
with the same vehemence with which they opposed village
schools. In the drafting of the General Inclosure Act, note
was taken of the 1843 report of the Select Committee on the
Labouring Poor (Allotments of Land) which declared that:
'As it is desirable that the profits of the allotments should be
viewed by the holder of it in the light of an aid and not as a
substitute for his ordinary income accruing from wages, and
that they should not become an inducement to neglect his
usual paid labour, the allotment should be of no greater
extent than can be cultivated during the leisure moments of
the family.'[19] But in fact, 'the labourer, even when in
employment, was as likely as not a pauper who depended for
part of his family income on the parish'. This is the
conclusion of Hobsbawm and Rudé in their study of the
'Captain Swing' explosion of discontent, threats, petitions
and arson in 1830. 'In extreme cases,' they remark, 'it could
be said with little exaggeration that the farmworker could
no longer strictly be described as a wage-labourer ... It does
not take much imagination to picture the situation of

famished dependence of the sixty per cent of *all* inhabitants of Hitcham or Polstead, or of almost the entire population of Wattisham and Whatfield (all in the Cosford Hundred, Suffolk), or the 958 out of 1746 inhabitants of Benenden, the half of those living in Biddenden or Goudhurst (Kent), who were paupers.'[20] Yet the Select Committee on Allotments was obliged to report that: 'It was not until 1830, when discontent had been so painfully exhibited amongst the peasantry of the southern counties that this method of alleviating their situation was much resorted to.'

The Hammonds sought an explanation for the antagonism of farmers towards the spread of allotments:

It had been to the interest of a small farmer in the old common-field village to have a number of semi-labourers, semi-owners who could help at the harvest: the large farmer wanted a permanent supply of labour which was absolutely at his command ... The strength of the hostility of the farmers to allotments is seen in the language of those few landlords who were interested in this policy. Lord Winchilsea and his friends were always urging philanthrophists to proceed with caution, and to try to reason the farmers out of their prejudices. The Report of the Poor Law Commission in 1834 showed that these prejudices were as strong as ever. 'We can do little or nothing to prevent pauperism; the farmers will have it: they prefer that the labourers should be slaves; they object to their having gardens, saying: The more they work for themselves, the less they work for us.' This was the view of Boys, the writer on agricultural subjects, who, criticizing Kent's declaration in favour of allotments, remarks: 'If farmers in general were to accommodate their labourers with two acres of land, a cow and two or three pigs, they would probably have more difficulty in getting their hard work done – as the cow, land, etc, would enable them to live with less earnings.'[21]

This resentment of allotment schemes by farmers was bitterly expressed by one of them when the rector of Hitcham proposed allotments in 1845: 'I am sorry to say that it appears that you are one of those philanthropical gentlemen who wish to make themselves popular with the lower class of society at the expense of the farmer; him you would crush and stamp underfoot if possible . . .'[22] Hitcham in Suffolk was 'populous, remote and woefully neglected'. Its poor rate and its crime rate were among the highest in the county. Heading the list of its sins were arson and crimes of violence. 'With industry and frugality' the diet of its poor consisted 'principally of bread and potatoes'. To this village, in 1837, came a new rector, John Stevens Henslow, after 'the farmers had harassed the former incumbent until they broke his spirit'. Henslow was an unusual clergyman. He was Professor of Botany at Cambridge, was a friend and mentor of Charles Darwin, and was an active campaigner for worthy causes. On 20 March 1842 he preached a sermon 'on the occasion of three persons of the parish being condemned to fifteen years' transportation for sheep-stealing', and had it printed at Hadleigh, in Suffolk, for circulation. By that year he had set up a variety of clubs and societies in the parish and had started a school, even though 'the cause of popular education was not well received by the wealthy of Hitcham'. In 1844 Henslow began campaigning for allotments in a series of letters, 'To the Public' and 'To the Landlords of Suffolk' in the *Bury and Norwich Post*, followed in 1845 by an 'Address to landlords on the advantages to be expected from the general establishment of a spade tenantry among the labouring classes'.[23] He drew attention to successful allotment schemes elsewhere in the county, as at Barton where Sir H. Bunbury had 'allotted half an acre [of] sites as near as possible to the labourers' own cottages'. This proposal, too, was met by hostility, and the first allotments were in the glebe – the land that was part of the rector's benefice. 'Your Allotment scheme seems an excellent one',

Darwin wrote to Henslow, but local antagonism was not abated, and Henslow's biographer explains that:

When the Hitcham Charity Land became available again in 1849, he was able to secure sixteen acres for eight years and it was this land that he allocated as quarter-acre allotments. The farmers had not relented and continued to make it very difficult for Henslow. Thus, when he acquired twenty acres the following year, some of the allottees had to withdraw their names because the farmers 'by whom they were pretty generally employed, would not allow them to hold an allotment under the pain and penalty of being refused further employment on their farms'. Henslow's brother-in-law, Jenyns, reported that in his own Cambridge-shire parish he too had run into farmer opposition to an allotment scheme on the grounds that 'the men would give their masters short time and easy work' to reserve their energies for allotment work later in the day! Allegations of stealing the masters' seed were also made. In Hitcham, however, the opposition was much stronger and based on social fears. Jenyns explained that '... the farmers are apt to think that the holding of an allotment will give the labourer a spirit of independence that will interfere with the service he owes his master.'[24]

Shrewdly, Henslow made the two annual shows of the Hitcham Labourers' and Mechanics' Horticultural Society, held from 1850 onwards, the crowning events of the village year, with sideshows, sports, lectures and high teas. He invited the good and the great from the world of Victorian science and horticulture to attend and to donate prizes: tools, barometers, teapots and fertilizers. The celebrated professor of botany, John Lindley, donated the recently dis-covered phosphate manure, Chilean guano. Lindley wrote in 1859, after distributing the prizes at the vegetable show: 'It is the practice at Hitcham, twice in the season, to inspect the

𝕮𝖔𝖓𝖉𝖎𝖙𝖎𝖔𝖓𝖘,

On which Mr. GIBBARD consents to let GROUND for GARDENS,
in *Church Field*, in the Parish of *Sharnbrook*.

I. EACH Allotment shall be let for one Year only; namely, from
the *tenth* of *October*, 1830, to the *eleventh* of *October*, 1831,
at which time possession shall be given up, without any previous Notice being required.

II. The Rent shall be paid half-yearly to Mr. GIBBARD's Agent,
Mr. *George Church*; namely, on the *sixth* of *April* and
the *eleventh* of *October*, in each Year.

III. The Straw, on being converted into Manure, shall be returned to the Land, and at least   Load of Manure
shall be laid on each Allotment in every Year.

IV. No Occupier shall underlet his Allotment.

V. No Occupier shall be allowed to trespass upon another's Land
in going to and from his own Allotment.

VI. Every Occupier will be expected to attend some Place of
public Worship at least once on every Sunday, and should
he neglect to do so without sufficient cause, will be deprived
of his Land.

VII. The Land shall be cultivated by each Occupier by Spade
Husbandry only.

VIII. Any Occupier guilty of dishonesty, or theft, will be deprived
of his Land.

IX. If any Occupier neglects to manage his Land properly, he
will be deprived of it.

JOHN GIBBARD, *Esq. of Sharnbrook, in the County of Bedford,
agrees to let to   of the said
Place,   of Land, in Church Field,
at the yearly Rent of   and the said
                             agrees to take and rent the
same on the above Conditions, to which the said Parties
have hereby set their Hands this   Day of
                    in the Year* 1831.

cottagers' allotment and to award some gardening imple-
ments to the owners of those best cultivated. Here too the
improvement is steady and marked, year by year the inspectors find less fault, while the best are like neatly kept gardens. The first prize man had forty-six crops on his
allotment, yet of this variety none were neglected, as was
proved by his also taking ten prizes for different articles.'[25]

Allotment history is full of remarkable innovators like
Henslow of Hitcham, combining the sponsorship of allotment societies with a concern for education and an interest
in horticultural science and its improvement. Thus one of
those who sought to influence the Select Committee of 1843
was Mrs Mary Ann Gilbert of Sussex, who 'demonstrated
that pauperism could be diminished if the unemployed were
provided with ground on which to grow their own food. She
put paupers to reclaiming and cultivating waste land near
Beachy Head, and sent Lord Liverpool some specimens of
the potatoes grown "on the beach". By 1835 she had 213
allotment tenants and she provided them with much good
advice on the use of liquid manure, forking the soil, and
stall-feeding of cows, while her two agricultural schools
offered the children of the allotment-holders an opportunity
of learning the rudiments of cultivation as well as the three
Rs.'[26]

Another pioneer of scientific horticulture, keenly concerned with the allotment movement, was Sir John Lawes,
who in 1843 had turned his inherited estate in Hertfordshire into the Rothamsted Experimental Station. He had
established allotment gardens there and in 1857 it occurred
to him that a club might add to the comfort and enjoyment of
the plot-holders. 'It need hardly be said,' Lawes remarked,
'that a club-house receiving barrels of beer direct from the
brewer did not meet with the approval of the publicans.' He
also noted that: 'Labouring men are rather apt to imagine
that if any one does them a kindness, his motives are not
altogether disinterested. If they had thought one of my
objects was to know more about their ideas and acts; if, in

fact, they had fancied that they did not possess entire freedom of action, they would not have abandoned the public
house for the club.' So he provided a club-house with a stove,
a verandah and a thatched roof, and then 'for the rest of the
year rarely, if ever, went near the place'.

Twenty years later, Lawes wrote with satisfaction about
both the survival of the club, with around 180 members, and
the healthy state of the allotments. 'To become a member of
the club, it is necessary to possess an allotment-garden, the
ordinary size of which is one-eighth of an acre (twenty rods),
and the rent five shillings per annum, although some allotments are only half that size. I occasionally give prizes for
the best cultivated gardens, and every second year we have
a show of vegetables. The men take immense interest in
these gardens, and should the Royal Agricultural Society
offer a premium for the best set of allotment gardens, we
should stand a very fair chance of carrying off the prize.' He
reproduced the elaborate series of thirty-one Rules of the
Rothamsted Allotment Club, of interest because they had
been evolved by the members over a considerable time by
trial and error, and because they were rigidly enforced.
Among them, many are familiar items in the rules of modern allotment societies, others deal ingeniously with trans-
gressions or reflect the sabbatarianism of the time:

Any member getting vegetables in the garden-fields
after nine o'clock on a Sunday morning, by Rothamsted
time, will be fined sixpence.

Any member taking tools from another man's garden
without leave and not returning them the same day,
will be fined one shilling.

Any member laying dung on the gravel roads, will be
fined one shilling for the first offence, and for the second
offence he will be expelled from the club.

Any member who sells the produce of his garden to a
stranger, must be present himself – or some of his
family must be present, or he must give notice to the

man who attends to the walks to be present – when the produce is cut or removed. If the purchaser removes the produce without a witness, the owner of the garden will be fined one shilling.[27]

Another set of rules from the same period is provided by Richard Jefferies, in describing the allotment gardens at Lyddington, near Swindon, where the local clergyman had turned part of his glebe land into allotment gardens on a site 300 yards from the village.

Each plot of ground is divided from the next by a narrow green path: no hedges or mounds are permitted, and the field itself is enclosed without a hedge to harbour birds. The soil is a rich dark loam, yielding good crops, with very little manure, and the surface is level. There are sixty-three tenants occupying plots varying in size, according to circumstances, from 48 'lug' downwards – 25, 30, 16, etc. A 'lug' is a provincialism for perch. The rent is 5d per 'lug' or perch, and each occupier on becoming a tenant receives a card on which the following rules are printed in large type: –

1. The land shall be cultivated by the spade only, and proper attention shall be paid to its cultivation.
2. No allotment, or any part thereof, shall be under-let or exchanged.
3. The rent shall be due on 1 September in each year, and shall be paid before the crop is taken off the ground.
4. All tenants shall maintain a character for morality and sobriety, and shall not frequent a public-house on the Sabbathday.
5. If any tenant fail to pay his rent or to perform any of the foregoing conditions he shall immediately forfeit his allotment, with his crop upon the same, and the landlord or his agent shall take possession and enforce payment of the rent due by sale of the crop or otherwise, as in arrears of rent.

All the tenants are earnestly requested to attend regularly at the House of God during the times of Divine Service, with their families, to the best of their abilities.[28]

At Rothamsted, Sir John Lawes had concluded that the licensed club was the best way of lessening and arresting the evils attendant on drinking. 'If any one,' he wrote, 'will picture to himself the limited accommodation of a labourer's cottage on a winter's evening, with one small fire entirely surrounded by his wife and children, he will hardly blame the man who seeks warmth, quiet, and the society of his fellow-labourers elsewhere. Some attempt made by me to substitute coffee for beer was not successful. It is true the men drank it, and pronounced it very good, as long as I supplied it gratis, but they could not be persuaded to purchase it as a substitute for their beloved beer.'[29] But at the Lyddington Garden Allotments, the Reverend H. Munn sent a private circular to his tenants saying that:

Sad reports have been brought to me lately of the conduct of some in the parish, and among them, I am sorry to say, are tenants of the Allotment Gardens. Such conduct is contrary to the rules on which the allotments are held, and also contrary to the intentions of my predecessor in letting them out to the parishioners. They are intended to improve the conditions of the labourers and their families, giving them employment in the summer evenings, increasing their supply of food, and withdrawing them from the influence of the public-house. But when drinking habits are indulged all these benefits are lost, and the allotments, which were intended to do the labourer good, only increase his means of obtaining intoxicating drinks.[30]

A political struggle

An amendment to the address about allotments, moved

by Mr Jesse Collings in January 1886, and carried by the votes of the bulk of the Liberal members, obliged Lord Salisbury to resign and restored Mr Gladstone to power, who forthwith gave Mr Jesse Collings a subordinate place in his new Administration. Once in office, however, Mr Gladstone did nothing whatever to promote the extension of allotments, the urgent need of which had been the plea for that Government-displacing amendment; and when Mr Jesse Collings refused to assist him in carrying Home Rule for Ireland, which both had till then opposed, Mr Gladstone contemptuously, and I must add ungratefully, described his ex-Secretary to the Local Government Board as a 'certain Mr Jesse Collings' ... The question of allotments has thus acquired a somewhat factitious importance, and has been brought rather more prominently forward than it probably would otherwise have been.

> Lord Fortescue,
> 'Poor Men's Gardens',
> *The Nineteenth Century*,
> [March 1888]

At a local level it was often the clergy who persuaded landlords to provide land for allotments. Pamela Horn records that 'In south Lindsey it was only after a lengthy campaign by the curate of Swaby that the reluctant agents of the Ancaster estate granted five acres to the parish "to keep him quiet", while the Reverend W.M. Pierce saw to it that "almost every poor man in his parishes has an allotment of land". In defiance of the wishes of the farmers he let three acres of his glebe at Fulletby to labourers and helped to provide them with tools.'[31] But the characteristic attitude of country parsons was to support the devastating changes in access to land resulting from the Enclosure Acts. They were enlisted in the army of the powerful to persuade the rural poor that the rights they once possessed were dissolved by Act of Parliament. Not only this, but even charitable bequests of land for the benefit of the poor had, over the years, been diverted from their original purpose.

It was thus that Joseph Ashby of Tysoe found himself involved in reclaiming ancestral rights. In her celebrated biography his daughter explained how the Tysoe Labourers' Charity Lands Allotment Committee had to struggle to win control of the land originally intended for their use:[32]

> In October the Vicar invited the holders of the ten-pole allotments to a tea-party and made a speech to them on their duties. Allotments, he said, might be rightly cultivated by them, under certain conditions. They must have the necessary leisure to till them; they must apply manure; the produce must be consumed at home (which meant they were not free to sell it). A sixteenth of an acre was the right extent. Possibly if a man had no garden at all, it might not be wrong to have two sixteenths. They must on no account spend too much time and strength on the allotment to the neglect of what was due to their masters, not forgetting that their Heavenly Master required spiritual work of them on Sundays.[33]

The campaign of Ashby and his associates led to the Allotment Extension Act of 1882 which required the trustees of charity land in a parish to provide a suitable portion for allotments. If they failed, the Charity Commissioners *could* enforce the law.

Pamela Horn tells a touching story of local determination faced by the entrenched arrogance of the landowning class:

> The seriousness with which many labourers regarded the allotments issue is illustrated by a letter which disgruntled cottagers at Hoggeston, Buckinghamshire, sent to the agent of their landlord, Lord Rosebery. The latter had promised that a suitable plot would be provided to meet the men's needs, but they felt that the agent was responding tardily to that undertaking.

Eventually they plucked up courage to write and tell him so: 'In our humble way we uphold the integrity of his *Lordship's pledged word* at least equally with yourself; we claim at your hands the redemption of his Lordship's kind & unmistakable promise, nor shall we abandon our suit until the latter has been made good.' Nor did they, for they even wrote to Lord Rosebery himself on the subject. In the end their persistence had its reward with the granting of the necessary plots more than a year later. But most villagers lacked the stubborn determination they showed in approaching their social superiors.[34]

A century later the sixth Earl of Rosebery died, and his stately home at Mentmore, which 'glittered with gold' according to the author of *Save Mentmore for the Nation*, was offered to the public. The government declined, and after its treasures had been auctioned at Sotheby's for £6 million, the house was sold to the Maharishi International College for transcendental meditation. 'Lord Rosebery, the good and patriotic aristocrat, even withdrew a few items from the sale in order to present them as gifts to faithful but now sadly departed servants.'[35] There was always a grotesque disparity between the claims of poor people for a patch of land and the response of their masters, and the truth is that the legal owners of rural Britain managed their subject races in exactly the same way that their younger sons managed the colonial empire. They bankrupted the local shopkeepers because it was beneath them to pay bills, but the people they abhorred most were the 'educated natives' with their 'uppity demands'.

The dispossessed 'natives' pursued their campaign in the face of every kind of discouragement. If they were too demanding they could simply be sacked. Land could be offered which was too far away from home to be useful, and as a landlord's *coup de grâce* the rent could be too high. 'The care and cultivation of allotments at considerable distance from a man's home is generally tedious and difficult, while the rent charged for accommodation land near a town or village is often exorbitant.'[36] An exhaustive analysis of the rents actually charged for allotments shows that they were 'from 40 per cent to 500 per cent above the surrounding rents'.[37] Finally, no landlord was under any obligation to provide any allotments at all, except to any good or faithful servant who was suitably deferential. 'In comparison with the rights of more privileged peoples, the English labourer's right to his allotment would be seen more as a symbol of his dispossession than of privilege.'[38] Not all observers of the crisis of agricultural labour at the end of the century were as sanguine as the campaigners on the value of the allotment to alleviate the farm worker's lot. 'Again and again I was informed that one man cannot work an allotment, and do full time at his regular work. A few times a year you must take two or three days off work, or hire someone.'[39] And the investigator of the *Daily News* stressed the lengthening of working hours it implied. An Oxford labourer who had dreamed of a smallholding had a threequarter-acre plot which helped him a great deal to get through the winter, but: 'Jest when the master wants 'e is jest the time when you wants to be on your own ground.' Another man told him: 'I sometimes think I likes the winter better nor summer. In winter, when you done your work, you can go 'ome and rest a ha' a bit o' comfort. But in the summer you has to do yer day's work and then go on the allotment.'[40]

It may have been a political accident that the allotment question brought down a government a century ago, but it was no accident that allotments had become a political issue. It had become important for a whole series of reasons. One was the fact that Gladstone's Franchise Act of 1884 had actually given the vote to the male agricultural labourer, an event that seemed incredible to his employer, confident that his faithful old Hodge would never want to be involved in abstractions like politics. Another was the influence of Joseph Arch's National Agricultural Labourers' Union, which in the face of threats to the livelihood of those who dared to join, had enrolled 86,000 members by 1874. Among the union's aims were both the provision of smallholdings and 'the securing of suitable allotments'. Its treasurer was Jesse Collings, who devised the evocative slogan, 'Three acres and a cow', which won the support of the Liberal Party in which he became an increasingly prominent member as the extension of the franchise enabled his party to make a bid for the new rural vote. Smallholdings and allotments were, as a future Conservative prime minister, Arthur Balfour, noted, entirely unrelated. 'A Smallholdings Bill aims at creating a Peasant Proprietary; an Allotments Bill aims at improving the position of the agricultural labourer while leaving him in the position of an agricultural labourer.'[41] In practice the two campaigns complemented each other. A gain for one was an opportunity for both.

Gladstone declared that the agricultural labourer was practically divorced from the soil, and that immediate legislation was required to reinstate him, but it was the incoming Conservative government that pushed through Parliament the Allotments Act of 1887, which enabled local sanitary authorities to provide allotments and if necessary to acquire land for this purpose by compulsory purchase.[42] The procedure was, however, so cumbersome and expensive, that the initial effect of the Act was to encourage voluntary provision for fear of more effective legislation. Allotment campaigners continued to press the issue, one of them stressing that: 'It is only by persistent, fearless and determined agitation, on the platform and in the press, and by using all the levers that local election contests give, that the existing authorities can be forced into providing allotments ...',[43] and with the establishment of county councils in 1888, the opportunity came. Halley Stewart had been elected to Parliament as an allotment candidate in 1887, and: 'Light began to dawn with the county council elections for January 1889. Allotments were made the test question, and upon "allotments" or "no allotments" every constituency was fought. The allotment party won by a small majority . . .'[44]

More effective legislation followed, and in 1907 the responsibility to provide allotments was imposed on urban local authorities. The consolidating Small Holdings and Allotments Act of 1908 became the basis of the modern responsibility of local councils to provide allotments. Like the population it catered for, the allotment had moved from being part of the fabric of rural life to being part of the pattern of land use and social relationships in towns and cities.

Woodcut by Henry Iles from the *New Statesman*

4
Town gardens

'In those days Nottingham was surrounded by allotments, not
in their hundreds but in their tens of thousands, and the great
Dean Hole, the man who really transformed rose-growing in
Britain, estimated that in his day, about a hundred years ago,
there were some 20,000 of them scattered around what was
then an important town but not yet a city, and the home of
under 200,000 people – an allotment for about every third
family. Most of them, I imagine, were like our family a few
decades later, growing virtually all their own vegetables and
thereby making themselves independent of everyone else for
at least a large portion of the daily diet.'

Harry Wheatcroft,
My Life with Roses,
Odhams, 1959

When Richard Jefferies described the allotment gardens of
the agricultural poor, he noted that in his nearest town
there were allotments of a different kind, let at 1s 6d per
'lug' or perch (thirty square yards) or £12 an acre, and at
that price were 'eagerly caught up' by 'every class, from
labourers and mechanics to well-to-do tradesmen'.[1]

Old maps of medieval towns and cities show that, before
pressure of population filled every vacant space, they were
full of gardens both around and detached from houses. Then
the horticultural areas of intensive cultivation spread
beyond the city walls. All gardeners, rich or poor, amateur
or professional, grew surplus crops for sale since yields were
so uncertain. In London, from the early seventeenth
century, the charter of the Gardeners' Company and the
Fruiterers' Company forbade non-guild members from
selling without permission within six miles of the city. At
the beginning of the ninteenth century, westwards from the
City, vegetable gardens began at Tothill Fields, and

'Chelsea still included a large slab of "common garden land" as well as private market gardens ... Earls Court also had several "common gardens" and from there through Fulham, Parson's Green, Walham Green and Hammersmith the land was almost solid with gardens, much of it common land on which the gardeners rented strips.'[2]

The most famous and most extensive of these urban commons is the Town Moor in Newcastle-upon-Tyne, whose origins are lost in the mists of time. It is said either to have been given to the townsmen by Adam de Jesmond in the thirteenth century, or to have been held by the burgesses 'under a certain fee-farm rent paid to the crown from time immemorial'.[3] For centuries it was under an uneasy dual management of both the Corporation and the Freemen, with each body claiming the right to dig for coal and other minerals, and to graze cattle. 'On the eve of the new year, 1772, part of the Moor ... was advertised, by order of the common council, to be let for purposes of cultivation and improvement. The result was a violent protest, and an action laid by the freemen against this invasion of their alleged rights.'[4] Parliament passed a Bill establishing the right for resident freemen and their widows each to graze two milch cows on the Moor, for the race-course and Cowhill (where fairs are held) and booths, tents and meeting places to be retained, while allowing other portions to be granted to the highest bidders for cultivation. 'Annually, on Guild day, the Stewards of the Freemen elect a herbage committee to superintend the Moor and Leazes; and the rents of the intakes are distributed amongst the poor resident burgesses and widows of burgesses.'[5] A whole series of 'in-takes' and 'out-takes' are today's Town Moor allotments.

In Leicester the ancient Freeman's Common, on land near the city centre, was less fortunate. It was parcelled up into ownership by the freemen of the borough, in perpetuity. One plot-holder explained to us that: 'As these were handed down over the years they came into the possession of descendants, working folk, who used them as allotments. Then, lamentably, the land became valuable real estate and was built on.' But that is not the whole story, for in the 1930s it was possible to claim that: 'There was a period when every third householder in the city possessed an allotment, and when the movement reached its highest point over 16,000 allotments were being cultivated. Leicester is fortunate as far as the obtaining of land is concerned, as Simon de Montfort bequeathed some land situated right in the centre of the town, a condition being that if any part of it were sold the proceeds should be re-invested in land. This has enabled the Corporation to buy a huge belt of land nearly all round the city.'[6]

As early as 1731 in Birmingham, 'a flourishing allotment system existed within the urban boundary and immediately adjacent to the urban core'.[7] Known as 'small gardens' or 'guinea gardens', they were celebrated by a historian of the years 1810–20 as 'a "hobby" with the Birmingham working man' in which 'the cultivation of flowers was carried to great perfection by him',[8] and in 1825 the author of *A Picture of Birmingham* recorded that 'from the west end of this area (north of the town centre) we enjoy a pleasing and lively summer-view over a considerable tract of land laid out in small gardens. This mode of applying plots of ground in the immediate vicinity of the town, is highly beneficial to the inhabitants ... They promote healthful exercise and rational enjoyment among families of the artisans; and, with good management, produce an ample supply of those wholesome vegetable stores, which are comparatively seldom tasted by the middling classes when they have to be purchased.'[9]

But Elizabeth Galloway stresses that:

There was little similarity in either function or appearance between the 'guinea garden' and its successor, the allotment. 'Guinea gardens' had provided a recreational opportunity for middle-class citizens living nearby, and appear to have been cultivated as both ornamental and productive gardens in developing industrial towns such as Coventry and Sheffield, as well as in Birmingham. By contrast, urban allotments arose out of their rural counterpart, providing non-agricultural labourers (many of whom had only recently moved from the country into the town), with the opportunity to supplement their low wages by growing fruit and vegetables. Allotments were introduced into urban areas from the early eighteenth century onwards and so existed alongside 'guinea gardens' for at least fifty years, but the two concepts were so different in character and clientele that neither seems to have exerted much influence on the other.[10]

The most ancient of Nottingham's allotment sites, Hunger Hills, has been in the hands of the Corporation for many centuries. In 1605 it was divided into 'burgess parts' and rented to thirty burgesses or freemen or their widows. In 1842, on the petition of the Nottingham Independent Cottage Garden Society, the land was formed into 400 gardens, let for about £1 per annum each, whose tenants were usually stockingers or 'twisthands' in the local hosiery industry. The rent was considered high, but apart from fruit and vegetables the Hunger Hills gardeners grew flowers, and particularly roses, for sale. These became famous and were sent twice a week to the Manchester and Liverpool markets.[11] In 1885 the Corporation sought, unsuccessfully, to make the site available for house-building. 'They tried to persuade garden-holders to leave with compensation so that destitute "respectable working men" out-of-work due to the depression in many trades, could be employed building new houses.'[12]

With their sunny slopes, tall hedges and brick-built summerhouses, the Hunger Hills allotments were always secret gardens, hard to find and easy to be lost amongst. A local historian reported in the 1920s that the sixty acres were divided into 540 plots averaging 540 square yards each and that: 'There is one main avenue, and many small ones, presenting on a map the appearance of a great maze, and greatly puzzling a spectator on his first approach, for they seem to run in all directions.'[13] In his day the hedges were 'well-trimmed, and are planted with fruit trees, currant and gooseberry bushes'. Fifty years later another visitor found them unkempt and hanging down with untaken fruit:

> Seeing some of the decaying huts, complete with little cupboards and mantelpieces, and large windows, it seems strange that they were only used as summer-houses. Then, on talking with long-term gardeners, it turns out that many people actually lived on the gardens. One man's wife had been born and brought up with a family of eight in a house on the patch he now uses, and her family had lived there as far back as anyone knew. They carried water from the taps, but had no light except incandescent lamps. In 1929 they were told that when the current occupier died they would have to make the house uninhabitable in a fortnight or pay for the Corporation to do it – so they pulled it down in 1940.[14]

The period when the Hunger Hills were converted to allotment plots was a time of depression in the knitting trades, and in Nottingham, just as in rural areas, allotments were recommended as an alternative to the rigours and expense of the Poor Law. In 1841 James Orange, pastor of a nonconformist chapel in Nottingham, published his *Plea for the Poor*, setting out what became known as 'Orange's Cottage Garden Plan'. 'His intention was to transplant a measure of peasant husbandry to the midst of industrial society. For many years framework knitters had worked their allotments in the outlying villages, but Orange wanted to benefit working men in the town ... The first step was to obtain land and divide it into allotments of one-quarter of an acre, an area which Orange considered to be no more than supplementary to an industrial occupation. It should support a small family for about thirteen weeks, sufficient "to carry them through any necessity which may be forced upon them in a depression of trade or a time of sickness".[15]

Within the city the Burgess Rights Committee refused his request for a few acres of common land, preferring to rent at £25 an acre, 'which only the better paid artisans and tradesmen could afford'. In the industrial villages on the fringe, land *was* available. At Caunton a site bequeathed for the benefit of the parish was converted into allotments, a hundred plots were contributed at Arnold, and at Basford the Duke of Portland let seventy-five acres. But the scheme failed at Beeston, Lenton, Radford, Sneinton, Hyson Green and Ratcliffe, until the Nottingham Enclosure Act of 1845 and the Nottingham Freemen's Allotments Act of 1850 made land available.[16]

Other towns and cities had a similar pattern of *ad hoc* provision, ancient freemen's rights and local Acts of Parliament, until, by the turn of the century, allotment gardens were more an urban than a rural phenomenon, simply because of the huge expansion of the urban population. The fringe of every city was becoming the kind of mixture of rural pursuits and land uses that is described in the Nottinghamshire-set novels of D.H. Lawrence. Thus a woman born in 1895 recalls her father's allotment among the cornfields of what is now urban Nottingham:

You know the corner of Radford Boulevard and Alperton Road, opposite Gregory Boulevard corner? That's where the cornfield was ... My dad put produce into the shows on Churchfield Lane on a field – two days, Saturdays and Sundays, where he used to win prizes for his marrows and potatoes. Well, this cornfield, when they'd cut the corn a lot of we kids used to go in gleaning, and we'd eat the corn that they'd left. Yes, it was so near to town that you can hardly think it's true, can you? But we used to go and play most of the two days at the show field where he got prizes for his marrows and his potatoes, and sweet peas.[17]

The Small Holdings and Allotments Act of 1908 consolidated the previous legislation obliging local authorities, urban as well as rural, to provide allotments for the 'labouring population' where it could not be obtained privately, and 'the provision of allotments in *urban* areas began to show a significant increase, both in the public and the private sector. In 1913, evidence given to a Land Inquiry Committee showed a keen demand for allotments in almost every urban area'[18]. Soon afterwards this demand grew overwhelmingly because of the First World War. 'A few days after the outbreak of war, the Board of Agriculture and Fisheries made an appeal to the owners of private gardens to preserve their surplus stocks of vegetable seedlings for distribution to allotment holders; and the Royal Horticultural Society appointed a committee to assist in the distribution of these surplus plants.'[19] But drastic measures to increase the number of allotments were not taken until dangerously late in that war, as, like the delayed introduction of food rationing, such a measure was thought bad for morale in revealing the success of the German blockade and the huge shipping losses. Finally, in December 1916 powers were given to local authorities to take over unoccupied land for allotments without the owners' consent. In February 1917, unrestricted U-boat warfare began and the Kaiser threatened to 'starve the British people, until they, who have refused peace, will kneel and plead for it'.[20]

Common land, parks and playing fields were subdivided, dug and planted. The government's Food Production Department appointed horticultural advisers everywhere and after the 1917 campaign inspectors were appointed to seek out more land. 'These representatives resorted to considerable ingenuity to revitalize flagging interest and succeeded to a striking degree. It generally sufficed to intimate to a lagging local authority that it was tumbling down the record of achievement. Its *amour propre* was wounded, and it rebuckled into its task with enhanced vim ... Headmasters of public and secondary schools, commandants of auxiliary hospitals, and the authorities in charge of work-houses, infirmaries, asylums and reformatories were urged to let themselves go and to turn all available land to account.'[21] The nation's leaders made their token efforts. 'The King directed that potatoes, cabbages and other vege-tables should replace the normal geraniums in the flower-beds surrounding the Queen Victoria Memorial opposite Buckingham Palace and in the royal parks; Lloyd George let it be known that he was growing King Edward potatoes in his garden at Walton Heath; and the Archbishop of Canter-bury issued a pastoral letter sanctioning Sunday Work.'[22] It is recorded that: 'Lloyd George had stormy meetings with Britain's "landowner Junkers", men who were fiercely patriotic in their fashion but saw the order as the biggest challenge since the break-up of the feudal estates. Was it for this that their fathers had enclosed the family lands?"[23]

The results of this campaign astounded everyone. The number of allotments in 1913 was variously estimated as between 450,000 and 600,000. By the end of the year they numbered something between 1,300,000 and 1,500,000. In 1918 it could be claimed that 'for every five occupied houses throughout the two kingdoms there is one allotment! Truly we have become a nation of gardeners to be able to record such a startling result ... which culminated in the produc-tion of 2,000,000 tons of vegetables.'[24] In 1914 there were 27,680 railway allotments on 2,102 acres. By 1918 the figure had grown to 93,473 on 6,081 acres.[25] But the war had spread allotment gardening beyond any limits of occupation or class. The phrase 'the labouring population' was dropped from the legislation in England and Wales, and in Scotland in 1919. The war introduced a vast new population to the habit and the techniques of vegetable gardening. This was essentially an urban population. 'The greatest individual additions had, of course, taken place in the towns, especially in those centres which had previously been addicted to the movement. Many urban centres trebled and quadrupled their allotments, whilst the country districts added at most two-thirds to their previous total.'[26] And precisely because of this, the First World War gave the allotment movement, as Thorpe noted, an urban emphasis it has never since lost.

'Allotments', wrote the enthusiastic F.E. Green, 'have now become woven into the texture of our national life', and he declared in 1918 that this 'new short-sleeved army, numbering now over 1,300,000 men and women', had 'held the pass with the spade while the country was in danger of semi-starvation. There is something more due to them than a notice to quit in 1920.' They had achieved miracles of food production and had 'done this without any allure of high guaranteed prices such as have been held out to farmers before they would put their hands to the plough ... They have converted wastes of urban lands, which have produced nothing but coarse grass for years, into a condition of high fertility.' Having done all this, they would not be 'content to see their work undone in 1920, and their allotments producing good food for the nation slip back into derelict sites where tuffets of twitch and water grass will once more claim possession of land which had grown potatoes and beans.'[27]

Although to this day there are many allotment sites and local societies that owe their origin to the First World War, it was evident that the 50,000 requisitioned acres would have to be returned to their owners. The Conservators of Epping Forest, which includes large East London open spaces like Wanstead Flats and Chingford Plain, had unwillingly surrendered land for allotments during the war, and as soon as it was over fought long and bitterly contested legal battles, taken as far as the High Court, to get the land back for public recreational use.[28] The allotment-holders claimed that allotment work was also a recreation and that they were helping to combat profiteering in vegetable prices. It was in fact an embarrassment for government that the allotment gardeners who had served their purpose in the war effort, insisted on going on growing. Thorpe explains that the demand for allotments, particularly from returning ex-servicemen, continued unabated:

In 1919 it was estimated that no less than 7000 new applicants were coming forward each week, but the number of vacant plots was not nearly enough to accommodate them; moreover, as soon as the holder of an allotment left, his neighbour would certainly try to seize the opportunity to enlarge his plot. Various theories were advanced to account for this unprecedented demand. First, the welter of free advice and help which had been available during the war had created a widespread interest in gardening among those who had not previously considered the possibility of taking an allotment. Second, there was, immediately after the war, a steep rise in the price of fresh vegetables, and third, the closure of munitions factories and a general ban on overtime had given many workers more leisure without offering any means of spending it profitably. Lastly, and perhaps this was the most important reason, there were in 1919 large numbers of returning ex-servicemen whose resettlement in civilian life was posing many problems.[29]

Various measures were taken to protect the rights of owners of land requisitioned in war-time and to allay the worries of plot-holders. Through the Agriculture Act of 1920 allotment tenants gained the right to demand compensation for disturbance, and, by the Allotments Act of 1922, they were further safeguarded with provisions against arbitrary ejectment, while local authorities were compelled to appoint an allotment committee with tenant representation. Some 4490 acres of land were made available through that Act, to provide 62,112 plots. But by 1929, 'the number of allotments in England and Wales had fallen below one million, and the area under cultivation was less than 150,000 acres', and 'by 1939 there were only about 815,000 plots covering about 109,000 acres'.[30] Numbers remained higher than the pre-war level, and the decline is usually explained by the return of emergency land to its owners and to the demands of inter-war suburban expansion and house-building. It was claimed that: 'The enemy of urban allotments is not sloth, but the builder.'[31] This comment ignores the fact that the inter-war building boom gave millions of families a domestic garden for the first time. The majority of the houses built in the twenty years between the wars, both by local authorities and by speculative builders, were laid out to the formula of 'twelve to the acre' which had been 'woven into the law' by the Garden City architect Raymond Unwin, whose convictions dominated the Tudor Walters Report of 1918.[32] This was a lower density than that of the bye-law housing typical of the period beteen 1875 and 1914, and was certainly lower than that of almost all the housing built, whether publicly or privately, after the Second World War. It was deliberately intended to meet most families' gardening ambitions, and it did.

However, the experience of the dream years of the 1930s was varied by class and by place. There was actually a small boom in the middle of the decade, described by the Ministry of Agriculture, which was then the government department concerned with allotments, as 'a recent revival of interests'. This rise was the result partly of special measures taken by the Ministry and by local authorities to provide sites; partly of the activities of the Society of Friends in the especially depressed areas of primary industry to fund plots, tools and seeds;[33] and partly of the formation of the Land Settlement Association, whose prime aims were to turn the urban unemployed into smallholders and to provide 'stock' allotments, giving an opportunity to those people who wanted to revive an ancient pattern of self-sufficiency, long frowned upon officially, to keep animals like pigs and poultry on their plots, providing cheap food and a ready supply in manure.[34] The changes during this decade proved to be very different in different parts of the country and across the same city. Some people lost their sites in areas which were redeveloped, but those able to move to the new estates on the fringe of the city were able to enjoy the large allotment sites that many councils provided at that time.[35]

On the outbreak of war again in 1939, the government was ready to avoid the belatedness of the allotment campaign of twenty-two years earlier. A broadcast by the Minister of Agriculture on 4 October 1939 proclaimed that: 'Half a million more allotments properly worked will provide potatoes and vegetables that will feed another million adults and one and a half million children for eight months of the year, so let's get going and let "Dig for Victory" be the matter for everyone with a garden or allotment and every man and woman capable of digging an allotment in their spare time.' The campaign closely resembled that of the First World War. A Cultivation of Lands (Allotments) Order 1939 empowered councils to take over unoccupied land, and the events of 1940 led the Minister to make a further broadcast appeal for 'half a million more allotments'. A barrage of propaganda urged the nation to turn its lawns into vegetable gardens and local authorities to encourage new allotment sites. The first Ministry 'Growmore' bulletin with a cropping plan for a ten-rod allotment was issued in 1939, and by 1942 ten million instructional leaflets were being distributed annually. The Ministry organized Dig for Victory exhibitions all over the country and urged local authorities to set up demonstration plots, which 'proved of first-class educational, propaganda and psychological value'.[36] The results, as expected, were phenomenal. 'A survey of manual workers about the middle of the war indicated that over half kept either an allotment or a garden. By 1943–4, domestic hen-keepers were producing about twenty-five per cent of the country's officially known supplies of fresh eggs, and by the end of the war the Domestic Poultry Keepers' Council had over one and a quarter million members owning twelve million birds. Pig-keeping was another craze – there were eventually six thousand, nine hundred "Pig Clubs" with hundreds of thousands of members, feeding their beasts on kitchen waste.'[37]

The government estimated in 1944 that the food grown on

allotments, private gardens and plots of land cultivated by service personnel amounted to ten per cent of all food produced in Britain.[38] There were probably 1,500,000 allotment gardens by the end of the war. Many of today's veteran gardeners look back fondly to those wartime days that introduced them to the habit of keeping an allotment. But an inevitable decline followed. An attempt was made, in the austerity of post-war Britain, to popularize the slogan 'Dig for Plenty', and in 1948, addressing the assembled plotholders of the then National Allotments and Gardens Society, the Minister of Agriculture declared that: 'Today we are digging for our very lives, for food, for dollars and for our self-respect.'[39] But this mood was temporary.

Apart from the return of the wartime emergency sites to their peacetime uses, post-war reconstruction and the wholesale redevelopment of city centres brought great pressure on urban and suburban land for new housing, schools, hospitals and industrial sites. Repeating the history of the 1930s, people were moving to new homes with larger gardens. The exact shifts in land ownership and use are difficult to aggregate, but Thorpe calculated that while one-fifth of council allotment plots were lost in the 1950s, the loss of private plots rose from one-fifth in that decade to one-half during the next.[40] Ambiguities pervade council data as to whether the land lost was 'statutory' or 'temporary' allotment land. But the variation between places that was seen between the wars was repeated. In Leeds and Birmingham private sites declined dramatically: in Leeds between 1948 and 1963 from 5000 plots to 500, from 400 acres to 43; in Birmingham the number was halved from 4000 plots in 1948.[41] At the same time some cities lost the bulk of their temporary plots, the figures for Birmingham falling from 8881 in 1948 to 2395 in 1963, while statutory plots in the same period fell by only 150 from the 1948 figure of 8968, though the data provided by local authorities are very ambiguous.[42] Sites within city boundaries were redeveloped for housing. The people who wanted plots had

Allotment Demand and Supply 1935–78

Year	total plots	acreage	vacant		waiting list
1935	609352	59403	18130*		(no info)
1950	1039233	105281	62839	(6%)	33744
1960	801061	85169	101512	(12.6%)	6573
1970	532964	58242	111126	(21%)	5870
1973	467755	52300	36274	(7.7%)	27208
1975	439750	47455	24965	(5.5%)	83298
1977	497793	49873	20572	(4.1%)	121037
1978	479301	49105	23178	(4.7%)	(not available)

(source DOE; *approximated from acreage given)

none nearby and were the very citizens without the mobility to reach sites further out, while other sites remained next to areas developed for industry with no housing around them. Their survival could not be justified.[43]

Quite separately, plots on railway land were reduced by a quarter in the 1950s and by a further half in the next seven years. The rationalization of the lines in the 'Beeching' years was responsible, and numbers fell from 75,306 plots on 4321 acres in 1948 to 38,094 on 2128 acres in 1963. A total of 2963 acres (over 30,000 plots) of the most protected (or 'statutory') council land was disposed of in the seven years before 1967.[44] Pressures for development made all allotment land vulnerable, and a decline in interest made their loss harder to resist. While 5.6 per cent of all plots were empty in the 1930s, 20 per cent were vacant by the mid-1960s.[45] Landlords may carry some responsibility for this, and there is evidence that many thousands of people were fed up with working plots that were on poor ground, badly located, had no adequate water supply, were unfenced, and under threat of development with the loss of many years' invested effort.[46]

Advances in living standards and aspirations, as well as the machinery of social welfare and the prospect of full employment, had released people from the financial *need* to produce their own food. Changes in technology and marketing were promoting convenience foods as a symbol of liberation from drudgery. The prevalent image of allotment gardening suffered from associations with poverty, charity and wartime needs. Allotments became the butt of jokes when people wanted to distance themselves from these conditions and associations, especially in the years after rationing in the 1950s and then during the period of affluence and the youth culture of the 1960s. When Harold Wilson's reforming government of 1964 commissioned Harry Thorpe's Committee of Inquiry into Allotments, the intention must have been to straighten out an antiquated, backward-looking activity, selfishly squatting on valuable urban land. But neither the government nor Thorpe anticipated the changes that would follow, nor the new impetus for 'the greening of the cities' that was to arise in the 1970s and 1980s. Nor indeed did the allotment movement.

The aggressive institutional modernity and the 'white heat' of new technologies of the 1960s remain the dominant culture in the 1980s, but a whole series of undercurrents have changed not only our perceptions of the allotment, but actual demands for plots. A book by Rachel Carson on the environmental and ecological dangers of modern food production and land use, published in the early 1960s, had reached, through the diffusion of its message, a vast audience.[47] This new ecological awareness was linked with the anti-consumerism of the various alternative cultures that arose from the commercialization of life in the 1960s, and with the paradox that rocketing land prices were accompanied by a continual spread of vacant sites in the cities. Like the empty office blocks, sites were too *valuable* to be used.[48] The oil crisis of 1973, apart from all its other consequences, made people more aware of the transport and packaging element in food prices, which rose steeply in the following years, and this combination of trends sharply affected the demand for allotments. The disposal of sites was cut by eighty-four per cent between 1970 and 1977, though railway allotments continued to dwindle from 18,564 plots on 1142 acres in 1970 to 8885 plots on 670 acres in 1978.[49]

Some councils developed huge waiting lists in the 1970s: 4060 people in Avon alone, 15,533 in Greater London, 5697 in Essex and 5559 in the West Midlands in 1976. Humberside recorded one vacant plot out of 4792, and Bedfordshire six out of almost 4000 in that year.[50] As ever, the pattern was different in other localities. Derbyshire had nearly a thousand 'empties' out of 7000, a quarter of the vacant plots being in private ownership, including those of the National Coal Board. The Department of the Environment ceased its collection of data in 1980, but it is possible to build up a picture of the course of change in the 1980s by looking at a number of places around Britain. Between 1971 and 1987 the London Borough of Haringey increased its plots by a third, although the land used decreased by five per cent, as average plot sizes were reduced. The waiting list was 520 in 1976 and 68 in 1977.[51] Newcastle-upon-Tyne had 3319 plots in 1963 and in 1987 still has 3100, with few vacancies.[52] Places as diverse as Wigton in Cumbria, Bedworth in the West Midlands, villages in the Stratford on Avon district and around Chester le Street in Durham and the London Borough of Hackney all have few or no vacancies.[53]

However, in the London Borough of Hounslow (where there were 2887 plots in 1976 and much the same, 2780, in 1987) the waiting list in 1976 was 640 with 108 vacant plots, while in 1987 there were 45 people waiting and at the same time 740 vacant plots.[54] In Rochford, Essex, where there are only 145 plots, there are 24 people on the waiting list. In Thurrock in the same county, there are 1537 plots, few unoccupied, and 265 people waiting. There is a flourishing allotment community in Chelmsford, but there are only 20 on the waiting list and one-third of its 1250 plots are vacant.[55] In Birmingham there was a waiting list of 2000 in 1976, with no vacant plots; by 1987 there were only a few dozen people on the list for its total of 8000 plots.[56] Bristol had hardly any vacant plots in 1976 and a thousand would-be plot-holders. In 1987 one-seventh of the city's 7000 plots were vacant, with 250 on the waiting list. In 1975 Irene Evans conducted a survey of allotment provision in Scotland. She found that nineteen Scottish districts had no allotments at all, and that: 'As far as the cities are concerned, Dundee has the best allotment provision. It provides one allotment per 270 people, Aberdeen provides one per 350, Edinburgh has one per 420 and Glasgow one per 950.'[57] She told us of her conviction that with allotments, as with other aspects of social provision, there was an *acceptance culture*: people used what was available, but would seldom express a demand for what was not available. In those places where provision was best, as in Dundee, waiting lists were longest.[58]

The allotment scene at the end of the 1980s is clearly diverse. It seems reasonable to infer a slight fall over the decade in the overall number of cultivated plots, although such is the variety of local experience, many will deny this. Our experience, and that of allotment-holders and local authority officers we have talked to, confirms the survival of the '1970s influx' to a considerable degree, although the acute increase following the potato price rise in the mid-1970s was not sustained. The build-up of new plot-holders has levelled out. Several council officers told us that there was a failure to attract 'upwardly mobile people' into allotment gardening because they preferred recreation with more glamour and panache, sedulously promoted by commercial interests including councils themselves with lavishly equipped leisure centres, for those who can pay. Others said that families preferred a day in the country. A few of them actually stressed the importance of allotments for unemployed people and the steps their councils were taking to help. The most remarkable result of the cultural changes of the post-war years is the sheer diversity of today's allotment-holders.

The century began with the shift in emphasis from the cottager's plot to the garden site for the urban labouring poor. It ends with the allotment raised in status and recognition, and used by a cross-section of the whole community. Demographic changes and the huge outward movement of population have brought a new demand for village plots, where many old charitable sites remain, even though the trustees told us that it was frequently hard to observe strictly the original donors' intentions ('It's often difficult to find the local poor these days'). There are also many thousands of people in village, town, suburb and city for whom holding an allotment is, and always has been, part of the ordinary fabric of family life, taken for granted until it is threatened.

But the amazing fact is that the number of people who cultivate allotments, added to those on waiting lists in 1978, was practically the same, at 650,211, as in the original boom days just before the First World War, and that the number of council plots is 50,000 more *today* than in the next-best peacetime peak in the 1930s.[59] There must be something like half-a-million allotments now, a remarkable figure for a movement whose imminent death has been prophesied for years.

5
A family affair?

'The women never worked in the vegetable gardens or on the allotments, even when they had their children off hand and had plenty of spare time, for there was a strict division of labour and that was "men's work". Victorian ideas, too, had penetrated to some extent, and any work outside the home was considered unwomanly. But even that code permitted a woman to cultivate a flower garden . . .'

Flora Thompson
Lark Rise,
Oxford University Press, 1939

Although the saying, 'When Adam delved and Eve span', dates from the fourteenth century, Flora Thompson, recalling village life in Oxfordshire in the 1880s, was probably right in seeing as particularly Victorian the idea that in the families of the poor, women should not cultivate the soil. A government report of 1867 on 'The Employment of Children, Young Persons and Women in Agriculture' declared that working on the land would 'almost unsex a woman' and that it would generate 'a further very pregnant social mischief by unfitting or indisposing her for a woman's proper duties at home'.[1]

In fact, of course, women have always worked on the land, out of necessity, and allotments – though seen traditionally as a male preserve – have often been, from the same necessity, a focus of activity for the whole family. When Raphael Samuel compiled his remarkable account of Headington Quarry in Oxfordshire, one old informant, Fred Tolley, told him how potato-pulling was 'treated like a harvest; the whole family was roped in, and the mother and the boys spent more time on it than the old man himself'. He remembered how:

The old man used to march us up there. I can hear him now, when we were picking up 'taters. 'Take 'em up, don't tread the buggers in.' ... We used to have a couple of days off school, when we got the 'taters up. We used to ... borrow the old man's pony and cart, to get them home ... We used to go up, mother and us boys, and dig up all day and when the old chap come home from work, he come straight up and load them up and away we come. Once we dug up the wrong plot – someone else's potatoes – and the old man come up at night; he swore, but he took them round to the fellow ... it ended all right.[2]

The grand-daughter of another man at Headington Quarry recalls how: 'All the boys had to help, mind you, even though they went to work. When they come home their work wasn't done, and his wife used to go up there.'[3] Spike Mays tells the story of an allotment tragedy he caused as a small child before the First World War:

Sunday was always the best day at Glemsford, because my father would take me to his allotment. I used to sit there in the sun ... and watch his feverish hoeings, diggings and plantings, to grow us food. He was very good at gardening and used to grow parsnips so sturdy and long that they won prizes at the Flower Show ... Even today I associate the word 'vegetables' with my father's rolled up sleeves, his toil and sweat.

'We must watch out fer the weeds, young feller-me-lad, an' pull 'em up,' he used to say. 'Weeds don't never do nothing useful ... They choke the life outer the good things by stealin' their food ... They're just like a lot of wicked men in this wicked old world. Growin' fat an' strong by stealin' from others ... If we don't keep a sharp lookout an' pull 'em up the minute we see 'em, we shall starve.' Watching the big blade of his shut-knife slice through bread and raw onion, I sat on his knee and put my finger into one of his sweat bands, then into my mouth ... I remember the salty taste, the shock of his emphasis on the word *starve* ...

One Sunday, instead of going to his allotment my father went to sing his solo in the church choir for the Harvest Festival. Perhaps concerned that the wicked weeds might win if my father was not there to do them mischief, I went to his allotment alone, and without permission.

Hours later my mother, who had been driven to distraction by my absence, found me. I was weeding, wantonly. She arrived in time to see the last juicy carrot uprooted from its tilthy bed; to see too, that every bold and bulbous Spanish onion had suffered a similar fate. Her hands flew to her face to hide her distress. 'You wicked, wicked child ... Your poor father's been a-slavin' to grow us food ... Now look what you've done ... Look at it! Jest you wait till I get you indoors ... jest you wait!' ...

I knew no words to tell her my fear of starvation; my fear that because my father was thanking God at the top of his voice for all things safely gathered in, instead of being at his plot fighting the weeds, starvation was imminent ...

'I were only weedin', I said.[4]

And Ken Ausden, remembering the years just before the Second World War at Swindon, where his father was a railwayman, tells how:

Our allotment was about a mile from our house, along the canal tow-path, across the other side of the town near the railway sidings. It was a big allotment, about twenty lug, and in the spring we'd often spend all day there on a Saturday. Mum and Dad and all the kids and a great basket of jam sandwiches, a thermos of tea and a bottle of Tizer. We all had jobs to do – Dad digging, Mum putting in the peas and beans and cabbage plants, and us kids hoeing and weeding and fetching cans of water from the brook when we weren't watching the trains go by. I hated it. It put me off gardening for life.[5]

If he hated the family outings in the spring, it was even worse being sent alone to pick the family's greenstuff for the week in the frozen January of 1939. 'Dad being poorly with his cough and Mum washing and cooking and me being the eldest and the only one with a bike. Ignoring the notice "Cycling prohibited on the Canal Path", I'd belt along on my drop-handlebar skid-iron, pick sprouts and kale and broccoli and cabbage till there was no feeling left in my bloodless, frozen fingers and then pedal laboriously back home with a bulging bag swinging from each handlebar and a heavy saddle-bag behind . . .'[6]

In the late 1960s, Paul Thompson and Thea Vigne conducted a study of 'Family Life and Work Experience before 1918' based on life-history interviews with 444 men and women born between 1870 and 1906 in various parts of England, Scotland and Wales. When asked about their parents' leisure interests, one or two mentioned their mothers as allotment-holders. A woman born in 1890 explained: 'Yes, me mother was a keen gardener. Very keen. Had a plot in Mill Lane. Yes. Down by the railway wall you know. And she did it until she died. At eighty-five she did. Yes, it was her – you know – well you thought it was her one delight.'[7] And a waggon-builder's wife, born in 1888, recalled that, 'I had a friend, and she – they – had their allotment next to ours and she kept two goats. I used to go and help her hold them. I used to hold them and she used to milk them.'[8]

But many of the respondents mentioned the allotment as a commitment that structured their fathers' lives, especially in the families of men in occupations particularly associated with allotment-holding – miners, railwaymen and gas-workers. 'My father used to have a garden. Yes, what they called a pit garden. All the pitmen had them.'[9] 'Dad always had an allotment. Being in the gas company they all had a

piece of ground.'[10] 'Well my father, of course, had an allotment. And lots of men would have allotments they would
work. O yes.'[11] 'Father had an allotment down on the railway line, so much a year.'[12]

One respondent explained that: 'Father spent an hour or
two on the allotment every night',[13] while another mentioned that her father worked there 'until dusk'.[14] Where did
father spend his time? – 'out on the allotment'.[15] 'On a
Saturday you did your allotment', explained a joiner born in
1879 in Edinburgh.[16] And a woman born in 1878 in Melton
Mowbray, where her father was a pattern-maker, described
how: 'He was very fond of his greenhouse – and gardening
and he – also had a piece of allotment and he had a pig. And
of course, Sundays, they used to – friends used to come up
and have a look at the garden and talk about these things
you see ... what they grew and what they did. Sort of
homely affairs.'[17] Another remembered her unemployed
father: 'He had his allotment up here on Pewley Way which
was his hobby. That was his hobby. No, he more or less
broke up after he – they – well you know – you know what a
man is when – er – the work stops.'[18]

A tin-miner's son from Camborne recalled how his father
would make use of every scrap of land: 'Well - he did have a
bit of a garden up Town Moor, but he had the biggest garden
at Porkellis. But up Troon Moor he never left anything
unturned that he could turn – in the vegetables, for the
house, you know what I mean, doesn't matter how small he
would utilize the land ...'[19]

Often these Edwardian children mentioned that their
parents had several plots. One recalled how his father was 'a
big gardener' so that 'all his time was devoted to the garden
you know. In fact he had several allotments, he was as big as
that ... two or three – even four – I remember him with four
allotments. In fact he used to talk about half an acre you
know.'[20] And a man born in Arnold, Nottinghamshire, in
1894, who had fifteen siblings, reckoned that his miner
father grew enough vegetables to last this big family for

about one third of the year. 'You see, me Dad had got three –
what they call club gardens – up Spout Lane, besides that
one at home.' Three extra ones? 'Three. Three hundred
yards each. So we had nine hundred yards as he were gardening for his vegetables and gooseberries ... and rasp-
berries. Apple tree or two and a plum. And me Dad bred
pigs.'[21]

A theatre-orchestra musician worked every night, but, as
his daughter recalls, 'he managed to keep three allotments
going ... I often wonder ... Mind you, we children did a bit
of weeding and setting out and things like that, you know,
we helped him, but ... He kept us in vegetables and flowers.
Yes. Mind you he had plenty of children to go down and
weed, and do all that, and he would give his orders...'[22]
Other children of that generation remember a more limited
role: 'When you went up there did you ever do any planting
or anything?' 'No, we never did any, no.' 'Would you help
your father?' 'Yes, we might watch him and – he would tell
us about it, you know, what he'd grown, and proudly give it
to us to take home for our meal the next day [in] which we
always had our own vegetables.'[23]

The daughter of a maker of hand-sewn shoes who came
from Luton remembers happy picnics on the allotment: 'And
they always had allotment gardens where they used to grow
all the vegetables and they used to grow beautiful flowers,
used to show in the flower shows. Yes, my father used to win
cups and medals, gold medals and carvers and all sorts of
beautiful things. Showing flowers ... My mother used to
take tea for all of us to the garden. We had a garden about a
mile from home. And she'd pack up all the stuff you know
and we used to have lovely picnics at the garden. And my
Dad used to give me a penny a day to tie his sweet peas
up...'[24] Similarly, the daughter of a Greenwich waterman
who always had an allotment says: 'he was a very good
gardener. So he kept us up with beetroots and lettuce and
onions'. 'Did you help in the garden?' 'Oh yes, we used to go
and help him to weed it.'[25] 'Was it your father who tended

the allotment?', an Edinburgh woman was asked. 'Yes, yes,' she replied, 'And my mother. And the family.'[26]

Phyllis Reichl looks back to 1921 in Birmingham when: 'The harvesting and consumption of all those delectable products from Father's allotment concerned us children closely and we had to help ... One of my most treasured memories is of long summer evenings or Sunday mornings (he worked on Saturday morning and Saturday afternoons were for watching football and cricket), when my young sturdy father wheeled his wooden barrow back with his spade and fork on top of the week's supply of vegetables.'[27] But a man born in 1898, whose father was unemployed, recalled bitterly that he and his brother used to do all the allotment weeding and turning over, while his father collected the money from people who came round on a Sunday morning to buy flowers. He explained that 'his father used to grow flowers and sell them round the district. But even though they helped in the garden they never received any benefit from the proceeds – his father always kept that, as he put it, for boots. He seemed to think that this was very, very unfair and obviously still felt very resentful about it. He said it was very hard work for children, weeding.'[28]

That some of these memories should be continually cherished, but that others should still rankle after many decades, or that Ken Ausden can claim to have been put off gardening for life by his childhood experience, indicates that the allotment cannot necessarily be seen as a reinforcement for the cement of family affections. Many more old people, whose childhood was spent in Edwardian or inter-war Britain, remember not that Dad was down on the allotment producing food for the family, but that he was down at the pub or club drinking up the week's wages. Both were retreats from the overcrowded family home.

In the 1950s, when Norman Dennis and his colleagues surveyed a South Yorkshire mining town, Ashton (recognizable as Featherstone), they found a society where boys were destined to be miners and girls were destined to be miners' wives. They were in a male society with its leisure centred around the pub, the working-men's club and the bookies' office. 'Institutionalized leisure activities are predominantly for males, and there is a virtual and definite exclusion of women from any social activities.' There was plenty of money around, and it was spent on gambling, 'sprees' and outings, while 'fresh fruit and vegetables are often neglected when preserved foods, much more expensive, are bought'.[29] Allotment-holders, survivors from an older culture, remained, but: 'Among men who have allotments there are those, a minority, who spend so much time there as to separate themselves from their families for considerable periods.'[30] By the 1980s, Ray Garner, interpreting the meaning of the allotment sheds of South Yorkshire, concluded that: 'For some men the "gardens" are considered as being their natural home, when the house is considered as a place to experience the shared activities of family life.' To him, 'Allotment gardening, or to be more accurate, activities conducted on allotment gardens, are almost without exception male oriented. This is not because women are not interested in gardens but simply that established attitudes and working patterns dictate that the allotments are almost exclusively a male domain. It is considered as an annexe to the working-man's club or the betting shop.'[31]

In many places and on many sites this would be vigorously denied. There are more and more women working on allotments, often with their partners and often alone. Nick Allen, whose wife is the registered tenant, recognizes the plot as an important part of conjugal solidarity, and maybe family solidarity too. He is able to 'contribute heavy labour, as a task valued by the rest of the family in a way that jogging is not'. Sheila Allen follows her father, a keen gardener for many years.[32] In other households, nowadays, there is a team relationship, with both immersed in the allotment. Joan and Harry Bone work closely in preparation for the Pot Leek exhibitions, measuring and making tallies of their likely competitors for the World Championship.[33] Even in the archetypal male bastion of the pigeon loft, there are women's pigeon clubs, women sharing the time on the site and men and women contesting their pigeons alongside each other.[34]

But in 1986 it was regarded as news, not just that a woman should win prizes with her garden produce, but that, in Lancashire, she should have an allotment at all. The style of reporting this is as revealing as the story: 'Up North – where men are men and women are expected to know their places – Mary Ellis came as a bit of a shock. For the petite Ms Ellis ... has been invading the traditionally male stronghold of the allotment. What's more, she's also made something of an assault on showbenches around the Lancashire town of Colne – with resounding success. In 1984 she won the cup for the best exhibit in the Earby show with her three seed onions and last season came up with numerous first prizes and the top trophy in the members' section.' When she took over the allotment because her husband was 'fed up' with it, the 'average age of males then on site was seventy-ish and the reception accorded to the pretty 23-year-old was slightly bemused, if not a little hostile in parts. "My neighbours on the site thought I was a joke and because they reckoned I was just going to mess about, they didn't have any time for me", says Mary. "Once they saw I was serious about it everything changed though." Eleven years after she started allotment gardening, Mary is no longer the only woman on the site and she says there are several couples who work their plot together and even bring the family along as well.'[35]

Thorpe's committee found one local association whose members included 'getting away from the wife and childen' among their reasons for taking a plot, and they remarked that: 'We wonder whether a fairly large number share something of the feelings of the one anonymous allotment-holder who bravely told us that his *only* reason for taking an allotment was to get away from his wife! It is clear that the majority of allotment-holders receive little assistance from their families, and it seems unlikely, on present evidence, that the nucleus of the next generation of allotment-holders might emerge from the children of those who have allotments today.'[36] The committee's reasoning for this statement was based on two of the facts it found. First, that although eighty per cent of allotment-holders lived in urban areas, almost half of these had spent their childhood in the country; and secondly, that over fifty per cent were the sons of former allotment-holders and the great majority of these had worked on their parents' allotments as children. 'There is only a fifty per cent overlap between these two groups of people, and almost seventy-two per cent of today's allotment-holders were either born in rural areas or are the sons of allotment-holders. In this appears to lie much of the movement's strength, for the majority of allotment-holders obviously possess a deep-rooted affection both for gardening and the open air. Indeed, one allotment-holder described it as "inherited enjoyment".'[37]

Thorpe's committee found that only 3.2 per cent of allotment-holders were women and that a mere 1.8 per cent were housewives. They admitted that the figures might present a slightly false picture because of the tendency for tenancy agreements to be made in the husband's name even when the wife spends more time than the husband on the plot, but 'only in a minority of cases do the wives of married allotment-holders help their husbands in the cultivation of the allotment'.[38] Since there was no evidence to suggest that *gardening* was less popular among women than among men, the reasons must lie, the committee concluded, in the nature of *allotment* gardening itself. First, they thought, 'women generally prefer the cultivation of flowers to vegetables and often reach a tacit agreement that they will take charge of the home garden while their husbands look after the allotment'. This was of course the same customary division of horticultural labour that had the force of law in Flora Thompson's village a century ago. The committee did not comment on the fact that it is still far *easier* for husbands to be out of the house for long periods than for wives, but they suggested that vegetable growing demands a greater physical effort than the cultivation of flowers.

Their final point in explaining the relative absence of women from allotment sites was very significant. They thought that 'women tend to be more fastidious than men about the conditions under which they will engage in their hobbies, and the lack of decent facilities, the absence of any strong *social* activity and the general air of dereliction on many allotment sites probably act as considerable deterrents'. This opinion was supported by the important observation that: 'On the relatively few sites which possess good amenities *and* a community spirit, women allotmentholders are much more in evidence than elsewhere.'[39]

Harry Thorpe felt strongly on this point and later remarked on the incredibly poor provision of amenities on most allotment sites when compared with those on, say, school playing fields, municipal bowling greens and golf courses: 'Although watering the garden is a well-known chore, only about fifty per cent of urban allotment sites (many of them having been under cultivation for half to three-quarters of a century!) had acquired a piped water supply. But the fact that less than two per cent had a WC, and only seven per cent a toilet of any kind, makes one wonder whether close parallels might not exist in some respects between the productivity of British allotment gardening on the one hand, and of Chinese horticulture as described in F.H. King's classic work, *Farmers of Forty Centuries*, on the other!'[40] Numerous inquiries had convinced him that if it was hoped to attract younger people – husband, wife and children – to allotment sites, we needed the improved kind of 'leisure gardens' his report recommended, and which had so impressed him in other parts of Europe; proper sanitary facilities, an adequate water supply, car parking and play areas for children, a communal club house and permission to erect summer houses or chalets were all required.

He thought it self-evident that unless such essential

services were provided, most women would remain unwilling to spend all day with their families on the plot. Of course, whether or not there are parking facilities on the site, growing numbers of plot-holders use a car to get there and modern mobility partly compensates for the lack of amenities.

Several local secretaries remarked to us about the different gardening traditions of families of immigrant origin, among whom it is not taken for granted that the *paterfamilias* is the only one working on the allotment. Michael Hyde noticed that among Latvian and Ukranian immigrants in Hull, the whole family would come to work on the plots at Newlands Park. Those Newham film-makers in the 1970s found that 'there is a West Indian man with his English wife and five children, who are fairly unusual on the site as their visits to the allotment are a family outing'. Ted Harwood of the Walthamstow Town Allotments Association saw the same thing among plot-holders of Afro-Caribbean and Asian origins. 'Once they had the offer of a plot, they would all come down, including the tiny children, to clear the ground. And they'd go on coming, the whole family.'[41]

We also take for granted the stereotype of the allotment as an exclusively male side of family life in Britain, opening up only in the 1980s. Yet Raphael Samuel, gathering recollections from the turn of the century, noted how: 'Children still played a big part in the family economy, though compulsory school-going inevitably curtailed it. As for women, their role as housekeepers was a very much more active one than it is today, for the household was to some extent self-supporting: production and consumption, so far from being separated, went hand in hand, bound together in the day-to-day necessities of substance.'[42] And in 1934 a report on the allotments held by unemployed people in Sheffield described how: 'The wives and families constantly visit the allotments and the plots are frequently alive with simple picnic parties, especially at holiday times.'[43] The allotment was always much more of a family affair than we supposed.

6
The gift relationship

'It was now the season for planting and sowing; many gardens and allotments of the villagers had already received their spring tillage, but the garden and the allotment of the Durbeyfields were behindhand. She found, to her dismay, that this was owing to their having eaten all the seed potatoes, – that last lapse of the improvident. At the earliest moment she obtained what others she could procure, and in a few days her father was well enough to see to the garden, under Tess's persuasive efforts; while she herself undertook the allotment-plot which they rented in a field a couple of hundred yards out of the village . . .'

Thomas Hardy,
Tess of the D'Urbervilles, 1891

Hardy's Tess was able to 'borrow' from each of the neighbouring plot-holders a few seed potatoes, and she and her sister 'worked on here with their neighbours till the last rays of the sun smote flat upon the white pegs that divided the plots'. The plots were divided, but the villagers were united in their individual but communal labour. 'Nobody looked at his or her companions. The eyes of all were on the soil', but 'something in the place, the hour, the crackling fires, the fantastic mysteries of light and shade, made others as well as Tess enjoy being there'.

The scene that night on 'the high, dry, open enclosure, where there were forty or fifty such pieces, and where labour was at its briskest when the hired labour of the day had ended' was an epitome of the combination of self-help and mutual aid that characterizes the allotment world. The two phrases are familiar because each was the title of a celebrated book from the Victorian era. *Mutual Aid*, by the Russian anarchist Peter Kropotkin, was a celebration of the propensity to co-operate, whether in insects, animals or humans, intended as a rebuttal of 'social Darwinism', the misinterpretation of Darwin's theory of natural selection which claimed that in the struggle for survival the weak go to the wall. The survival of the fittest did not work that way, Kropotkin claimed, just because, instinctively, we help each other.[1] The adjoining plot-holders automatically shared their seed potatoes with Tess.

Samuel Smiles was a radical journalist whose much-reprinted *Self-Help* exhorted its readers to apply thrift and self-improvement to their lives and not to neglect practical skills. He was outraged that his book had been regarded as a manual of ruthless individualism, declaring in the preface to his second edition that this was 'the very opposite of what it really is ... Although its chief object unquestionably is to stimulate youths to rely upon their own efforts in life rather than depend upon the help or patronage of others, it will also be found ... that the duty of helping oneself in the highest sense involves the helping of one's neighbours.'[2] Tess of the D'Urbervilles had earned the support of the other plot-holders through her willingness to make good the misfortunes that her family had suffered by her own efforts and 'as evening thickened some of the gardening men and women gave over for the night, but the greater number remained to get their planting done, Tess being among them, though she sent her sister home'.

The novelist gave us a passing glimpse of the domestic and communal economy which, below the level of landowners, merchants and industrialists, actually sustained the poor, who were the greater part of the population, rural or urban. And when we compare the Victorian antecedents of our public institutions with the organs of popular mutual aid, the very names speak volumes. On the one side the Workhouse, the Poor Law Infirmary, the National Society for the Education of the Poor in Accordance with the Principles of the Established Church; and on the other, the *Friendly* Society, the Sick *Club*, the *Co-operative* Society, the Trade *Union*. The allotment, with its intimate network of sharing relationships, was one of the nearest and closest of these.

Throughout history the greater part of any population has lived in a culture of this kind of reciprocity, both because of and in spite of poverty. The only thing poor people have been able to give each other has been food, the most important commodity of all. Every gardener has, during the season, gluts and scarcities, and through the year is both a donor and a recipient. The transaction is, as David Riesman puts it in discussing the concept of the gift relationship, 'anchored deeply in the social fabric and cultural orientation of the collectivity'. He explains that: 'In the ritual exchange system the gift is neither a profit-motivated economic transaction nor a totally disinterested unilateral transfer. Rather, it is a moral nexus, bringing about and maintaining personal relationships between individuals and groups. Gift leads to counter-gift (so that to give is also to receive, albeit possibly after a time-lag) or at least to a thank-you; and there are social sanctions such as shame if one refuses to give.'[3]

Few allotment-holders would recognize their behaviour in this description, yet it permeates the whole culture of the allotment. It is second nature. It is a tradition not only to share seeds, seedlings and produce with other plot-holders, but also to bring a basket of vegetables to a neighbour at home known to be in bad times, always careful to avoid the notion of charity. 'Our Dad told me to bring these round, as they'd only go to waste otherwise' was the formula. It was the normal and understood way to behave. Thus a woman, born in 1897, whose father had an allotment in the First World War, remembers how 'he grew beautiful stuff and anybody that hadn't an allotment or a garden, he used to bring barrowloads home and give them away'.[4]

This gift relationship was so accepted that it was often institutionalized for good causes. It was frequently decided that the exhibits submitted for the fruit, flower and vegetable show should be donated to a local charity, and a plot-holder's son remembers how: 'Father was on the committee for the Longton Cottage Hospital for years. At the Tam o' Shanter, which was a pub, they had a stall at the front of the public-house and the money went to the cottage hospital ... And certain members that went into the pub, they used to be allotment-holders. They'd bring vegetables, and it all went to the same cause. And anyone that knows the Longton Cottage Hospital, and they've ever been in for any out-patient treatment, they'll find a plaque on the wall in there that tells you when and how much the Tam o' Shanter gave to that hospital.'[5]

Ken Penney, who grew up in the East End of London around the period of the Second World War, recalled how it was automatic for the men to return from their allotments on Hackney Marshes on Sundays and distribute vegetables to all the neighbours;[6] and, remembering a much earlier period, Fred Tolley told Raphael Samuel how: 'Those old chaps never reckoned to buy seed potatoes – they used to swap with someone else ... make a change ... he'd save some seed out of his and I'd save seed, and then we'd change them over. Perhaps he had a bit of ground that was heavy, and you had some ground that was light...'[7] This sense of reciprocity is built in to the patterns of behaviour expected on the site. Thus an anecdote told in an allotment journal in 1986 tells how:

'You won't get any digging done this afternoon', said Bill.

'Why not?', I asked belligerently. 'They'll be a row if I don't.'

'Well, see for yourself', said Bill casually.

I looked down the allotment. It had all been dug and raked and was ready for setting.

'What's been going on?' I asked in amazement.

'Well,' he began, somewhat diffidently. 'I saw you were behind hand last week, so I thought I'd finish it off for you.'

What with a feeling of bewilderment and a small lump in my throat, I could hardly speak. 'It's very good of you, Bill,' I said at last. 'Thanks a lot. Here, have a pipe of my bacca.'

But he was already busy hoeing. 'Mustn't waste time,' he said with a grin. 'Or you'll never get those peas in!'[8]

The story could be dismissed as a sentimental homily, but not within the allotment world, where gardeners thoroughly aware of the sheer dreadfulness of human behaviour, plagued by theft and vandalism, the deliberate destruction of their crops, and the depredations of other people's pet animals, carefully cultivate this kind of relationship. It was also in 1986 that the Newcastle quantity surveyor, Harry James, when asked why he was an allotment-holder, told us of his happy memories of helping his father on the plot and of his admiration for the 'caring attitude' he found among his fellow-members of the Fenham Allotments Society, and of the 'willingness to help out the old chaps' whether with seed potatoes, digging or anything else. A seventy-seven-year-old plot-holder from Oxford was voicing a universally expressed view when he remarked that: 'One of the best memories of the war years was the great friendship that existed between gardeners, sharing of views, seeds and time to help others.'[9] Some plot-holders even reflect that it is as though the allotment culture preserved patterns of social relationships that had been buried in other fields of life.

Conventionally there is a gulf between this gift relationship and the sale of allotment produce for cash. The rules of many an allotment society cite this as grounds for expulsion and the proscription is still solemnly included in the conditions of membership, even though nowadays no-one would have the time, the nerve or the energy to pursue the issue. Its existence was always based on a misunderstanding of the way poor people get by in life, and always have, as well as a failure to see that the gift relationship is bedded in reciprocity, and that if people could not reciprocate in kind, they would be only too anxious to do so in cash. John Benson explains that: 'In fact it was probably difficult to avoid entering the market at some level: "If you'd got a lot of fowl, anybody 'ud come to your house, and ask if you'd got half a dozen eggs: they'd come to you for them." Sometimes the difficulty of distinguishing production for domestic consumption from production for the local market is reflected in the confusion of the surviving oral testimony.'[10] And he relates the testimony of a girl from Barrow-in-Furness who remembered with bitterness how her step-grandfather 'had a garden on Greengate where the nursery school now is and he used to bring all the vegetables, potatoes, cabbage, beans and the most beautiful tomatoes anybody had ever tasted and, believe it or not, he used to charge my mother for it.'[11] Her admiration for his skill as a gardener was mingled with her resentment that he had turned what should have been a gift relationship into a cash transaction.

Plenty of allotment-holders would 'make a bit on the side' as they put it, including hawking vegetables around back doors in the neighbourhood. Alan Sigsworth of East Anglia University told us how, when he was a boy in South Shields in the 1940s, his mother would invariably go down to the allotments for her vegetables, continually offering to pay for the little extras the seller insisted on throwing in, and continually being refused. It was a social as well as a shopping occasion. There are still allotment-holders in the Fens who supply the local markets, some with their own stall, and we met one man who claimed to live off his allotments. He was a trained gardener who had been employed by the corporation parks department. In the early 1970s, paid at the standard agricultural rate, he felt he could earn more by producing organically-grown food for the health food retailers. Today he has three allotments on two different sites, and the use of part of a friend's smallholding for soft fruit. He supplies three shops and has a round of private customers. When cash is very short he does building repairs. If he priced his labour and the cost of running a van economically, he would still be found to have an income below the figure the government considers to be the poverty line. Asked to describe the rewards of his work he replies, 'Satisfaction.'

Perhaps more important than the actual money value of the produce gleaned from an allotment is the *apparent* value. Reporting interviews with pensioners, Helen Marshall noted that 'it was the view of one that "pensioners couldn't do without it", whereas many, especially amongst those who had been gardening for several years, felt that it probably "broke even". One pensioner who had been gardening for twenty-eight years said that it was "a toss-up as to whether it pays", because of the price of fertilizers and seeds, and that it really depends on the season.'[12] There is obviously a relationship between the way you cultivate and the harvest you reap. Several old people told us that, while perhaps they could *survive* without their plots, their living standard would be reduced considerably, and there would be little room for things beyond the necessities.

In times of economic distress allotments have always been advocated, usually from outside the ranks of the poor, as a means by which they could, through diligence and self-help, both feed their families and add to the family income. This is why John Stuart Mill claimed that allotments were 'a contrivance to compensate the labourer for the insufficiency of his wages by giving him something else as a supplement to them', and that in fact they were 'a method of making people grow their own poor rate'.[13] The introduction of allotments has also been seen as one more step in the development of 'capitalist social relations', bearing down on the wage relationship of employer and employee, securing wage labour by the pittance, 'the minimum necessary' of an allotment. 'When tiny plots of land were allotted in the early-nineteenth century ... strict rules were attached to the holdings to ensure that the possession of a little piece of land did not detract from the performance of wage labour.'[14] The basis of Mill's misgivings, as well as the reason why others thought him wrong, can be seen in an account from 1830 of the allotments at Cottingham, outside Hull:

> ... in the year 1819, the parish officers of Cottingham took a piece of land consisting of twelve acres, which they divided into twenty equal parts, and sublet to so many poor families who had been accustomed to receive parochial relief. The rent charged to them for their allotments by the parish, was two shillings a year each family. The individuals to whom the ground was allotted, were selected from the mass of paupers for their industry and good character, and as having the largest families, most of them being burthened at the period with from eight to ten children. The agreement was that they were to trouble the parish for no kind of relief whatever, and were liable to be ejected from the land at a fortnight's notice, on improper behaviour or otherwise, as might appear advisable to the parish officers. Fifteen or sixteen of them have since been enabled to build cottages, partly through their own expenses and exertions, and partly through the means afforded them by the wealthy and benevolent of the neighbourhood, from observing the industry and orderly conduct of these poor people, and the good effects of the plan; but without any additional expense whatever to the parish. The parties in their present condition exhibit every appearance of cheerfulness and content. They have even improved in industry, and are more independent in fact and in behaviour, as they are now never compelled to submit to the degrading practice of dunning parish officers for relief.

This report could have been written to uphold John Stuart Mill's opinion, but it also provided support for those who felt he had missed the point about the importance of the allotment movement, for it went on to say that:

The actual saving to the parish is calculated at £200 a year, for it is estimated that a labouring man and his wife with eight or ten children, under ordinary contingencies as paupers, seldom receive less from their parish than ten pounds per annum: thus, on twenty families the saving will be the amount mentioned. This, however, is within the mark; the probability is that the same number of persons, if left in their former state of pauperism would have cost the parish a far greater sum. Many of the families from the facilities afforded by the Hull markets, make, it is stated on the best authority, thirty pounds a year by raising of fruit and garden stuff, and selling it in our town. The members of one family, whose name had been communicated to us, were at the period in which the allotments were made, in the most extreme state of indigence and privation: they now inhabit a comfortable tenement, are the owners of five cows, are pig dealers, and supply the town with sausages on an extensive scale. – What a contrast! Had this plan not been adopted by the parish of Cottingham, they would in all probability be still struggling in irremediable poverty!

It is explained that this allotment site was first known as 'Paupers' Gardens', 'but the parish officers, considering that a sort of stigma was attached to this appelation, which might have injurious effect, and tend to counteract the feeling of independence they felt it to be in their interest to inculcate amongst these poor people, had boards placed and inscribed with the more respectable title of "New Village", by which latter name the little colony is now known'.[15]

Pamela Horn records that: 'At Haddenham in Buckinghamshire, by the 1880s, the allotment had become the most significant part of a cottager's life ... Most families consumed the produce themselves, but sometimes surpluses were sold in nearby towns or disposed of to occupiers of neighbouring smallholdings. The latter would then retail

these with their own vegetables. This happened in the
Woburn area of Bedfordshire, for example, while at Corsley
in Wiltshire Maude Davies found one woman who had
earned more than eight pounds in a year by selling soft
fruit, apples, poultry and vegetables, all produced on fifty
poles of ground.'[16]

Other students warn us that: 'However working people
chose to dispose of their produce, it is of course extremely
difficult to estimate profits or losses which they made from
the gardens and allotments', but that: 'Justified suspicion of
the arguments advanced by late-nineteenth and early-
twentieth-century proponents of working-class allotments
must not be allowed to obscure the fact that both gardens
and allotments could be made profitable'. It was necessity
that drove rural labourers to add long hours on the allotment to their working day, and 'to these ends every available hour – except Sunday – throughout the spring, summer
and autumn was given to their cultivation; and often, when
the work was in arrears, the husband would rise early and
put in an hour or two before beginning labour on the farm at
seven'.[17]

Allotment-holding in Victorian and Edwardian England
was most common in those counties where wages were
lowest. 'Only in the north of England and in Wales was
interest in allotments minimal. There, even at the end of the
century, payments in kind were still common, at a time
when perquisites had been phased out for the ordinary
labourer in much of central and southern England ... Men
who had potato ground in an employer's field naturally had
little interest in cultivating that vegetable in an allotment',[18] and as cash earnings were higher, they could afford
to buy or barter or exchange gifts when they needed extra
vegetables. The Edwardian agricultural economist, F.E.
Green, made the same point:

It is perfectly true that in counties like Oxford, Suffolk
and Norfolk, where wages have been low, allotments

have been popular, which rather points to the sinister fact that they are to some extent 'a contrivance to compensate the labourer for the insufficiency of his wages'. Further evidence to support Mill's contention is adduced by the fact that in 1909, whilst the Royal Commissioner on the Poor Law was sitting, Oxfordshire was one of the counties in which the percentage of pauperism was highest; and it is interesting to note that where wages are highest, such as in the Lothians and the English Border Counties, allotments are little in demand by farm workers.[19]

He saw the allotment for the rural worker as 'a base to fly to, as labourers say, when times are hard and labour troubles have to be fought out. To the labourer the allotment is the castle behind the walls of which he can bargain more manfully with his heavily armed foe – the farmer', whereas the urban allotment-holder in his experience was a man of the artisan type: the railway worker, the mill hand, the carpenter and the brick-layer. 'It is doubtful whether these men with their ten or twenty rods have ever thought much about their allotments as supplementary aids to wages. The love of gardening and the desire to be in the open air, besides the ambition to grow vegetables for their own table, have been their incentive rather than cash returns. Probably overtime at their own particular trade would have been financially more remunerative.'[20]

Today, there is a delight in the eye of the holder who finds willing purchasers of gooseberries, cabbages or grapes, and, with the sales, can at least pay for manure or seeds. There are still those who supply cauliflowers or incurve chrysanthemums to a local shopkeeper, and others who have a small stall near their home, often left over from times when the financial return was more significant. Many more now refuse to do this, and others have stopped the practice, not through rules imposed from outside, but since they found out the mark-up price. They prefer to give away their surplus, and hundreds actually grow surpluses to give to older and poorer people than themselves. 'I used to sell my flowers, until I saw that they were being sold for five times what I got,' one grower told us, 'so now I give them to the old people's home.'

In the early years of this century philanthropic attention was once more focussed on the plight of the farm worker in the agricultural depression. Then in 1906 'land-grabbers' occupied vacant sites at Plaistow in East London,[21] and in Manchester, Leeds and Bradford, with the intention of cultivating them so that 'the hungry could grow their own foods and obtain a living from their own methods'.[22] It was a conscious echo of Winstanley and the Diggers, and the result was the same. The Manchester occupation was quickly broken up with police support: '. . . the turf buildings were knocked down, the crops uprooted and the cooking utensils thrown into the highway'. The same thing happened in Leeds. The Bradford occupation of derelict land owned by Midland Railway, and known as the Girlington Klondike, petered out after three months because of lack of money and the approach of winter.[23] But these demonstrations did serve to dramatize the plight of the unemployed, and the return of large-scale unemployment in the 1920s revealed the desperate need of the 'supplementary aid' of allotment gardening for a growing number. The Society of Friends began exploring ways in which the 'scourge of unemployment' could be alleviated, noting that 'the Dole, while seeming to the general public to be a sufficient answer to unemployment, was in fact at times almost a deterrent to more satisfactory arrangements for relieving distress'.

It was widely believed for example that the 'Means Test' would take into account access to home produce. *The Times* reported in March 1934 that:

In Durham villages one sees that men are genuinely fearful of taking on an odd job to earn a shilling or two, doubtful whether their weekly means of livelihood will be cut down if they are found to be keeping a few hens. The policy of the commissioners, stated in their report, is to make no deductions for paid earnings of this sort; on the contrary they will encourage them; but that knowledge has not yet sufficiently filtered through to the men, and because their all depends on their Dole they take no risks and blame the Means Test . . . friends and relations cannot help one another because all are straitened in the same way. Everything superfluous has been pawned or sold by the time unemployment has continued for many months, and the necessities of life are largely worn out or broken . . .[24]

Even in mining areas, with their deep-rooted traditions of allotment-holding and of self-help and mutual aid, 'members of the Society of Friends ascertained that some allotments were going out of cultivation because the plot-holders just did not have the money to buy seeds and fertilizers'.[25] In South Wales, 'it is related of one man who had been accustomed to grow his own potatoes, but had become too poor to buy the seed, that for a time he received seed from his companions, and when that was no longer available he went to the rubbish heaps for peelings and took out such "eyes" as he could find in order to plant his allotment'.[26]

On the Means Test issue: 'The Friends Committee was enabled to get clear statements from the Ministry of Labour that the small amount of produce which a man could sell from his allotment would not affect the amount of his dole. This was a great gain (even although the feeling of suspicion on this point ceased only very slowly) . . .'. On the question of supplies, 'the Friends Committee decided to supply (at first free of charge) small seeds, seed potatoes, tools, fertilizer and lime, costing about 10s per plot'.[27] Their scheme 'was so successful that it was taken over by the government and during the winter of 1930, 64,000 families were helped. Owing to the demand for national economy in 1931, the government dropped this scheme, but it was again taken up by the Society of Friends, who got the government to agree to make a pound for pound grant. During 1931, 62,000 plot-holders were helped, and in subsequent years this number rose to over 100,000.'[28]

By 1934 the Sheffield Allotments for Unemployed Scheme was stressing that this enterprise owed as much to self-help as to charity:

> The scheme offers to every unemployed, partially unemployed, or seriously impoverished worker, the seed potatoes, vegetable seeds, lime, fertilizer and tools, requisite for planting a 300 square yard plot. In order to receive this benefit the men are asked to group them-selves into Societies, affording opportunities for mutual helpfulness and co-operation. The officers of these societies, numbering nearly 2500, collect contributions from the men to pay for their portion of the cost of supplies. In the season 1933–4 over 117,500 men were assisted and 27,000 have been helped to new plots – nationally. It will be remembered that this is a scheme to help men who help themselves – how substantial is that self-help is shown by the amount the men have contributed towards the cost of supplies – no less than £24,700 collected week by week by over 2000 secretaries.

The report from Sheffield stressed the importance for local industry, since 'last year over 56,000 spades, forks, etc were supplied nationally, and these were all made in Sheffield'.[29] The Second World War brought full employment and Dig for Victory, and the scheme for aided self-help for unemployed allotment-holders was replaced by government support for allotment gardeners as a whole, a subsidy for allotment societies and subsidized purchase of fertilizers on the same basis as the support given to farmers.

With the return of large-scale, long-term unemployment in the 1980s, outside well-wishers have once again suggested that people without jobs could improve their lives by taking over neglected allotments for both sustenance and income. Trevor Skeet, MP for North Bedfordshire, proposed this to the young unemployed in his constituency in 1986. Asked whether this would affect their right to draw unemployment payments or social security benefits, he replied: 'That's a matter that will have to be worked out',[30] a rather less specific answer than the one the Friends Committee was able to obtain from the government in 1929. His views were challenged by a local greengrocer who is also a councillor, who said: 'Let's suppose a man grows a hundred cabbages on his allotment plot and sells them at 30 pence each. He's earned £30, and then . . .?' But in parts of Britain there are surviving signs of the value of allotments to people without jobs. The council at South Tyneside established a special waiting list for unemployed people at a reduced rent, and over four years this list jumped from 20 to over 200. At Pontypridd in South Wales nearly half the plot-holders are unemployed. Birmingham offered a rent-free period to unemployed people and found a hundred new plot-holders in no time. The council dare not undertake a survey of existing unemployed holders for fear of the rent income it would lose. Town and parish councils in Cumbria and Durham organize cheap or free materials for their high proportion of unemployed tenants.

People who become unemployed are urged to use their enforced leisure being 'creative', and some do seize the opportunities, the allotment being one of them. But not all unemployed people find it, or other recreations, attractive.[31] In some parts of Newcastle, known locally as UB40 estates, there is the opposite experience. Allotments are associated with recreation. Spending time on the plot is something you do *after* work, and if there is no work there is no recreation. 'The essential criteria for satisfactory leisure experiences are highly likely to be missing . . . the freedom to choose activities, curtailed by financial and material constraints . . . the psychological effects of being jobless can often lead to a lack of interest and feelings of worthlessness.'[32] Moreover, working an allotment is considered by some people to be an admission of giving up hope of a job, settling into a long-term activity at a slower pace instead of feeling 'ready for work'. Finally, the unemployment culture of the 1980s is far removed from the experience of the 1930s. This is less due to the 'easy relief' provided by the state than to the wider culture of material and commercial success and possessions that measures a person's performance through short-term material gain and the achievement of particular styles that can only be paid for. There is also the view that marks the allotment as cissy. It is bad enough having to stay at home while the wife or mother works, without having to do that – or so runs the argument.[33]

Where the allotment has been built into local traditions within the peer group for generations, it has become the focus for many in the culture of redundancy, a dominant feature in many coalfields, steel and shipbuilding areas in the 1980s, dominantly etched in the landscape of Durham mining villages. In Horden, dozens of men have reorganized their lives around their plots and pigeon crees,[34] falling back, as their grandparents did, on the reciprocal give and take of the gift relationship.

7
Not much of a voice

'If we were to attempt to calculate the economic value of the immense amount of time, materials, resources and simple cash which goes into communal leisure, the figures would be astonishing. Yet the very suggestion is in a way an insult to the thousands who contribute their time – either as members or organizers of clubs – in making such a diverse range of leisure activities possible. It is precisely this freedom from economic measures, and from the trappings of the commercialized world of leisure, that attracts people into such groups and enables them to consider what might seem to be work (twenty hours a week perhaps for a club secretary) as leisure. However, leisure is fast becoming a new focus of interest for many sections of society ... Local government is beginning to co-ordinate its various leisure activities – almost every week there are advertisements for the post of "Director of Leisure" in newly created departments. A new leisure "profession" is emerging ...'

Jeff Bishop and Paul Hoggett,
Organizing Around Enthusiasms,
Comedia, 1986

Most allotment gardeners pay their rent, yearly or twice yearly, to the local council, either directly to a department labelled as parks, recreation or leisure services, or indirectly to the local association to which the council may have delegated management responsibilities, or which may for a century or more have run its own affairs through many a change in local-authority powers, boundaries and nomenclature. Self-management, however fragile, since it depends on the circumstances of individuals, is always cheaper than professional management, which depends on current pay scales in public employment as well as on the attitudes of council officers who may regard this responsibility as just one more dreary chore, or may be in the vanguard of opinion in developing 'model' allotment sites. Gardeners and council clerks alike can be completely unaware of the network of legislation, 'ambiguous to the point of incomprehensibility',[1] the Thorpe report commented, and it went on to show how: 'An allotments authority must refer to the 1908 Act to learn of its obligations, and to the Acts of 1922 and 1950 to discover their extent; it must turn back to 1908 to understand how it may acquire the land to fulfil those obligations, and on again to the 1925 Act to find the rules relating to the disposal of such land.'[2]

If councils are confused about their duties, so are tenants about their rights, until some decision by a council officer or committee draws everyone's attention, first, to the legal distinction between sites which are *statutory* – provided specifically for allotment use which may not be changed without central-government consent – and those that are *temporary* – provided for allotment use while destined ultimately for some other purpose – and then to tenants' right to compensation for the losses involved in closure of a site, and to the various legal precedents as to what is and what is not a reasonable rent increase.

Adequate organization of plot-holders, both locally and nationally, is thus particularly important. Yet Thorpe's committee reported that 'we have spoken to allotment-holders who not only failed to attend meetings of their association, but professed to be unaware that an association even existed'.[3] There is a paradox here, for the characteristic ethos of the allotment site, which we describe elsewhere, is one of spontaneous mutual aid. But this is much less evident at an organizational level. Maybe the necessary tedium of meetings and decisions takes too much out of people's gardening time, but it is a continual complaint of site secretaries that everyone leaves the donkey-work of management and representation to someone else. Plenty of instances contradict this view. Some allotment sites are the focus, or the excuse, for a rich social life with the annual

Dinner and Dance as its culmination. Some have a licensed bar in their clubhouse, and this results in their having an income available for every kind of expenditure. (The trite comment that this implies that the members will spend their time drinking rather than digging is answered by the fact that the local allotments society with its famous bar in Liverpool also carried off the local annual horticultural prizes.)

If we were obliged to nominate the allotment capital of Britain, we would have to name Birmingham. This would not be because the city has some of the most ancient as well as some of the newest of all allotment gardens, nor because they range from the most rudimentary of sites to the most sophisticated leisure gardens, nor even because Meadow Road, Edgbaston, is the most immaculate allotment site that anyone could imagine, and where the work of site maintenance is done by the tenants, not the city. The reason why Birmingham is a model for other allotment-holders as well as for other local authorities is because both sides have found a formula for effective administration. On the city council's side, allotments are the responsibility of the Land and Property Officer, assisted by an Allotments Officer with a long experience of the sites themselves, and an Allotments Clerk. On the plot-holders' side, there are over a hundred societies, federated into the Birmingham and District Allotments Council (BDAC). The city council has an Allotments and Smallholdings Sub-Committee with four co-opted members with full voting rights, and as well as the meetings of this sub-committee there are meetings every two months between the BDAC and the council's officers. There is an agreed planned budget of spending on allotment sites to cover several years ahead, and although the plot-holders would obviously like to see more money spent on some sites, the arrangement works well. The energetic secretary of the BDAC, a teacher by profession, has had to give up his own plot, to find the time to do his secretarial duties effectively. Not all towns and cities have their allotment systems as well managed as those of Birmingham, nor are the affairs of landlord and tenants always conducted in an atmosphere of mutual respect.

Over a century ago it was recognized that to win the right to cultivate a patch of ground it was necessary to organize both locally and nationally. 'In fact not even allotment legislation, let alone a Small Holdings Bill, passed Parliament until allotment candidates won elections to a local government body and to Parliament. These victories came only after the development of political organization in the allotment and smallholding movement.'[4] In 1882 Jesse Collings founded the Allotments Extension Association in Birmingham, and this body became 'the parent of the most active of the organizations devoted exclusively to political promotion of alloment legislation.'[5] Collins and his associates were 'thrown out' of the Association when they sided with the Unionists in the convolutions of Liberal-Unionist politics and started a rival body, the Rural Labourers' League, which outlasted the parent body and had 'twenty-five paid organizers and three thousand voluntary organizers, mostly rural persons'.[6] At the turn of the century an Agricultural Organization Society was formed to give both allotment-holders and smallholders the advantages of bulk buying, and in the latter case, co-operative marketing. It was financed by government grants.[7]

The huge expansion of allotment gardening in the First World War led to the formation, in October 1918, of the National Union of Alloment Holders. An enthusiastic report at the time explained that: 'Allotment-holders have grouped themselves under one great National Union which is not only the governing lever to influence Parliament . . .'[8]. The emphasis had moved to the towns and this was reflected in the Allotments Acts of 1922 and 1925 which removed the words 'for the labouring poor' from the legislation and required that one-third of the members of the allotment committees that urban authorities were obliged to appoint should be co-opted to represent allotment interests. Councils were also required to provide for allotments in town-planning schemes and were authorized to subsidize allotments to the extent of a penny rate. These were important gains, needing new activity, down on the site and nationally. Earlier historians observed that:

> ... their effectiveness depends on lively local agitation to admonish the authorities of their powers and duties; and therefore this period sees a rapid growth of allotment associations and their first combination into town and district federations ... Their formation failed to stop the decline in allotments, though it retarded it, and between 1919 and 1939 many societies disappeared simply becuse their allotments disappeared. Nor was there any corresponding growth in national organization. On the collapse of the Agricultural Organization Society in 1924, the Allotments Organization Society [AOS] was formed to carry on this, the most flourishing, part of its work. But the shock of the change was too great, and whereas the Agricultural Organization Society had had in 1923 over a thousand societies on its books, the Allotments Organization Society could only collect about 350 in 1925 and not many more by 1929. But the AOS was not the only national organization. The other was the National Union of Allotment Holders (NUAH), a brisky proletarian body formed during the Great War. At its prime it had perhaps a thousand affiliated societies, but it too fell on evil days, and by 1929 had about the same number as the AOS.[9]

In that year, through a triumph of diplomatic negotiation, the two dwindling bodies agreed to amalgamate. The NUAH had been founded 'more or less in ignorance of the work of the AOS',[10] and many plot-holders had no knowledge of the existence of *any* national body representing their interests. We can testify that this is similarly true in the 1980s. The present National Society dates its foundation from this amalgamation on 10 March 1930 as the National

Allotments Society Ltd, with G.W. Giles, who since the early 1920s had been serving the allotments executive of the AOS, as its general secretary. (He was still on the scene in 1950 as a member of the government's Allotments Advisory Committee.) This rebirth was largely due to the organization of allotments for the unemployed by the Society of Friends, mentioned in Chapter Six. A Central Committee of that Society and of the NAS, whose offices were in Drayton Street, London, backing on to the Friends' House in Euston Road, administered the government grant and the donations gathered by the Friends, and distributed them through local officers and Societies. The birth of entirely new local societies through the Friends scheme, with the unification of the two national bodies and the belated effects of the 1922 and 1925 Acts, combined to increase the number of affiliated societies from some 600 in 1930 to 1800 in 1939 and 2300 in 1941, 'and was accompanied by rapid progress in the grouping of local societies into district federations'.[11]

Then the vital importance of allotment-holding in the Second World War led to a government grant of £1500 a year, matched by a similar sum raised by the National itself, to help form and encourage new allotment associations. By the 1970s the old hands of the allotment movement were remembering this sum as £10,000 per annum,[12] and of course, allowing for inflation, were right. At the end of the war, with nearly 4000 affiliated associations, the National prepared an Allotment Holders' Charter, and submitted evidence to an Allotments Advisory Committee of the Ministry of Agriculture, urging four acres (1.6 hectares) of allotment gardens per thousand of population as a general target, and 'after three years of agitation, a Bill was brought before Parliament which resulted in the Allotments Act of 1950'.[13] It had the staff, the energy and the income to make its opinions felt. Since many home gardeners had been enrolled in local associations, the words 'and Gardens' were added to the National's name, and after a further merger it became the National Allotments Society and Village

Produce Association. Its slogan was 'The Right to Dig', the title also of a crusading manifesto published in 1951.[14]

But once the wartime and post-war food emergency was considered to be over, the National was, by comparison with many other bodies in what is usually called the voluntary sector, very unfortunate in its attempts to secure continuing grant aid from government departments and agencies. It failed to persuade the Ministry of Agriculture that it was in the national interest to reverse the post-war decline in allotment-holding, and it failed to persuade the Department of Education and Science that allotment-holding was as much entitled to Exchequer support as any other form of recreation. Not only this, but in the 1940s and 1950s when grant aid *was* forthcoming, the grants 'were made subject to stringent and peculiar conditions which probably made it impossible for it to use the money to the best purpose'. All through the post-war years it has rankled with the allotment movement that, even though market research and government social surveys continually reveal that there is more interest in gardening than in any other form of active recreation, expenditure on the provision of and improvement of allotments is seldom given comparable official solicitude as that afforded to sports of all kinds. Hence the importance it gives to the Judge's ruling in 1981 that: 'Allotment gardening is a recreational activity'.[15]

The National Society wholeheartedly welcomed the appointment of the Thorpe committee. 'For many years the Society has been begging for a Committee of Inquiry to be set up because we believe that its findings will help our members to maintain their right to dig.'[16] And Thorpe's recommendation of the leisure-garden concept had been anticipated in its own propaganda. At the end of the war it had employed a landscape architect, Richard Sudell, to prepare plans for the model site of the future, with club-houses, paddling pools, something to attract all the family and an abandonment of the traditional grid-iron layout.[17] Years later, driven out of its London headquarters by rent rises, the National moved its office to Flitwick, Bedfordshire, and set up two demonstration leisure gardens. Thorpe noted with approval that: 'The emphasis is on beauty, recreation and cultivation. Vegetables and bush fruits are still prominent, but the neat little summerhouses, bordered by flowers, invite the tenant and his family to spend some of their time relaxing in pleasant surroundings.'[18]

Thorpe's report was, however, deeply critical of the allotment movement. His committee found that, on the majority of sites, 'the few public-spirited allotment-holders who exist find their efforts stifled by the general air of indifference and sink all too easily into the apathy which surrounds them . . . Our first major criticism of today's recreation-oriented allotment-holder . . . is that he is primarily an individualist who considers his allotment to be as private as his home garden, who is seldom interested in anything beyond its boundaries, and is blind to his further responsibilities.'[19] The committee noted that the National Society, whose total membership had fallen from 296,098 in 1949 to roughly 170,000 in 1969, represented a minority of allotment-holders, 43.7 per cent in urban areas and 20.9 per cent in rural parishes, and it found that 30 per cent of members of affiliated associations were not even aware that they were members of the national organization.[20] The committee considered that the poverty of the National Society was the fault of the movement itself, and it was scathing about the annual conference which should have been the forum for 'a forthright exchange of views and a series of important decisions which the association representatives could take back to their sites', but where in fact most of the conference was devoted to 'discussing a series of resolutions which have often seemed to us to be vague, repetitive, poorly phrased and ill-conceived . . . Similar resolutions tended to appear on the agenda each year, the same ten speakers monopolized the rostrum, and almost the same speeches were made.'[21]

It is a tribute to the personality and persuasiveness of Harry Thorpe that the National Society, far from resenting the damaging criticism made at length and in detail in the committee's report, immediately invited Thorpe to become a Life Member and Vice-President. He was elected President in 1973, the year in which the organization changed its name, as specifically recommended in his report, to the National Society of Leisure Gardeners. He also became President of the International Federation, *Die Grüne Internationale*, and engineered the necessary support to enable an International Leisure Gardeners' Congress to be held at Birmingham University in 1976. He was gravely ill at the time, and died in the following year, sincerely mourned by the activists of the movement into whose history he had been catapulted by a chance government decision twelve years earlier. It has to be said, however, that two decades of governments have failed to implement the detailed recommendations for changes in the law that the Thorpe committee recommended, and that the National Society has similarly failed to take notice of his criticism in order to become a more effective voice for the allotment movement.

Thorpe himself was not disconcerted by the failure to promote a new image through fresh legislation. He thought the new designation of 'leisure gardens', in the name of the Society itself, and adopted by 'many progressive local authorities of their own free will' establishing leisure gardens of one design or another (Birmingham, Coventry, Bristol, Cardiff and Manchester), showed that 'we have not required the lash of government legislation to make us do this (perhaps we would then have done so reluctantly with resentment, instead of spontaneously of our own free will)'.[22] He was similarly delighted that since the publication of his report, 'the decline in the number of plots has slackened considerably and there are now long waiting lists for plots on most sites'.[23] But there was a deep irony here. Thorpe set out ten points associated with the 'new image': Good Design, Beauty, Amenity, Good Maintenance, Productivity, Family (with its neat little Summerhouse), Community (with its fine Pavilion), Grow for Pleasure, Grow for

Quality, and Grow to Show.[24] Many of the new influx of the 1970s on those lengthening waiting lists belonged to a generation, however, who, yearning for some degree of self-sufficiency in an environmentally conscious world, didn't want to sit around on the site. *They* wanted to grow for a quite different range of reasons, and with the puritanism of the newly converted, good design, beauty and amenity were not high among *their* priorities.

Nor has the simplification of allotment law been accomplished. Thorpe was confident that one of the several Secretaries of State for the Environment in the early 1970s would introduce a Bill. None did, and in two important ways legislation has been to the detriment of the allotment movement. First, the 1972 Local Government Act removed the obligation for local authorities to have allotment committees with at least a third of their membership consisting of gardeners. Then, the 1981 Local Government Planning and Land Act removed from the Department of the Environment the obligation to collect local-authority statistics on allotment gardens and on waiting lists. In 1976 Lord Wallace of Coslany opened a debate in the House of Lords on allotments and home food production in anticipation of a new Bill.[25] None resulted and, in 1984 and 1985, Lord Wallace in the absence of any hint of government legislation, twice attempted to pilot a Recreational Gardening Bill through Parliament.[26] He explained to us that 'I have now introduced two Bills and although each passed through the Lords without dissent, each time the government have obstructed it in the Commons by the non-democratic method of shouting "object".'[27] In fact, answering a specific question about the implementation of the Thorpe report, Lord Skelmersdale, for the government, told Lord Wallace that: 'We have looked at it and we have decided that it is not appropriate for modern times', and he added that 'recreational gardening is a matter for education and not for legislation'.[28]

No other interest group with up to half a million adherents could be dismissed so easily but for the fact that only a hundred thousand or so of them are organized, and those ineffectively. To that extent Lord Skelmersdale was right: before it can expect a modern replacement for its antiquated legislation, the allotment movement will have to educate itself to become an effective pressure group. The comparison is sometimes made with another formidably successful land-use lobby, the National Farmers' Union. For example, at the 1986 conference of the National Society, one resolution proposed that the Society should draw to the attention of Her Majesty's Government the grave concern with which the conference viewed 'the continued reduction in financial resources available to vegetable research', and in the debate on this motion a member made the interesting point that cuts in vegetable research hit allotment gardeners harder because 'while the NFU represents 3500 vegetable growers, the National Society represents 100,000'. Discussing this motion, another delegate remarked to us that 'the difference is that the farmers know perfectly well that it makes sense to subscribe enough to maintain a fulltime staff simply to negotiate continually with government and with members of parliament. *We* aren't willing to subscribe enough to run our own affairs efficiently.' And later, another veteran of the allotment movement said to us that: 'Experience has shown me that in general we're a mean and narrow lot.' Asked to explain this, he went on: 'We're mean in not making adequate contributions to our own organizations. The allotment-holder who looks beyond the end of his nose gets on to the management committee and finds his time taken up in running horticultural shows. These are a great morale-booster and encourager, but even the committee members are narrow because they won't get into the business of fighting for their interests with councils and the government.'

The local association may or may not be affiliated to the National Society, and may or may not have joined a city-wide or county-wide federation of allotment gardeners. The National Society's income is derived from a small *per capita* levy on membership of the local associations, with a rebate to encourage them to amalgamate locally. 'Under this system a local urban or rural federation can claim a refund of 25 per cent of all fees paid by its member associations, and a further 8½ per cent will be refunded to a *county* organization ... It justifies this system of rebates on the ground that when the area offices are well versed in organization and allotment law, they can attempt to do locally what ought to be done nationally if adequate staff and funds were available.'[29] Dependence on membership fees for income, in a period when the ordinary costs of maintaining a secretariat and an office are rising steeply, was – and continues to be – a disaster for the National, both as a co-ordinating body and as an effective lobby. 'Until 1959,' Thorpe reported, 'it employed a full-time administrative assistant and a national organizer, but the services of both were then dispensed with on the ground of economy. Its salaried staff now consists only of a full-time secretary and four assistants.' That was in 1969. The clerical back-up in 1988 for the sole secretary is half that, and the decision to sell the premises at Flitwick and move to a purpose-built office on part of the former steelworks site at Corby, Northamptonshire, hard to reach by public transport, three miles from a post office and five miles from a bank, means that it is difficult for the secretary to retain *any* assistance. In the period since Thorpe the National has had two long-term secretaries, one a retired army officer and the other a retired policeman (and keen allotment gardener), two very brief occupants of the post and, as the National Chairman Ted Smith ruefully explained, 'sixteen months when we existed without a secretary'.[30] As disinterested observers from the outside, we have to add that the Society's history shows that the most ardent publicist for the allotment movement would not stay in that post if every decision made provokes an argument with the Management Committee.

The permanent dilemma of the National is that if it raises the *per capita* fee to local societies, membership falls. As this membership (which in 1986 was 103,593 plus a few hundred life members and independent members and thirty local authorities) represents a small proportion of allotment gardeners, it affects the credibility of the Society in speaking for *all* allotment-holders. At the time of the Thorpe committee, when the fee was 1s a year, the National explained that: 'The fee is still very low, but to the association struggling hard to overcome the inherent attitude of a gardener who is interested only in his own small plot of land, and who cannot believe that this age-old right of a man who wishes to have an allotment will ever be challenged, the sum total fees for a large membership that the association is asked to transmit to the national body must seem high, particularly when it is borne in mind that the movement itself was bred out of poverty. The attitude unfortunately persists to the present day.'[31] Thorpe continually stressed that the fee (then one old penny a month per member, and to this day 2½ pence a month) was absurdly low. It resulted in an obvious limitation on the National's ability to serve its members but also had 'a number of psychological aspects whose importance could scarcely be exaggerated.' First it perpetuated the image of the allotment movement as a form of charity for the deserving poor. 'Secondly, it suggests to the individual allotment-holder that the value of National Allotments and Gardens Society is minimal. Finally it implants in the minds of those who might otherwise be prepared to help the movement a strong conviction that the movement is not prepared to help itself.'[32] The committee's response was that:

> Either the allotment movement *needs* a national organization which on the one hand can protect its interests and on the other can assist the individual and the association in the successful management of their allotments, or it does not. It *cannot* need a national body which, through lack of funds, is incapable of

filling either role satisfactorily ... It is, in our view, imperative that NAGS should resolve at once to increase its fees considerably. If, in consequence, some associations withdrew their allegiance, this would be both short-sighted and unfortunate; but the additional services which it would subsequently be able to provide would almost certainly draw the majority back, and the withdrawal of some parsimonious associations would be no great loss either to it or to the movement as a whole.[33]

Twenty years after Thorpe's foray into the allotment world, the same arguments are still used on both sides. Lord Wallace, the octogenarian Labour peer who tried to introduce new legislation, complains that 'one of the main problems is that gardeners are peaceful and complacent, only becoming militant on greenfly, blackfly, slugs, cats and wood-pigeons. Any action is left to old Tom, Harry or somebody else.'[34] The names were not picked at random. Harry of course was Professor Thorpe. Old Tom is in fact Tom Hume, who for years has been the secretary and consultant of the London Association of Recreational Gardeners. This is an example of the phenomenon well-known in the world of voluntary organizations, the splinter group that becomes a ginger group through doing its job more effectively than the original parent body. When Tom Hume was a boy in Blythe, Northumberland, in the First World War, his ex-miner father took on an allotment on a site which had been prepared for house-building, with permanent roads and water laid on. This gave him an early appreciation of the value of a well-serviced site. Over fifty years later, when as a retired post-office engineer he was secretary of the Middlesex Allotments and Gardens Council, he recorded a high level of 'member dissatisfaction with the way the National Society of Allotment and Leisure Gardeners was organized, managed and financed, the latter particularly with regard to grants for financing on behalf of the Society locally'.[35] The dispute arose because Middlesex felt discriminated against in the National Society's rebate system.

On legal advice, Middlesex disaffiliated from the National Society, *against* (according to the gardening press) Tom Hume's advice.[36] Having withdrawn, he and his members set up in 1974 the London Association of Recreational Gardeners, which grew to sixty-one member organizations, paying a standard fee, not on a *per capita* basis, as well as seventy independent members. The response of the National Management Committee was to expel Mr Hume from membership,[37] and finding that this did not take away his rights as a Life Member, to expel him from that too.[38] A decision was subsequently made to rescind this resolution, and we mention this sad little episode to indicate the validity of Thorpe's criticism of the level of discussion in the National Society.

Mr Hume is endowed with a formidably sharp analytical brain which he has applied single-mindedly to the problems of the allotment movement. No one else can match his mastery of the minutiae of local-government law, and certainly no one else would keep a high-quality photocopier in his front hall so as to bombard the mailing list with bulletins, journals, fact-sheets and background briefings on how the law and decisions in the courts and at planning inquiries affect plot-holders. Not only this, but members are kept in touch with new findings from the Vegetable Research Station and the National Vegetable Society. It was inevitable that it should be *his* expertise that lay behind both the drafting of the various Private Members' Bills which have sought to put into effect the significant recommendations of the Thorpe committee, and the High Court's decision to overturn a local authority's unreasonable rent increases, as well as successes at public inquiries to resist the resiting of allotment-holders on less suitable land adjoining motorways.

By the time of the National Society's annual conference at Redcar in 1985, both sides were obviously yearning for a

124

rapprochement. Mr Hume attended (as of right as a Life Member and shareholder) and was enthusiastically welcomed with verses and embraces to congratulate him on his eightieth birthday. What was needed, he declared on that occasion, was 'a National organization with status and dignity – to this could be added strength in numbers and a fair and economic fee structure to replace the existing *per capita* system'.[39]

Thus, ironically, the most important landmarks in the organizational history of the allotment movement in the last twenty years have been a government-commissioned report whose recommendations have not been followed, and the emergence of a dissident group 'motivated by the frustration of trying to get progressive ideas accepted by the National body's management . . .'.[40] At the 1985 conference, Tom Hume, the gadfly of the movement, reminded members of his endlessly expressed view that 'management should concern itself less about patching up an obsolete fees system and more with those members lost or never had. This can only be achieved by a more attractive fees structure.'[41] But that year the national chairman, commenting on the grave financial situation, declared that 'raising affiliation fees is not the answer, this needs very little research to prove that the opposite effect would most probably result'.[42] And at the 1986 conference the treasurer said that 'only as a last resort' would the National increase the membership fee of 25p per member. 'Every time we put the fee up, we suffer a massive loss of membership.' It had been found, he said, 'that a twenty-five per cent increase in the fee produced a ten per cent increase in income. Twenty-five years ago there were 2600 member societies, there are today 1400.'[43] At the 1987 conference a proposal to increase the fee by 5p was carried by a narrow margin.

The allotment movement is not alone in facing organizational problems. When Jeff Bishop and Paul Hoggett looked into the incredible range of self-organized leisure enthusiasms in two particular localities, they eventually came across the existence of corresponding national or regional 'parent' or 'umbrella' bodies which offered six distinct forms of support. The first of these was *organization* itself, which is a major task, whether for 'a large netball league or a series of gardening shows', and which often involved 'a national or regional tier of paid employees – in the Caravan Club, the Lawn Tennis Association and so forth'. The second was *judging*, 'the training, registration and organization of judges, referees, umpires and so forth', and the third was *newsletters etc*, ranging from 'an occasional, one-page, photocopied newsletter to regular, properly printed journals with illustrations and advertising'. The fourth was concerned with *supplies*, where 'naturally there are many occasions on which membership of a group can bring simple financial benefit, bulk purchase of photographic materials for example', and the fifth was *insurance*, 'often available at cheaper rates if one's group is involved with a league or association'. The final, and very important form of support, was found to be that of *aid and advice*.[44]

Aided by this identification of universal categories, we can examine the National in terms of the six distinct forms of support offered to local groups:

Organization. The big event of the National's year is the annual general meeting and conference, held early in June over three days in a succession of seaside resorts, and conducted in strict accordance with rules of procedure and standing orders with motions proposed in advance by accredited delegates. Its important function, as with other bodies, is to serve as a get-together and reinforcement of commitment among the activists of the movement. We have heard the usual dark hints that everything is fixed in advance by the Management Committee but there is plenty of evidence that decisions are made against management advice. This affects basic issues like the name of the Society itself. By the early 1980s a trend known as 'the Yorkshire backlash' had gathered enough strength to rewrite it as the National Society of Allotment and Leisure Gardeners. Thorpe's effort to change the image had failed. However, if the unofficial function of national conferences is to re-energize the local activists, it is equally important that the reports of the national management committee and the resolutions from the floor should be communicated to the local membership more effectively than the word-of-mouth impressions of the hundred or so delegates. The National's resources do not permit this vital task to be done. The same unpalatable truth affects the movement's international relations. In spite of an impassioned plea from Clive Birch, secretary of the Birmingham and District Allotments Council, that such a move would be absurdly narrow and insular, the 1986 conference passed a resolution 'that this conference considers the expense of sending delegates to the International Conference in Europe is totally unjustified and proposes that this Society withdraw from membership of *Die Grüne Internationale*'. In the following year, the Eastern Regional Panel of the Society urged it to 'immediately seek renewal' of international membership, and their resolution was defeated. Once again the unpalatable truth is that if there is no way of telling British allotment gardeners of other people's achievements, international connections are fruitless.

Judging. This is not a function of the National, but local associations do not find it difficult to find judges for shows and exhibitions. We were disturbed to hear from one local secretary that his association considered that it gets more from its affiliation to the Royal Horticultural Society than from its membership of the NSALG.

Newsletters. The National Society in a long history has produced journals in various forms. From 1965 to 1967 its well-presented monthly magazine, *Garden*, was on sale to the public. But, said Thorpe, it was 'destroyed by the apathy of the allotment movement itself. The publishers provided 3500 free copies of each issue for distribution to Associations affiliated to NAGS and additional cut-price copies could be provided for members. Almost without exception, however, the free copy for each association was passed from hand to hand among those members who cared to read it, and few extra copies were called for.'[45] The publishers withdrew from what Thorpe saw as an 'unequal struggle', and *Garden* became a quarterly bulletin, amateurishly produced by the secretary, but filled with reports from the counties, from head office, and on parliamentary and governmental matters affecting allotments. The same was true of the London breakaway journal, *The Recreational Gardener*. More recently another attempt was made to produce a general-interest magazine, *Allotment and Leisure Gardener*, published, allegedly quarterly, by a commercial firm for advertising purposes. Its failure to reflect real issues in the allotment world was much discussed at the National's conferences. The Society's publicity officer, Len Parnell, explained that of the 9500 copies received by him, he personally had distributed 6000. He said that the publisher told him that 'as long as you're not paying, you get what you get'.[46] Having extricated itself from one disastrous adventure, the Society sought in vain for an alternative publisher. In the days of instant magazine production, it and its members have both failed to keep in touch.

A similar sad story has to be told of the *Gardeners' Companion and Diary*, published annually by the National, with sales at one time of over 20,000 copies. This has all the usual features of a gardeners' pocket diary, with additional material on the structure of the allotment movement, addresses of the management committee and of area and district officers, model rules and advice on how the legislation affects plot-holders. It had been discontinued for several years, but was re-introduced for 1986 as a result of the 1985 annual general meeting. Ten thousand copies were ordered at 75p each, for sale to members at £1 (cheaper than the cheapest diary of any kind on sale at W.H. Smith). Sales were 3500, with a consequent loss of £4000. 'The great majority of societies don't order diaries,' explained Mr Greer, the treasurer, 'yet all you have to do is to walk round among plot-holders on a Sunday morning, and they sell like hot cakes.'

Supplies. One of the National's successes has been the Seeds Scheme by which members order seeds through the Society at a discount. It provides income for both local societies and the National. The current scheme was introduced by a former secretary, John Farmer, precisely in order to overcome the impasse over membership fees. The National's income from it has grown from £360 in 1974 to £17,000 in 1986. This leads the treasurer to ask: 'Are we properly structured to be a business organization?'

Insurance. Apart from insurance for property on the plots, the National takes a commission on providing ordinary household and car insurance for members. This service is under-used, and the treasurer sadly explained that in many local societies the forms are just not distributed. The Seeds Scheme provides a profit for the local societies but, like the diary, the insurance scheme simply benefits the National. 'Because there's nothing in it for them, they don't want to know.'[47]

Aid and advice. The National has always offered advice to affiliated members and societies, and will provide arbitration services and representation at public inquiries. It will also arrange legal aid in circumstances where the interests of the allotment-gardening community as a whole are involved. But undoubtedly the constrained circumstances of the National in the last few years have affected its ability to promote these interests positively, which is why one 1986 resolution called for the Society 'to improve its national image and become involved with legislators to alter and improve allotment legislation'.

That perennial resolution echoes the hopes of all those local enthusiasts, battling against an ocean of national indifference in a sea of automatic mutual aid on the site. Society secretaries often apologized to us for the fact that their own plots were not the best maintained, just because so much of their time was spent on paperwork, running the stores, and so on. Allotment gardening is not the kind of hobby that can be dropped for a while and then resumed, nor one which can fill in odd moments between other activities. A second point relates to the age of plot-holders and of the officers of local societies. If we conceive of 'leisure careers' (in the sense that people who are gymnasts at fifteen may be bowls-players at seventy-five), then it can be admitted that gardening is *the* leisure activity that most appeals to the old. 'More people are interested in gardening as a hobby at retirement age than at any other time.'[48] Thorpe found that allotment-holders who were retired had almost always had a plot long before retirement, and that few had taken on a plot after they had retired. It would display an unpleasant 'age-ism' to blame the apathy on the age of allotment gardeners, especially since many of the most valuable and forward-looking among the activists are undoubtedly old. The complaint ought to be that so many of the new *young* entrants to the movement are unwilling to play their part in its organization. Thorpe believed in the 1960s that 'the present image of allotment gardening holds little attraction for the young',[49] but his view was overtaken by dozens of new initiatives for turning derelict urban sites into allotments.

One uncomfortable fact is that the new young ventures in the greening of the cities have often been undertaken in complete ignorance of the venerable allotment movement already in existence. And another is that the organized allotment movement has totally ignored its new potential allies. But the lack of contact between the long-established and the newly invented is a purely theoretical issue in a movement of this size and scale that expects to run its affairs centrally with one paid secretary and one-and-a-half assistants. The vital task of effective national represent-ation demands a local willingness to pay. The organized allotment movement has steadfastly declined to take note of Harry Thorpe's devastating criticism. One of his Dutch admirers remarked that: 'I still see him sitting in our drawing-room in Amsterdam, discussing allotment matters till deep in the night, sipping a Dutch Genever and eating a raw herring . . . was all the work of my friend Harry done in vain?'[50]

International connections

'On Sunday, we took a bottle of wine and went up to their allotment. Sitting up on the hill overlooking the sea ... drinking ... talking. The allotment was made by a Greek and had been left the same – a series of secret gardens with box hedges, and a little hut with a mirror hanging in it and a tiny cupboard and pin-ups and Greek family photographs. Oddly enough, the allotment hillside overlooking the sea is quite like Greece.'

Nell Dunn,
Living Like I Do,
Futura, 1977

Nell Dunn discovered a Greek allotment in Brighton, Richard Mabey sees Greek allotments on the hillside above Berkhamsted, Italian allotment gardeners are famous everywhere. In the far north of Scotland an Italian immigrant family of seventy years ago opened an ice-cream parlour and did exactly what they would have done at home. They sought out a patch of land to rent, hacked out the stones, brought in every scrap of organic matter they could obtain, planted bushes as windbreaks, and grew the vegetables that everyone knew could not survive in that climate.

In London, the Maccini family were just the same. Generations ago they were immigrants in Clerkenwell and once they had accumulated a tiny capital sum they bought a neglected patch of grazing land with its tumbledown cottage on the steep slopes of one of those tributaries of the Thames in a southern suburb and planted their garden. In 1929 the borough council decided to build an estate and bought out the Maccinis, agreeing as part of the deal to rent them the end house with a large triangular slice of land, not otherwise usable for building. Sixty years later the family is still there. Beyond the immensely productive vegetable plot, the vineyard they have planted, and the greenhouses, is the wisteria-clad summerhouse, decorated with coloured calendars, plaster cherubs and Chianti flasks, where the old man and his sons and daughters-in-law sit drinking their wine in the twilight, looking down on the valley and the twinkling lights of the Arndale Towers, where the modern tenants have few such opportunities unless they join the allotment society.

Sebastien Espada (his real name was Sebastiano Spada) was an Italian anarchist exile from Mussolini's dictatorship who fought on the losing side in the Spanish Civil War. He escaped to Britain in 1939 and found that it simplified life if he was accepted as a Spaniard. (He was right, considering the tragedy of so many impeccably anti-Fascist Italians, long settled in Britain, who were interned as enemy aliens and drowned when the ships taking them abroad were torpedoed.) At Victoria Station two English members of the Spanish Anti-Fascist Aid Committee invited him to stay in their house in Ealing. For a considerable time the Spanish refugees were forbidden to take paid jobs, so Espada did the cooking and took over the pocket-size back garden, building a greenhouse from scrap materials. Then his opportunity came. He rented an allotment from the Ealing Pittshanger Allotment Society, and profiting from his training at the school of horticulture at Syracuse in Sicily, and his reading of Kropotkin's *Campi, fabbriche, officine,*[1] he won, year after year, the Mayor's prize for the best allotment in the borough. Every year Espada fretted because he was unable to obtain a copy of his diploma to show the Mayor, as though the evidence of his prowess did not lie all around.

Espada became famous for his incredible output of gooseberries and tomatoes and his prize-winning onions, and after the war resumed his international contacts, procuring seeds and cuttings from all over the world. In 1947 he astounded his fellow plot-holders with his Spanish beans, peppers, aubergines and artichokes, and his fifty-four-inch-long Italian marrow (*Legenaria leucanta longissima*). From friends in California he got seeds of the Kentucky tobacco plant, and learned the process of 'curing' his crop. 'He grew 30 pounds of tobacco from these seeds, but not being in a position to pay the duty of 53 shillings a pound, he contented himself with 3 pounds, and the excise officers destroyed the rest.'[2]

His allotment had steeply banked sides, on which zucchini grew, and its general level was eighteen inches higher than that of the surrounding plots. For Espada had taken to heart Kropotkin's great eulogy of the *culture maraîchère* around Paris and the other French and Belgian cities, and continually added every scrap of organic compost to enrich his soil. Kropotkin tells how some gardeners at Evesham in Worcestershire, having learned of the results of what was known as French Gardening, invited a Parisian *maraîcher* to Evesham. 'After he had brought from his Paris *marais* his glass-bells, frames and lights, and, above all, his knowledge, he began gardening under the eyes of his Evesham colleagues. "Happily enough," he said "I do not speak English; otherwise I should have had to talk all the time and give explanations, instead of working. So I show them my black trousers, and tell them in signs: Begin by making the soil as black as these trousers, then everything will be all right." '[3]

Later waves of immigration brought the gardening traditions of many parts of the world to British allotment plots: Italians in Bedfordshire, Ukrainians in Humberside and Manchester, West Indians and Asians in several cities. On a number of sites at Sparkbrook, Birmingham, families of Asian and Afro-Caribbean descent have reclaimed derelict sites for the intensive cultivation of characteristically Asian and West Indian vegetables, using organic methods. They call their project 'Ashram Acres'.

It is often only when the British go abroad that they realize the importance of the allotment culture that they scarcely notice at home. Visitors to Amiens, for example, having seen the great cathedral, find themselves among the canals in the curve of the river to the east of the city, in the *hortillonages*; here, the allotment-holders and market gardeners who used to sell their produce from barges, just as is done in Venice to this day, actually have a museum among their chalet gardens, celebrating the history of their plots, where they have built a fairy tale landscape of dwarf-sized mansions with pedimented gateways among the artichokes and chicory. Similarly, visitors to Florence, having admired Michelangelo's Belvedere Fort and the Boboli Gardens, see allotments of the most prosaic English kind pressed up against the very walls of these sanctified monuments. The message of this juxtaposition is clear. Here is a culture that does not consider vegetable growing to be an unaesthetic activity to be hidden away, but one which, like the washing strung between the windows of the ancient *palazzi*, is part of the essential fabric of daily life.

The same feeling assails the visitor to the cities of Eastern Europe, where the windows of the coach or limousine from the airport to the international hotel reveal a landscape of tiny plots with chalets, cabbages and tomatoes. Likewise in America, the highway from Washington to Georgetown is bordered by 'Community gardens'. One of us was the solitary pedestrian on this road and was told by a plot-holder that: 'This is the only place in the District of Columbia where you'll find a fresh vegetable.'[4]

On the European continent the first conscious movement, as opposed to automatic habit, of allotment gardening probably arose in Germany, and had several different origins. The city of Kiel set up *Armengärten* in 1830. These were gardens for the poor, the equivalent of 'poor's allotments' in England, and Kiel's example was rapidly followed in Leipzig, Berlin, Worms, Frankfurt, Königsberg, Dresden, Stettin and Danzig. The traditional German name given to allotments is *Schrebergärten*, accidentally immortalizing Dr Daniel Schreber of Leipzig, who actually had no connection with allotments. He was an advocate of exercise and outdoor recreation for the young. After his death a Schreber Association was formed to continue his work, and in 1865 it leased meadows outside the city for a playground and games field, including gardens for the pupils to maintain. But the children neglected their plots, 'lacking the necessary endurance' says a sympathetic chronicler,[5] and the gardens were taken over by their parents. This aspect of the movement spread, and by 1869 there were a hundred *Schrebergärten* sites, divided into family plots, attached to playing fields, and equipped with sheds and chalets. The association of allotment gardening with physical health and as a resort or refuge for the whole family, grew in other parts of Germany.

Parallel with this movement came another growth of *Laubenkolonien* (summerhouse colonies) resulting from the rapid growth of Berlin and other big cities, and the ensuing housing shortage and overcrowding. Families wanted to escape from the notorious back courts behind the imposing facades of the city streets, either for the weekend or as an alternative residence. 'Forty-three per cent of the occupiers of small gardens had lived in completely inadequate housing and preferred to erect chalets on rented land on the fringe of the city',[6] and in *wilden Wohngebeite* (wild housing regions or squatter settlements). Something more like the British allotment movement arose at the turn of the century, with *Kleingärten* provided by workers' organizations, by factories for their employees, as well as by local authorities, and the chalet-garden with a summerhouse to sleep in, as well as the link with physical health, all becoming part of the German allotment culture. Attempting to regulate allotment use, the Allotment and Small-holding Ordinance of 31 July 1919 laid down that on each plot one-third should be devoted to vegetables, one-third to fruit-growing and the rest for lawn, flowers and chalet.

In the period of astronomical inflation and of mass unemployment, access to an allotment was a godsend, but of course the allotment culture also appealed to the 'Blood and Soil' ideologists of the Nazi Party, and was seen as important by its economists with their emphasis on economic autarchy. Two months after the Nazi Party took office it was

announced that a Reich Small Garden Day would be celebrated in July. The chairman of the National Small Garden
Association, Rektor Förster, a secondary school head-
teacher, failed to notify his 600,000 members of this, and
was consequently replaced by a Nazi appointee, Dr Kamm-
ler, who in a speech in 1934 declared that: 'The first task of
the National Association is to plant National Socialist ideas
into the small garden movement. German allotment gardeners and smallholders have a duty to fulfil. *They* are
chosen to dig our German soil. Thus they have a duty to
recreate the collective work of the Folk.'[7] But allotments
could also provide a refuge from the regime, simply because
they included habitable chalets. In the 1920s a group of
anarcho-syndicalists set up their own allotment colony outside Düsseldorf, and were criticized by their Marxist con-
rades for this 'flight from the class struggle'. In the 1940s,
however, their site was used to hide various victims of the
regime, including Jews and deserters.[8] The ability to maintain an undisclosed private life, centred upon the allotment,
became ever more difficult because of the wartime imperative to pull down the chalets to grow food on every inch of
the plot; but at the same time, summerhouses on the allotment became a refuge from nightly bombings.

As in Britain, the war brought a huge expansion of the
number of allotments, followed by a post-war decline. In
1949 a new national body, the *Verband Deutscher
Kleingärtner* (Association of German Allotment Holders)
was formed. Its membership was then 752,589, and by 1964
this had dropped to 476,754. There was a hasty re-
establishment of the culture of chalets and summerhouses,
but in the 1970s a survey conducted by the Federal German
planning ministry found the German *Schrebergärten* still in
demand, and also that the importance of these gardens as
providers of fruit and vegetables had by no means disappeared.[9]

137

From allotments to summer homes

The allotment gardener dreams of the green season of the year. In the grey autumn he lives on memories from the past summer, in the white winter on expectations of the melting of the snow. During the violet-brown spring he lives for his work in the garden. Then when the warmth of the sun has unshackled the buds, and the trees have opened their flimsy green parasol over the plots – then is the time for the real delights of life.

> *Fifty Green Years*
> Linnea Allotment Society,
> Bromma, Sweden 1967

The allotment movements of other West European countries have a similar range of origins and a similar evolution. They were a response to the sudden growth of cities and the urbanization of the population in the nineteenth century, and arose from concern with physical health and the hope that fresh air could alleviate the scourge of tuberculosis, from the urge to gain a respite from overcrowded city tenements, from the wish to overcome the problems of the new urban poor, as well as from the desire of new immigrants to the cities to continue the habits of generations, and grow their own vegetables and keep a few chickens or geese, even in the least promising surroundings. Allotment gardening spread from Germany to Holland, and from there to the 'garden colonies' of Denamrk.

This movement cane to Sweden via Denmark, being introduced to Stockholm by Anna Lindhagen, sister of the well-known socialist and Mayor of Stockholm Carl Lindhagen, who became the driving force of the allotment-gardening movement. When visiting Copenhagen in 1903, Anna Lindhagen saw allotment gardeners digging and immediately became interested. After arrival home, she found that a modest start had been made on a few patches of ground at Kungsholmen.

She set to work methodically, obtaining sites and organizing the enterprise ... In rapid succession, the state, the city and private institutions granted sites for allotment gardens. In 1906 ... the Association of allotment gardens in Stockholm was founded on the initiative of Anna Lindhagen, who became its first chairman. Its treasurer was Anna Åbergsson, an ardent soul, incisive in both tongue and pen, when fighting on behalf of allotment-garden activity. Sigrid Hård of Segerstad, who was educated in gardening and able to teach allotment gardeners how to attend to their patches, became secretary.[10]

Swedish allotment history provokes a whole series of reflections. The first is that, as in other countries and other places, the dedication of a handful of individuals brought it into existence. Of the many social issues to which they might have devoted their energies, the particular one they chose was that of allotment gardening. Everywhere these initiatives have been vital. The second is the fact that the Swedish initiators were women, in a field of activity which has been assumed to be male-dominated; and the third is that the movement they set in motion evolved over the years to become in fact the 'second home' culture so prominent in the Scandinavian countries today.

By the 1920s the chalets on the plots were increasingly used as summer dwellings, and although tenancies stipulated that they could only be slept in between April and September, housing shortages led to about 450 Stockholm families living there all the year round. The city was expanding and 'The suburban villas had just commenced their conquering march, and sites outside the boundaries were considered especially suitable. Two mighty men, who both wanted to work for "sunlight and fresh air" for ordinary people in society were rivals for the development areas. However, if the "small-villa" movement had its Alex Dahlberg, the allotment movement had its Carl Lindhagen, indefatigably submitting motions and proposals in which he complained that Director Dahlberg, commonly known as "the real-estate office", did not share the general enthusiasm over allotment gardens.'[11] The planning politics of many European cities reflect this disagreement between the town-planning and landscape-architecture establishment on the one hand and the plot-holders on the other.

However much the movement spread from the city in the world of weekend homes, in Stockholm itself it was tolerated not for its contribution to the lives of the plot-holders, but for the accidental fact that from a landscape architect's point of view, 'due to their floral splendour and cottages of a summerhouse character, these areas would make a nice picture in the surrounding parks'.[12]

In Holland there was a similar struggle to get allotment gardening accepted as an activity written into the town-planning legislation. The secretary of the umbrella organization, *Algemeen Vorbond van Volkstuinders Verenigingen in Nederland* (Dutch Society of Leisure Garden Clubs), explains that, while public parks cost a great deal to maintain, the low rents paid by his 200 member societies are comparable in cost because 'the garden sites are also open to the public'.[13] He sees a similar evolution for the allotment as first a necessity and then an amenity. 'In the beginning they rented a plot and started gardening. Later on they made it into a nicer site as far as possible. Once again later on, the authorities had the sites designed. Since the Second World War the garden sites became gradually a part of town planning. We see a continuing progress: along with higher standards of living gardens became more beautiful, huts and shacks gradually became little summer garden houses, women and children started to join the men, and it became an open-air recreation for all the family.'[14]

This evolution impressed the members of the Thorpe committee, visiting the countries of Western Europe in the 1960s:

The ratio of 'allotment gardens' to 'chalet gardens' varies enormously. In Sweden the allotment garden has virtually disappeared, possibly because many workers in that country can now qualify for a retirement pension equal to eighty per cent of their former salaries. In Denmark, the allotment garden is today largely confined to rural areas. In West Germany ... we were shown several examples in Hamburg where chalet gardens and allotment gardens flourish on the same site. In Holland, by contrast, the chalet garden represents only a minority of allotment provision ... It was emphasized to us in Rotterdam, that the dichotomy between the chalet garden and the allotment garden is by no means as great as one might suppose. Not only does the local authority adopt the same system of administration for both types of allotment, but there has in recent years been an increasing tendency for the occupiers of allotment gardens to graduate to chalet gardens by what is regarded as a natural form of development.[15]

The committee raised an important question: 'If the transition from "allotment garden" to "chalet garden" has been a natural process, it is pertinent to ask at once why no similar development had occurred in this country.' The paradoxical conclusion the committee reached was that:

... we are convinced that a major part of the answer lies in the complete absence of mandatory allotments legislation in every country which we visited. The fact that every publicly provided allotment site, whether it is composed of vegetable plots or of chalet gardens, exists as a result of voluntary action by a local authority, has generated between the allotment movement and the municipalities a spirit of harmony which has rarely existed in this country and is conspicuously lacking today. Within this atmosphere, there is ample room for experimentation with new ideas, which can be allowed to germinate both in the town hall and on the site without the constant fear that they will offend against some enactment . . . Throughout our tour, we formed the impression that the planner regards the provision and the effective siting of allotments as an *important* part of his work, not least because he is confident that the sites which he designates will add to the attractiveness of his town . . . The officials in every town decided voluntarily and as a matter of course that we must talk either to the planning officer or to private planners engaged on the town's development, and some of those planners were themselves chalet gardeners.[16]

There was one lesson that Thorpe's committee brought back from Europe which had no part in their recommendations simply because they knew that in Britain it would have been seized upon to dominate all the other issues in their report. This was the fact that European allotment gardeners take it for granted that they can sleep on their plots, something which would be regarded as outrageous by every public-health inspector and every council committee in Britain. Thorpe stressed that 'in the whole of our tour we found only one site where the gardeners *and their families* were *not* permitted to spend the night in their chalets during the summer months – and even there the rule is not rigidly enforced. It is today the general practice for the whole family to remain on its chalet garden throughout the summer weekends, and often for the duration of the school holidays. No local authority frowned on this practice . . .'[17]

These highly successful and confident allotment-holders are linked by a twelve-nation International Office of Gardens and Allotments, based in Luxemburg, and run for over forty years by a lawyer, Dr Aloyse Weirich. Known as *Die Grüne Internationale*, it was instigated in 1924 by the Abbé Lemire, who had struggled since 1896 to develop a sense of collective identity among French allotment gardeners.

The French experience

Maheu spent the afternoon working in his garden. He had already planted potatoes, beans, and peas, and now he began to plant out cabbage and lettuce seedlings which he had heeled in the day before. This bit of garden kept them in vegetables, except potatoes of which they never had enough. He was very good at gardening and even raised artichokes, which the neighbours regarded as mere showing off. As he was preparing his row, Levaque came along to smoke a pipe on his plot and have a look at some cos lettuce that Bouteloup had planted that morning, for if it had not been for the lodger's hard digging, nothing would have grown there but nettles ...

Emile Zola
Germinal, 1885

French allotment gardening links the traditions of southern and northern Europe. Zola's Maheu in his bleak little colliery village near the Belgian border was exactly like any English miner of his time. He made what he could of his allotment, as did thousands of railway workers. But as France industrialized in the nineteenth century, its new urban working class had closer links with the soil precisely because the revolution of 1789 had broken the power of the great landowners. As people moved to the factory towns in search of a living wage, they brought with them peasant values and assumptions, beautifully expressed by Proudhon, recalling how: 'In my father's house, we breakfasted on maize porridge; at midday we ate potatoes; in the evening bacon soup, and that every day of the week. And despite the economists who praise the English diet, we, with that vegetarian feeding, were fat and strong. Do you know why? Because we breathed the air of our own fields and lived from the produce of our own cultivation.'[18]

To this day there are allotment-holders on the fringes of

French cities who mix the *culture maraîchère* of producing vegetables for the market with that of the *jardins-ouvriers* producing for domestic consumption. This is similarly true in Italy where Philip Mattera reports how: 'There are even people who have been moonlighting in agriculture. Studies of employees of the few large factories of the South, especially the huge Italsider plant at Taranto, have found that many are using their free time to resume their prior occupation as small farmers.'[19] And it is true of Spain where, in the northern cities, the *huertos comunalos*, or publicly provided allotment sites, are dominated by new immigrants from the countryside, rather than by established city dwellers.[20] The same thing happens in France. In 1980 Michel Bonneau found that forty-five per cent of allotment-garden holders in Roubaix were immigrant workers, whose motivation was, above all, economic. Their situation, he notes, 'is in fact, exactly like that of the French working class at the end of nineteenth century'.[21]

Most French workers in those days were not city dwellers but uprooted peasants, holding on to rural habits of domestic self-sufficiency, and 'were nourished mainly on bread and on vegetables that they grew themselves'.[22] Abbé Lemire, who founded the *Ligue du coin de terre et du foyer* in 1896, was a liberal Catholic politician whose ideals were similar to those of G.K. Chesterton's Distributist movement in this country. He wanted a society of self-supporting family units. In founding the organization of allotment-holders, 'he wanted to construct a pressure group to promote his legislative aims: the guarantee for each family of the ownership of house and land'. This 'curious mixture of conservatism and progressivism' brought him 'hard struggles with the Catholic hierarchy',[23] but corresponded with aspirations that run deep in French daily life.

'The worker's garden is his countryside, the popular equivalent of the country villa where his boss spends his Sundays,' declared Louis Riviere at the Congress of Worker-Gardeners in 1903, neatly encapsulating a favourite theme in the Ligue's propaganda. A postcard issued in 1920 claims that: 'In his garden the worker finds: 1. A healthy leisure occupation which leaves him with an eight-hour day (The garden is the enemy of alcoholism). 2. A means of combatting the cost of living. A 200-metre garden brings the worker 500 francs worth of fresh vegetables: it increases his wages. 3. An opportunity to spend his free time with his family: The garden and its summerhouse is the worker's country home.'

The allotment societies federated in the Ligue had a busy calendar of shows, fêtes, processions and banquets, presided over by Abbé Lemire until his death in 1928. The government legislation for the provision of allotments that he had always sought did not come until many years later, with the 1941 law enacted by Pétain's Vichy regime. As in Britain and Germany, wartime allotments reached a record number, with about 600,000 in France as a whole, including 20,000 in the suburbs of Paris and 25,000 in those of Lyons. Françoise Dubost remarks that there is no need to attribute this to the Vichy ideology of Work, Family and Fatherland: the facts of acute food shortage were a sufficient explanation. After the war, however, the organized allotment movement was regarded with a certain suspicion in France. New legislation in 1952 provided support for 'family gardens', assuming that the purpose of such gardens was food production, even though the *jardin familial* in the post-war years might have been a kitchen garden, a leisure garden – or a mixture of both. Nevertheless, vast numbers of allotment sites were lost in urban expansion after the war. The *loi Royer* of 1976 sought to guarantee members of any gardening society against expropriation and to provide them with alternative sites. 'But in France we had to wait until 1979 for a decree from the Environment Ministry officially announcing a new allotment policy.' This provided government subsidies for the creation of new sites. The channelling of support through garden societies guarantees that they have a very large membership. The *Ligue du coin de terre*, in spite of its long-term decline, still has 45,000 individual members and 120,000 if the membership of affiliated societies is included. The *Societé d'horticulture et des jardins populaires de France* has 950,000 members, the Railway Workers' Gardening Society 120,000. These figures include both home gardeners and allotment-holders.

In spite of the growing popularity of the leisure garden, following what the French regard as the 'Swedish style', about forty per cent of French households grow vegetables.[24] When Françoise Dubost asked them why, the typical answers were: 'Just to eat something fresh'; 'It doesn't pay for itself certainly, but at least we know what we're eating'; 'they're natural, not treated with chemical fertilizers'; 'one can have beans, salads and peas really early'. She was also interested in the impact of the domestic freezer, which seven per cent of French households had acquired by 1972 and thirty-one per cent by 1982. Interviewing plot-holders aged between forty and fifty at Coudreaux in the Paris region, she learned that many did not use the freezer for conserving vegetables, precisely because their interest was in *fresh* food, or because they considered that the cost of freezing at the temperatures necessary for meat was too high to make it worth while conserving vegetables. She found that men tended to continue traditional ways of storing vegetables, like bottling, while women thought that it demanded too much work and was not worth the effort.

A survey made in the Paris/Ile-de-France region in 1985 confirmed that after a gradual decline in the post-war decades there had been an upsurge of interest in allotment-holding since the mid-1970s and a change in the type of gardener. Previously they tended to be retired suburbanites. Now the proportion over sixty-five had fallen to fifteen per cent, with the typical plot-holder aged between thirty and forty, having two children, and living in a flat. Few married women were tenants in their own right, while immigrant workers comprised only five per cent of plot-

146

holders in the region. As many as seventy per cent had a rural background in their own lifetime.[25]

Eastern gardens

It is common for legalized trade to be expanded far beyond what the state planners had intended when they lifted the prohibition. Perhaps most common is the growth of home production of fruits and vegetables into an extensive business. The travelling greengrocer and florist have become such familiar figures in the Soviet Union that there are popular jokes about them. Hedrick Smith recounts a tale about a flight from Tbilisi to Moscow that someone tried to hijack to the west. A Georgian man overpowered the hijacker and allowed the plane to reach its intended destination. As he was being decorated for his supposed heroism, the man was asked by a government official what induced him to act. He responded, 'What was I going to do with 5,000 carnations in Paris?'

Philip Mattera,
Off the Books,
Pluto Press, 1985

The collectivization of agriculture in the Soviet Union was like the Enclosure movement in eighteenth-century Britain, though it was accomplished with far greater suffering. It deprived the rural population of every kind of access to land, and in coming to terms with reality one of the first steps was to provide the precise equivalent of the 'fuel allotments' that arose in England 150 years earlier. The naturalist Mikhail Prishvin described one of these: 'This plantation had been allotted to the people of the village for firewood; for this reason it was known as the allotment. It has been divided, of course, into strips, and each man took what he required from his own strip. One peasant wouldn't cut anything at all, and his section stood out like an island. Another would only cut the big timber, leaving the small stuff to grow. A third would cut everything perfectly clean, so that all that would be left on his strip would be heaps of rotting twigs and branches . . .'[26]

After the fuel allotments came the famous private plots. The commissars grumbled, just like nineteenth-century English farmers, that more attention would be lavished on the personal plot than on work on the State farm, but notoriously, the private plots have been the salvation of the ordinary Russian's food supply. 'In 1963, private plots covered about 44,000 square kilometres or some 4 per cent of all the arable land of the collective farms. From this "private" land, however, comes about half of all the vegetables produced in the USSR, while 40 per cent of the cows and 30 per cent of the pigs in the country are on them.'[27] Those Georgian farmers who found it worth while to take suitcases of tomatoes, flowers and grapes on immensely long air journeys became famous.

But apart from the huge market for the private plotholders in the agricultural industry, there is an enormous demand among ordinary urban Soviet citizens for an allotment or leisure garden. As everywhere else in Europe, except Britain, the assumption is that it should develop into a weekend home. The economist Hugh Stretton remarked that: 'Pathetically, Russian town dwellers go out and comb the countryside for patches of neglected land they can plant, visit, enjoy, "make their own", however tenuously. Their masters, who own everything just as the masters did in Marx's day, discourage this petit-bourgeois practice.'[28] At the top of Soviet society possession of a dacha is normal of course and for many decades there has been pressure from below to democratize the chalet-garden trend. By the 1970s attempts were made to accommodate the demand with garden co-operatives. 'Land is frequently allocated in this way to factories whose workers are given their own plots of land. The plots are sometimes rented but are often treated as the workers' own with a right of sale either to another member of the co-operative or sometimes apparently to the general public.'[29] Even though 'vegetable growing on the English model is less widespread', these plots contribute very significently to local fruit supplies, but Dennis Shaw reports that the most significant feature of the garden co-operative is the 'summer garden cottage' or tiny wooden chalet which people are permitted to erect upon it. He quotes an article by a Soviet author observing the importance of gardening as the major leisure activity in the co-operatives of Estonia, while outside Moscow 'some summer garden chalets constructed in the 1950s already have central heating and an obvious air of permanency' – though around Leningrad 'many dachas are uncomfortable, poorly constructed, and situated either in areas which are aesthetically poor or on land that would be better put to other purposes'.

By 1985 it was reported that the Soviet government was catching up with the allotment boom 'which has been sweeping the country for some years'. The press was beginning to carry articles on the social benefits of allotment gardening.

For the average Russian city dweller, it looks as if the first symbol of the Gorbachev era will be an allotment. The Politburo has authorized a series of measures designed to increase the number of private gardens, to provide the gardeners with seeds and garden tools – and to produce a heavy boost to the state's production of fruit and vegetables ... In the past three years, 5000 shops have been authorized to start stocking goods for private gardens – and these have already proved too few for the soaring demand ... Once the plot has been dug, planted and harvested, the owner is allowed to put up a garden shed – and, with a little creative interpretation of the rules, a shed can become a small dacha. The state has a register of over five million allotment-holders, and estimates that they contribute each year over a million tons of fruit and vegetables to the Soviet diet.[30]

All the countries of Eastern Europe have variations on the Soviet experience. In Hungary two expensively unsuccessful attempts at collectivization of agriculture were followed by the introduction of private plots at the suggestion of other communist governments.[31] 'As it is, the prosperity of the peasants, if one could call it that, is to a considerable extent the result of their own efforts on small-scale plots.'[32] The landscape of chalet gardens can be seen on the outskirts of the cities of Poland, Czechoslovakia, Hungary, Romania, Bulgaria and Yugoslavia. The existence of peasant-owned land on the fringes of cities offers opportunities for piecemeal evolution – indeed even "overnight mush-rooming" – of "wild settlements", as in Nowy Dwor and elsewhere outside Warsaw or in Kozarski Bok and Trnje on the margins of Zagreb. Such communities are not encour-aged, yet they are tolerated and even provided with utilities and welfare . . .'[33]

In Bulgaria, families from Sofia have second homes on the lower slopes of Mount Vitosha, and these tend to become the permanent residences on their owners' retirement, while in Prague, every fifth household has a second home, many owners coming from the old industrial quarters of the city. Indeed, a situation has gradually evolved whereby large numbers of Prague citizens live during the week in new State or co-operative buildings, or poorly maintained inner-city apartments, and devote their energy and initiative to their second home and its garden outside the city. Juri Musil surveyed an urbanized East Bohemian region and found that three-quarters of households said they had a garden. Of these, 69 per cent were attached to houses, 13 per cent were on small allotments in garden colonies, 11 per cent at weekend houses and the rest elsewhere. 'Planners from many cities agreed that in recent years the demand for small allotments had grown rapidly. This interest was undoubtedly stimulated by a series of government decrees aiming at the exploitation of fallow land and at increasing auxiliary food production'; it was also linked with ideas of 'escaping from the cities and the back-to-the-land movement', ecological consciousness and the desire for uncontaminated food. He found that all workers on co-operative or State farms had small private plots. 'The motivation of these activities is predominantly economic, but not market-oriented. They improve the families' budgets and enable them to enter non-monetary exchange of products and services between relatives, friends and neighbours. Usually most family members take part ...' These transactions are in fact part of the informal economy of reciprocal mutual aid that is attracting increasing academic attention in both Eastern and Western countries. As Jiri Musil puts it: 'For very simple and understandable reasons ... in conditions where services are scarce and expensive, a non-formal economic as well as social network based mainly on locality, has to complement the formal economy ... a world of numerous local interactions, material and non-material exchanges and mutual support ...'[34]

American communities

The country has been mildly amused at the proceedings of the unemployed 'land-grabbers' who have seized pieces of waste ground in London and a provincial city and begun (rather late in the season) to plant vegetables upon them. The methods of these destitute men are, it is true, predatory and cannot be countenanced but their avowed object – namely, to grow food upon soil which at present is producing nothing – is one with which it is difficult not to sympathize.

Now at Philadelphia, in the United States, exists a Vacant Lots Association, which obtains from owners of building land lying uncultivated in the neighbourhood of the city permission to put it to its natural use until it is otherwise required. This land, under certain regulations, is handed over to the very poor, who grow vegetables upon it with results to their health, happiness and pockets that are very remarkable, as I can testify from personal knowledge and inspection. Could not the American example be followed in this country?

H. Rider Haggard
letter to *The Times*,
19 July 1906

The gardens on vacant lots in Philadelphia that impressed Rider Haggard were first initiated as a result of the economic panic of 1893. 'Urban gardens were a popular form of relief work because of the European tradition of kitchen and community gardening and the political success of promoting the self-help ethic. These community gardens, commonly called Potato Patches, provided both supplementary income for the participants and an escape from the stigma of being on the "dole" ... They worked well to assimilate the new immigrants and to moderate the severity of the economic crisis.'[35] Their continuing advocate was a New York lawyer, Bolton Hall, who had an unbounded faith in 'little lots well tilled', and was sure that 'all men could be producers with vacant-lot gardens and rural vegetable patches'. Agriculture is unique among occupations, Hall told his audiences, 'in that it can be engaged in without any particular experience'.[36] This was hardly the remark of a practical gardener.

With the entry of America into the First World War patriotism replaced poverty as a motivation. Largely to free the freight industry for the transport of war material, the virtues of local food production were urged by the federal government's National War Garden Commission. Posters urged Americans to be 'Soldiers of the Soil' and to 'Hoe for Liberty' by setting up Freedom Gardens. The campaign was very successful and long after the end of the war the phrase was still used. In the 1960s when Studs Terkel was compiling his oral history of the Great Depression he interviewed a woman in Marcus, Iowa, near the South Dakota border, asking her how she and her neighbours survived in the 1930s. She replied: 'We had our Freedom Gardens and did much canning. There was work to do, and busy people are happy people.'[37]

Her recollection is a reminder that before the days of the freezer, home canning of vegetables (as opposed to the industrial kind) was a commonplace in the United States to an extent that never penetrated Europe. As the effects of the stock market collapse of 1929 dug deeper into American society, a whole literature arose on the theme of escape from the city, or using the green patches that the city can provide.[38] As the Depression hit America, Herbert Hoover commissioned a report on unemployment relief, which urged the creation of 'subsistence gardens',[39] and in the years that followed, Roosevelt's Federal Emergency Relief Administration funded 'relief gardens'. These took two forms: allotment gardens, using the English phrase, which 'stressed the value of individual achievement as a way to prevent loss of morale and preserve self-respect', and industrial gardens operated by employed foremen of experience, where gardeners were 'paid' in vegetables and fruit in proportion to the number of hours worked. Scarcely had this programme been wound up, when the United States, like the other belligerent nations, reached record numbers of allotment gardeners. The Federal government's National Victory Garden Program sought to 'decrease the demand on the domestic food supply; to decrease the demand for tin cans; to decrease the use of railroads for non-military cargo; to sustain morale; and to alleviate food shortages by promoting gardening.' The result was remarkable. 'Forty per cent of the fresh vegetables consumed in the United States in 1944 were produced in Victory Gardens in the backyards and vacant lots of America.'[40]

The results, organized with infectious enthusiasm by a vast number of local pressure groups, federated in the National Gardening Association[42] and the American Community Gardening Association,[43] are even more impressive than the wartime efforts. It must be the least-known fact about the United States – just as the least-known fact about

153

the Soviet Union is that it has five million allotment gardeners – that community gardening is the nation's most characteristic pursuit. But that is what an annual Gallup Poll reveals:

Gardening maintained its rank as the most popular outdoor leisure activity of Americans in 1984, according to the National Gardening Survey. More people have flower or vegetable gardens than jog, swim, play tennis, golf, or fish. Forty per cent of all US households (an estimated thirty-four million households) had vegetable gardens in 1984.

Community gardening appeals to people of all backgrounds and ages. It is widely established and well-supported across the country. Each gardener's prime purpose is to get better-tasting and more nutritious food and at the same time to save money. Community gardens inevitably provide additional bonuses to their local areas. They inspire people to heightened social, educational and neighbourhood-beautification activities ... Community gardening is primarily an urban phenomenon and is now becoming integrated into city food policies and community development strategies. Cities providing secure land and some technical and financial assistance promote the self-help process of producing one's own food ... A need for permanent community garden sites (sites legally dedicated to gardening) was not seen as a major problem by those responding to the surveys quoted here. This is due in part to the fact that about half of all community garden sites are owned by non-profit organizations and are perceived as being secure. The popularity of community gardening over the last decade was for the most part a response to rising food costs. Many gardeners had a short-term goal: food production for the family. Today's community gardens are more diverse and are successful public amenities, many made beautiful by ornamental

plantings and public facilities of various kinds. Participants have developed a stronger bond to the land.
Recent experience proves that commercial development
on previously 'safe' community garden sites is a real
threat, as cities consider the maximum tax benefit they
could get from the land ... With more than twelve
million households (three out of four in urban areas)
expressing an interest in community gardening,
increased support for urban garden projects is clearly
warranted.[44]

These are remarkable findings. Canada has a similar range
of new urban initiatives, inspired by a non-profit Vancouver
society, City Farmer, which calls itself 'Canada's office of
urban agriculture', runs four demonstration plots and
claims that eighty per cent of all Canadians live on fertile
soil in urban centres, and that the cities can feed themselves.[45] Japanese cities have leisure gardens, small in size
(twenty square metres in Tokyo) because of the very high
price of urban land. They are rented from private landlords
and managed by local authorities.[46] Other cities of the Far
East are surrounded by a network of tiny holdings of incredible productivity, some of them market gardens, others
operated to augment their income by families with other
occupations. There are countries and cities in Asia, Africa
and Latin America where access to a plot of ground for food
production, whether for the household or the market, has
been and is today the factor that determines survival. And
of course there are cities where the poor are systematically
denied access to land. The international allotment scene is a
microcosm of the world itself.

9
Close to the earth

'One cold afternoon a strip was being made ready for the first planting of broad beans. When he thought it was done, Will fetched the beans and the line, but his grandfather had started on the strip again, moving incredibly slowly, raking and raking at the earth until it seemed he was trying to change its nature. Already there was nothing larger than a marble, but still endlessly, the raking and fining went on. Though he said nothing, Will doubted whether in the growing it would make much difference. It was less this, he thought, than some ritual of service ... the jobs which satisfied (Will) were those involving an immediate, sharp effect – hauling at a grubbed root, heaving a load of leaves to the heap, forcing along a heavy bundle of sticks. To (his grandfather) there seemed all the time in the world, though already the blue damp valley was thickening, and evening was drawing along the valley.'

Raymond Williams,
Border Country,
Chatto and Windus, 1960

For many of us, the only experience of the land is as an observer; enjoying a spectacle prepared for us. We share our participation at arm's length from the conditions that produce it; unaware of the circumstances and relationships involved. In the allotment, people participate in *using* the earth. Working the allotment is significant in a context of social relationships that we have already explored, and not separate from this there is a set of experiences, meanings and values of shared participation and individual activity in relation to the ground.

Germaine Greer feels that 'heaven is like Sissinghurst with turnips'. There is a rhythm in cultivation, a sense of postponed rewards rather than instant gratification ... a meaning frequently sought but unfulfilled in the wider world. People let their hair down on allotments, without the constraints of everyday conventions; here, even the bonfire becomes part of an absorption in an alternative world, typical of the intensity of individual experience it provides, while 'fashions' display a determined individuality. These activities are significant in being different from the mainstream ... There is an unusual sense of holding things in common, an alternative of low investment and a power of individuality. The allotment is part of a tradition of criticism of modern urban industrial society and the kinds of surroundings it creates. It provides a very practical, immediate alternative. Many features of the allotment seem to hold significant meaning in people's wider lives, and the visible allotment constitutes a cultural representation of these. It is an aesthetic adventure, whether this is in the pattern of leaves, the structural unity of the plot, the softening hawthorn hedgerow; the wind, the colour, the form of the opening flowers and the ripening fruit. There is a sensuality in growing things. 'Working outdoors feels much better for your body somehow ... more vigorous than day to day housework ... much more variety and stimulus. The air is always different and alerts the skin ... unexpected scents brought by breezes ... only when on your hands and knees do you notice insects and other small wonders ... my allotment is of central importance to my life. I feel strongly that everyone should have access to land, to establish a close relationship to the earth, something increasingly missing in our society, but essential as our surroundings become more artificial.'[1]

Back to the land

He seemed to get on better with his father, for they were often seen ... working diligently but ineptly, by local working-class standards, on a allotment. 'What he grew on it, I don't know, but he and Eric knew nothing about gardening ... They didn't have a clue – and owning an allotment was an odd thing for a man in his walk of life to do, none of the other retired civil servants did.' Such was the opinion of Mr Percy Girling, whose father owned a pub and rented the Blairs the allotment. When asked what he thought their 'walk of life' was, he replied: 'They were people who had missed their way somewhere, they weren't quite right, do you see? For instance, the allotment...'

Bernard Crick,
George Orwell, A Life,
Secker and Warburg, 1980

Theirs was 'the idea of a cottage where one grew one's own vegetables and lived on fifteen shillings a week', as Virginia Woolf put it in her novel *Night and Day*, in 1911. There have always been people for whom growing a portion of their own food has been a moral or ideological imperative, even though they might not be 'natural' gardeners. Orwell's acquaintances patronized his insistence on growing things and, whenever he had a chance, of keeping chickens and a goat. Filling in a literary questionnaire in 1940, he wrote, 'outside my work the thing I care about is gardening, especially vegetable gardening'.[2] That was the year when the geographer Keith Wheeler, then an eleven-year-old evacuee from Wandsworth in South London, fell under the influence of Harold and Amy, a middle-aged Fabian couple living at Petersfield in Hampshire. They had 'great simplicity, sympathetic intelligence, a quiet zeal for social reform, a sense of belonging to the people' and, of course, an allotment. Young Keith took on a plot himself on which he grew potatoes and gigantic sunflowers, and developed a lifelong concern for the human environment, both rural and urban. Getting into the country during the war influenced many attitudes like this.

The allotment epitomizes the back-to-the-land movement of the turn of the century, so far as it could then reach people of limited means. For the poor, disenfranchised from the land for over a century, the allotment offered a return to the land when no alternative existed. What did this mean to them? Since that time, the allotment has embraced a wide spectrum of people. It represents a stake in the land. While some people *choose* to live in parts of the city where gardens are small, others have been keen to contribute to the revitalization of land that had become unusable, returning it to cultivation. There is a growing interest in productive ways of using land.

People have also linked the allotment with the movement to encourage healthy eating and good sources of food. 'The allotment movement had certainly contributed something to the labourer's diet – Rowntree found that approximately one-twelfth of the food consumed was self-produced.'[3] Allotment holders' families at the end of the last century were found to have better diets than those who did not, even compared to unskilled labourers, whose earnings were several shillings a week more than theirs. To the labourer's diet of 44 lb. of bread and 25 lb. of potatoes, the farm labourer who had an allotment was able to have 40 lb. of bread, 40 lb. of potatoes and to add 20 lb. of fresh vegetables.[4]

The importance of allotments in the diet of the ordinary household was noted at the end of the eighteenth century: 'If we look at the average Englishman's diet we see that bread, cheese and meat were the principal sources of nourishment and the commons were perfect for providing cheese and meat. Vegetables were not a big feature of the average household economy except for onions, leeks, garlic and cole crops or members of the cabbage family.'[5] By the first half of the next century:

> The melancholy picture which emerges is of a population which spent its life in semi-starvation, existing on a scanty and monotonous diet of bread, potatoes, root vegetables and weak tea. Fresh meat was scarcely seen, unless the labourer dared to incur the severity of the game laws by poaching a rabbit or a hare: 'meat' meant

salt pork or bacon and a family was fortunate if it could afford these more than once a week. It is also clear that wheat flour was often of poor quality, and that rye bread and the even less attractive barley bread were still extensively used in the forties, especially in the Midlands and North. The one redeeming feature in the diet seems to have been the considerable quantities of fresh vegetables – potatoes, beans, onions, turnips, cabbages and so on – which the labourer willingly consumed.[6]

By the 1870s, Richard Jefferies in his well-known, and patronizing, account of the Wiltshire labourer, was explaining to readers of *The Times* that: 'His food may, perhaps, have something to do with the deadened slowness which seems to pervade everything he does – there seems a lack of vitality about him. It consists chiefly of bread and cheese, with bacon twice or thrice a week, varied with onions, and ... boiled cabbage, of which he eats an immense quantity. Vegetables are his luxuries, and a large garden, therefore, is the greatest blessing he can have...'[7]

Awareness of diet was not confined to the middle class; 'the idea of the gardens was to bring the family up. An' I'll tell ye ah divin't care what they say, we wa' healthier then that what we are noo. The stuff ye get oot of tins. Ye had to have a gardin te supplement the hoosehold.'[8] 'Commercially some fruits are picked unripe to decrease damage and spoilage during transit to distant markets and this results in a poorer product as does wilting and bruising.'[9] Just as was written on the situation in the Fens of over a hundred years ago, so it is considered that home-grown vegetables encourages early familiarity with fresh food, increasingly recognized as useful in health.[10]

The interest in healthy eating, fresh food and organic growing found its natural expression in the allotment. Tied in with this was the ideal of self-sufficiency, in itself an escape and an attempt at self-reliance in a society increasingly alien to the notion of an integrated community. And there was a renewed approach to food-growing for its own sake. Cultivation, as a source of interest as well as a practical activity, became the basis of a social culture enjoyed by all allotment holders. Added to this, they shared an appreciation of the landscape itself, peopled by its dedicated practitioners ... The allotment, then, represents a specific form of escape, embodying both the romance of a return to a separate way of life and a distraction from contemporary pressures in the outside world. On the allotment, the holder is in control, and his life is centred around how he treats the ground, the crops he grows in and on it, and any livestock he might keep.

The allotment had been the sole opportunity to reclaim one's 'own' life from the constraints of society after the First World War. It represented a haven of land that could still be cultivated in one's own way; there was a longer continuity. Many of these feelings found their expression in the allotment. Attachment to an allotment has become a much-prized, even ritualized undertaking. For many holders, 'the ineradicable peasant in the half-tamed Englishman' found in the allotment his true affinity, his 'uninterrupted pastoral' disturbed by employment 'at work'.[11] In this vision could be seen the peasant tradition of the allotment as a source of escape, contentment and struggle.

Leeks, whose image seems to revolve around cups, prizes and weird cultural tricks, are part of this escape. 'For the man of the house the leeks provide a quiet and relaxing release from the crowded family life of the terraced house ... In this way the miner can legitimately escape from both the family and the life underground, even if he often does little more than just sit and watch over his trench. But the leek offers more than just an individual reward to the grower. Leek growing is a *community* thing ...'[12] The same can be said of pigeon-keeping, which seems also to reflect a sense of liberation, caught by Keith Armstrong's poem:

... and only the flight
in his pigeons' wings
kept him dreaming
believing ... dreaming the dream
that his sons might fly
like his birds
escape out of hell

Keith Armstrong, 1985

It is no coincidence that many of the allotment-holders whom we talked to were concerned about healthy foods and the way in which they were grown. Frequently they had parents who worked the land and were dedicated gardeners, with or without allotments. There is a link between sustaining activity on the land, an escape and a concern simply for good health. Many allotment-holders combine these with a vigorous approach to rights. Ted Harwood is a committed allotment-holder whose attitude to cultivation and to the allotment movement is bound up with a wider awareness of a particular way of life. As he says himself, he is a fighter, and a keen observer of people's efforts at cultivation. He is very careful about what he eats, and has a caravan on a plot of land along the river Thames near Pangbourne. He and his wife live in Walthamstow, in a terraced house with a small garden. His early years were spent in Tower Hamlets, an environment too poor, and crowded, for a garden – and with no space available for allotments.

By trade he was a furniture maker. This took him and his wife to several parts of the country where they were able to have a large garden; this was especially so when they lived in Cornwall in the 1960s, where there was land that he could afford. Throughout his career he had been a strong Trade Union man, secretary to his branch. This has helped him to be an effective Secretary to the Waltham Forest Plot-holders Federation, and an active advocate for allotments in northeast London. When he was involved in a campaign to save a site from development, his attitude was to argue for a better location for the development proposed rather than simply to resist change.

By the time Ted retired they were living in the built-up inner suburbs of Walthamstow. The time retirement now allowed him he channels into his allotment. But this is not his only pastime. His urge to make things extends to making most of the furniture in his house, and, with his wife, furnishing and maintaining their plot in the country. The exercise working on the allotment affords him is just one benefit. Since suffering from bouts of ill-health Ted has turned enthusiastically to a more healthy diet and grows his crops organically. Only Growmore supplements his cultivation; Jeyes Fluid and calomel dust are the kind of treatments to which he restricts his crops. He saves as much seed as possible.

His concern about the value of well-grown food in people's lives, and his joy in growing things, as well as his personal reputation, have led to him being not only a well-known Secretary on the London circuit but a judge for the London Children's Flower Society. He believes that it is important for kids 'to appreciate what flowers mean, to know how to grow them'. He recalls sadly that some have a complete lack of understanding as to what to do, presenting a little bit of earth in the bottom of a pot and anticipating first prize. There is a desire to get involved, a love of the soil, and a unity in his life that are all reflected in the way he sees, and enjoys, his allotment.[13]

Dr Schwitzer has always been interested in gardening. Her mother's people had been farmers for generations, while her father's family were fruit farmers in Kent and in Essex. As a student she spent vacations doing farm work. Today, she is not only a very keen gardener but also a botanist. Her garden, steeply sloping in a wooded part of north London between Highgate, Crouch End and Muswell Hill, is not suitable for cropping, so when she chanced upon some neglected allotments by the railway near her home she was able to rekindle her enthusiasm for cultivation.

She recognizes that allotments – though in the main not a necessity – are of immense psychological value, as well as a source of pleasure through the growing of one's own crops and important in getting the holders out into the open air. She links the interest in allotments with the Open Air Farm Schools movement near her home, in Highgate, at the turn of the century. She is concerned about the way crops are prepared commercially, and stored. There is also a social interest in working with others on the site. A flourishing community has come into being around the allotments for whose survival she is largely responsible. Faced with a Railways Board looking for capital gains to be made from their land, Dr Schwitzer and friends pressed for, and achieved, the return of the site to allotments.

As well as a very practical interest, Dr Schwitzer's involvement stems from her curiosity about the way in which the environment has shaped history, and of how popular local views of places have been influenced. She is a professional historian whose career has been spent lecturing at London University, and in recent years she has made tapes of people's own histories, which have included reminiscences of work and play on the allotment, of tending the ground as a family affair. Her researches on the site she helped to save showed that it had a direct descent from common land, which it still was in 1816, the year a local farmer bought it. It may have been left as a fuel allotment, or as grazing land, but fifty years later it was sold again to provide allotments for railway workers, building the Highgate to Finsbury line, who lived in the Peabody flats nearby.[14]

Hilary Scuffham used to be an agricultural technician, but changed jobs because of his concern about the way that pesticides and other toxic chemicals were used. He is especially careful in the way that he treats the ground, favouring organic methods wherever possible. In his new job as a hospital porter he works with people suffering from the long-term effects of drug treatment and this confirms his bias towards more natural treatments.[15]

In wartime people like Eric Blair were seen as worthy citizens, in peacetime as harmless eccentrics. Then towards the end of the 1960s a change in the public mood began to be felt, and first a trickle, then a flood of articles, reports, pamphlets and organizations drew attention to what was perceived as a crisis of population and resources, of pollution and waste, energy and imbalance. It was stressed that the world's resources are finite, and that the rich nations have been consuming at a rate which the planet cannot sustain, with the result, not only that the poor countries could never hope to achieve levels of consumption previously taken for granted by the rich nations, but that the rich nations themselves would have to change course to survive. This was dismissed by some as gloom and doom, until the oil crisis of 1973 revealed the vulnerability of the western economies. In 1974 the environmental group, Friends of the Earth, issued a report called *Losing Ground* which declared 'people will be going hungry in Britain before the end of the century unless dramatic steps are taken within the next few years to step up domestic production of food, to limit the population and to develop agricultural systems that require less energy'.[16] It was a sign of the times, and in fact journalist Michael Leapman chronicled in *The Times* diary what he called 'the discovery of the allotment by the middle class'.[17]

Another literary participant in the allotment boom was Jeremy Bugler of the *Observer*, who reported in 1976 that: 'A national passion, suddenly conceived, for grow-your-own-fruit-and-veg is now accepted as the most striking change in British horticulture for three decades ... the Royal Horticultural Society's gardens at Wisley this spring had people hurrying past the rhododendrons to crowd into the "model vegetable garden". Every weekend, drought notwithstanding, doleful queues of families hang about allotment sheds, trying to get on the "list", and are turned away, often by the gardening gauleiters into whose hands allotment societies have a curious knack of falling ... Seedsmen like Suttons have had their sales go up by half as much again in the last two years.'[18]

With its necessary knack for dramatizing situations, Friends of the Earth declared 15 March 1975 as D-Day or Dig-In Day, to draw attention to the quantity of derelict land in the cities at a time when local authorities were acknowledging that the demand for allotments was continually rising, with a hundred per cent increase in London alone. Demonstration dig-ins were staged in half a dozen cities, often, as in Greater Manchester, with the support of the local authority.[19] In Cardiff and Southampton, breaking new ground, the local groups used horse-drawn ploughs 'just to make the point that it's possible to grow food without the help of oil'.[20] In Nottingham the city's Friends of the Earth took over two of the overgrown plots at Hunger Hills and put the produce on sale in the town centre to publicize the movement, declaring that 'Nottingham is one of the few cities in Britain where there is no waiting list for allotments. Instead of bewailing the waste of space, the public should count themselves lucky.'[21] In Birmingham three empty plots were squatted by the Friends of the Earth on one of the most ancient of the city's allotment sites.

Cultivation

Dear Pomona,
Uncle Harry has got an alotment and grows vegetables. He says what makes the mold is worms. You know we pulled all the worms out off our garden and chukked them over Miss Natchbols wall. Well you better get some more quick ask George to help you and I bring som seeds home when I comes next week by the xcursion on Moms birthday.

A. E. Coppard, *The Cherry Tree*

Whilst many families needed the allotment 'to fill their bellies',[22] even amongst the poor, there was a strong involvement in the activity of cultivation itself. The refinement of the art of cultivation, expressed in both the shows and in casual conversation, was not left to the specialist, the professional or even the home gardener.

Already in the middle of the century, gardening had become one of the major interests or pastimes of Britons. Gillian Darley went as far as to say that 'we do not sing, or dance, we garden'. Although maintaining a garden has become big business, it can still be done without much financial investment. It represented a different form of cultivation from the home garden. Although used as an annexe to the kitchen, it provided space without clashing with the wider uses of the garden. It was a place exclusively for cultivation and so it remains at the end of the century.

The distinction between the garden and the allotment goes further. As a place to go to, separate from the home, the allotment is more closely akin to the strip field; it represents a return to the land in more complete form. Of the cottage garden Hyams said it is 'no more than the vestige of the Elizabethan five-acre small-holding for the raising of food'.[23] In turn, whilst more cottages become weekend homes, this role is handed more exclusively to the allotment.

Gardening has provided an essential outlet for creativity, and has a central place in English folk art and culture. But this is by no means exclusively ours. Immigrant cultures, from the Caribbean, the Mediterranean and the Far East, have become represented in allotment cultivation, and shared their skills.

In his discussion of the planting of broad beans, Raymond Williams gets close to the actual feeling of attachment to the ground. There is a rhythm and ritual unique to cultivation. 'The cottagers worked in their gardens and allotments even after a long, hard day at the farm. Keeping a fine, clean tilth – touching 'er up a bit – was considered the most important part of good gardening.'[24] For Charles Tomlinson's father, 'John Maydew', the allotment, as for many people, was a challenge, hard work and struggle. Working with the land

167

after a day in the office was a hard-earned reminder of an earlier and happier time of his life. One allotment-holder, a professional person, told us of the 'challenge in its own right' that it represents to him. The procedures have to be carried out at certain times of the year. So, come what may, he is there nearly every Sunday.

'The men took great pride in their gardens and allotments and there was always competition among them as to who should have the earliest and choicest of each kind. Fat green peas, broad beans as big as an (old) halfpenny, cauliflowers a child could make an armchair out of, runner beans and cabbages and kale ... lettuces, radishes and onions.'[25] On their Sunday walks, it was difficult for Linda Thew's parents not to stop to chat with friends about their allotment: '... the walk ended with our going to the allotments. Here we walked up and down slowly while my parents pointed out the success (or, rarely, failure) of one crop of vegetables and fruit after another.'[26]

Christopher McLean is attached to his allotment. He visits his plot most evenings except Saturdays. He has a fine greenhouse on his plot, not a very familiar part of the scene nowadays. Edward Hyams said that 'the use of a small cheap greenhouse makes the allotment-holder his own nurseryman'. Christopher likes growing things because you 'can see the results'. He considers himself 'a lucky man having this (the plot), going fishing, having a drink'. He treasures this opportunity, with a place to sit to enjoy the view of his labours. He wins prizes, too. He lives in Liverpool, is still in work, and reckons that if he had no job then the allotment, much as it receives his attention, would only remind him that he had time to spare.[27] We were told by a woman in south London that her husband had been saved from a breakdown by taking on an allotment – the hope and rewards and interest that it had given him.

Mrs Sitch has always loved plants. This interest led her to attend a horticultural weekend near Oxford, then a weekly afternoon class. She was encouraged by the woman teacher to try an allotment. Hesitantly she took on a half plot. Ten years later and by stages, this became a double plot. She cultivates it herself – with her husband being content to enjoy the fruits of her labours. Encouraged by Mrs Sitch, several other women have started plots in the village where working on the allotment used to be seen more as a job for men. It has become part of Mrs Sitch's life, and she holds the position of Allotment Association secretary not because she is a woman but because she is an admired and effective allotment gardener. 'It is an absorbing hobby,' she says, and she like to make an outing of going to her site. She is keen to try out new varieties of seed, of asparagus, seakale and celariac, and gets supplies from the Isle of Wight and Cornwall. She is also experimenting with the seed of plants she has seen growing in Scotland.[28]

At eighty-two, John Francis cultivates four full-sized allotments, as he has done for decades. When we met him, in late October, in a valley site in Pont-y-Pridd, he was picking the last crop of Onward peas, and a second, late crop of broad beans. The previous weekend his son-in-law had helped him pick sixty-nine pounds of grapes from a thirty-foot-long greenhouse he built years ago. Next to the vinery stand his dozens of chrysanthemums, disbudded and perfectly staked. He left school at the age of twelve and went down the mines, at fourteen adding film-going as a pastime. Some years later he became a projectionist, which occupation he later turned to full-time. But for years the allotment has been his great love.[29]

The joys and the tribulations of allotment cultivation are well recorded in a diary kept by Lady Strawson, a Land Girl during the last war. For over ten years, her allotment has compensated for a large garden that was built over with houses. In the diary she expresses how neglected the site was on her arrival. The first day was spent cutting down the undergrowth. Several visits later there was still deep digging to finish, 'a slow process but probably the best'. With delight, in the following January she 'noticed beans just beginning to sprout'; there were soon peas, too. Later in the month, she records a 'lovely day. Bonfire going splendidly.' The bonfire is part of the ritual of the allotment, like sharing hints to contemptuous accuracy, and making a compost heap.[30]

There are ways of using the ground that are unique to the allotment. More akin to the cottage garden than the suburban and town garden of the late-twentieth century, the allotment's main crops are vegetables, though flowers are allowed to grow amongst them. The cottager had to put vegetables first; then later, in the nineteenth century, and very gradually, flowers were intermingled with them.[31] It was not until this century that back gardens became used, familiarly, for growing things, rather than as a backyard. It had been an extension to the house, not least the place for the lavatory and doing the washing.

Earlier, less conscious, arranging of the ground placed crops in informal patches and mixes. Gradually, through the influence of the horticultural magazines, good practice and increased yields encouraged row cultivation, neatly laid out and meticulously cultivated like Raymond Williams' committed figure. In the cottager's garden, the plants were set out in rows for ease of cultivation. It was only when the romantic design became the ideal, partly through its promotion in literature, that row cultivation gave way to the familiar curved layout of flower beds. In the 1970s, however, horticultural research argued for the greater ease of cultivation and sometimes improved cropping achieved by planting in squares; for the value of interplanting and of companion planting; and for the use of deep, and raised, beds. Flowers in the garden became useful to production.

Paradoxically, by the 1950s it had become increasingly the practice in home gardens to banish vegetables, aping the kitchen garden of the wealthy, and ignoring the initially decorative purpose of plants like the runner bean; 'cabbages can be decorative', too.[32] However, many vegetable varieties are now making a reappearance in the home garden, among them 'ornamental' kale and globe artichokes – and runner beans now adorn the patios of Belgravia. In contrast, we found vines common on allotments, occasional walnut trees, numerous globe artichokes, carnations and, more familiarly, rows of gladioli, chrysanthemums, and perhaps as 'companion planting', marigolds, especially calendula. If there was one vegetable that should be required planting it is the runner bean, for it gives a good return, provides visual interest, returns nitrogen to the soil and provides the ultimate opportunity for individual resourcefulness in cultivation in the use of supports.

John Carey appreciates that gardeners can be austere people:

> ... the sensuous gains that they look for are remote and devious ... parsnips ... an immense and exacting pleasure to grow. At the start of the season you grub out a row of pits ... poke into each soft dell about a dozen of the crisp wafers which are the parsnip's seeds, and pat earth over them. Come the summer, you pull out all but one of the seedlings from each cluster – pale golden pencils, with feathery tops, which it always gives you a pang to throw on to the compost heap. Then, as the winter approaches, the great spreading leaves of the survivors rot and yellow, and the parsnips withdraw into their subterranean existence until, some time after Christmas, the time comes to crack the frosty crust over them, and lug them out, gross, whiskered and reeking, from their lairs ...[33]

He explains a new slant on allotment aesthetics: 'As vegetable gardeners aren't primarily concerned with eating they harbour, like librarians, a tidy-minded dislike of anyone who actually wants to use the commodities they're in charge of. To have to uproot cabbages, say, from a row, and hand them over for cooking, is always an annoyance. The gaps look unsightly, like snapped-off teeth.'

During the drought of 1976, people learned techniques of

water conservation from Indian and Chinese allotment-holders. There are other distinctive qualities of cultivation, and of a general attitude to the allotment, amongst people from the Far East and the Mediterranean. English allotment-holders are filled with surprise and admiration at seeing Pakistani women plant their onion seeds whilst crouching on their haunches, and placing the seeds one at a time, with great care. They farm like that in Pakistan, and seeds are extremely expensive there. Growing things, and the earth, are more intensely important to them; they are more immediately matters of life and death. Well-organized and concentrated hard work is typical of the family approach of West Indian allotment-holders. Offered a plot during the week, several relatives will be on the site until dusk at the weekend to clear the ground ready for the season.[34]

Certain conditions make for a particular character of cultivation that is peculiar to the allotment: the journey from home, the size of the plot, the position of the plot on the site; the availability of water; potential vandalism; the likely openness of the site; and the presence of perennial weeds – of especial concern where one takes over a long-neglected site. The presence of many neighbours, the numerous varieties grown and crop practices used to have a big effect on cultivation. With the impermanence of many sites these influences mean that particular strategies are needed for dealing with tools, pests, weed and vegetable seeds; for drainage; and for cropping and effecting appropriate rotations. Strategies for postponing conversation with over-friendly neighbours might also be required ... Women holders have told us of their strenuous efforts on their plots whilst men spend their time bending over rotavators together, 'making the air blue'. Another told us of the man who came across and tried to show her how to make a furrow and sow seeds – ignoring her protestations! Men told us that topless allotment tenants added to the subtler sensuality of working an allotment.

In the new town of Milton Keynes, a hundred people moving in each year take on allotments. Many of these have moved from homes without gardens. Large numbers don't last the season. It is likely that some find the commitment required hard to sustain during the first year of moving, and later on it can be difficult to pick up the thread again. However, it is not only new movers who reach the point of calling it a day. There are real difficulties in cultivation, not to mention additional irritations like obtaining water and coping with vandals. The journey from home means that equipment and materials have to be carried or stored on site. There may be problems with the carriage, and the site may not be secure; indeed, sheds may not be allowed. The plot may be near a water supply, or the gate or the track, in which case transport, and especially water, are easy. If not, there is likely to be a great struggle. For generations, people with allotments up the steep sides of the Rhondda valley have survived this. On the hill site of the Rosendale Road allotments in south London, this causes trouble too, but people love the atmosphere high above the city when they finally arrive at their plots.

'It wasn't just the cost, it was getting it there by the wheelbarrow load. You tend to forget there are no roadways through allotments. Sandy worked on it during the day with help from their two sons, and at least two evenings a week ... the allotment had got to the stage where it was a chore rather than an enjoyment.'[35] The drought of 1976, following a dry summer in 1975, was responsible for many earnest newcomers giving up. The advice, 'more hoe less hose', is one that has to be taken on the allotment, where there is frequently no choice. The main problem is a naive belief that plants 'just grow'. 'Some dig the ground and try to crop it directly; they see the labour but not the progress,' Ted Harwood pointed out. They find it difficult to cope with the postponed rewards that come with allotment cultivation. But as Angela Harding wrote: 'Maybe the plot *should* be left bare until every rod, pole and perch has been blasted clear, but then every seedling set out nurtures hope ... any new allotmenteer (and old too?) *needs* dreams.'[36]

There is another struggle with the elements. In Liverpool, Chris Maclean found the weather too wet for some sweet corn; and mice had been a nuisance on his sweet peas that cheered up the wire netting by the compost heap. The greater problem of vandals is described graphically in a case from Harrow, west London. We found it repeated up and down the country. 'A nearby abandoned railway line gives the thieves and wreckers unobtrusive access. Whole rows of vegetables are torn up and scattered about, soft fruit bushes are stripped and damaged, while sheds are relieved of anything movable.'[37]

The problem with weeds is made worse by those species that thrive on persistent and careful cultivation of the soil. Horsetails, an antediluvian kind of clubmoss, grows best where the allotment is naturally well-watered, like the site in Oxford next to the river Thames. Some holders spend what they save on greengroceries on chemicals that don't seem to work; others double their cultivation time, thoroughly cleaning the soil of the finest rootlets. The nuisance is that they travel well over a metre underground, their roots poetically phrased to us by Allan Todd as 'a web of nature's pipes'.

> In the drought
> since your departure
> the marestails
> have gained ground
> plotting their mutiny
> to lay waste your bounty.

> Keith Spencer,
> 'Marestail' from *The Allotment*, 1982

Seven holders we know had at least seven remedies between them. One, Alan Todd, turned to his flame thrower to deal with persistent weeds. He left the plot safely that evening, only to be called the next morning by his plot neighbour. A spark must have rested somewhere on the ground, as not only his but his two neighbours' sheds had been burnt to the ground.

The allotment and the communal spirit it inspires often mean that seeds are shared and joint orders entered into. And then there is the magic of the variety names themselves – names like Chatenay Red Core and Wheeler's Imperial, 'full' as John Carey pointed out, 'of mysterious evocations like monuments to a lost culture. Who was Ailsa Craig, now immortalized as an onion? ... Who was the Lobjoit of Lobjoit's Green Cos?'[38] There is the surprise of someone else's seeds, of swapping varieties and, above all, hints. The observation alone that is available on allotment sites presents numerous examples of 'good practice'. Michael Hyde reported a unique approach to increasing soil cultivation and round-the-year operations:

> Bill Masser has made grass paths in his deeply dug, narrow-bed vegetable garden, rendering it pleasing aesthetically as well as practically viable throughout the year. He never has to tread on the soil ... (he) works the beds from the paths on which he can sit or kneel, if need be, to hand-weed the closely planted crops. The beds are 4½ feet wide and 15 feet long, interspersed with these green paths that are edged with 2-inch-thick concrete slabs along which, with careful guidance, the mower wheels can run. He finds rotation of crops easier with this system and he gets satisfaction by working one bed at a time: that way he can see where he's been, with a consequent sense of accomplishment.[39]

The freezer has had a significant effect on the value of the allotment, and this can be interpreted in two ways. It provides the chance to buy fresh food and *avoid* the cultivation. However, it also permits the allotment-holder to make use of a glut, and to take advantage of a limited range of crops that the soil, or his competence, allows him to grow. An allotment-holder in Nottingham put it this way: 'the advent of the home freezer has changed the economics of the allotment, since it copes with surplusses'.[40] It helps ease constraints on cultivation, too, in the form of what, when and how much you grow.

Composting is obviously a 'good thing' on allotment sites, for at least three reasons. It recycles plant material, so conserving food and the soil structure; it saves money and carriage of manure to the site; and it uses up otherwise 'waste' materials. It does not have to resemble the seamy picture that Flora Thompson gave a century ago: 'the house refuse was thrown on a nearby pile called "the muck'll"'. This was situated so that the oozings from the sty could drain into it; the manure was also thrown there when the sty was cleared; and the whole formed a nasty, smelly eyesore to have within a few feet of the windows.'[41] However, plot-holders compete for the product of allotment-site toilets, while in the cities local police stations provide cherished sources of manure. There are other solutions, and working to the contours on sloping sites is a means of conservation that we have learned especially from Mediterranean and Eastern cultivators.

The allotment is an admirable place on which to cultivate vegetables and flowers for display at a show, the individual plot-holder being a member of a wider competitive community, added to which there is simply more space on the allotment in which to grow a prize-winner. However, the actual day of a show is an ecstatic but tiny part of the whole experience. For Tommy Taylor, the showing was part of a wider enjoyment: 'On the allotment, you can feel everything there ... life is there.' However, he is unequivocal about showing. 'Being clean is a very important aspect of showing. There is a distinction between the grower and the shower – the competitive feel takes over.'[42] He gets no joy where the competition is very small. He maintains that big vegetables taste all right if they are properly grown. There is one leek-grower in the northeast who warms up for the championships by playing Johnny Matthis singing 'Let's do it' to his pollinating plants. 'If you've got the winners to put in the show, you get a lift; if not, down you go.'[43] 'The winners receive public recognition as the whole village, or seemingly the whole city, inspects the exhibits.'[44] There is a special 'Leek Card Calculator' to measure the size of the pot leeks in cubic inches, nearly as great a girth as critical length. Leek-slashing is one unfair competition, carried out at night by vandals – or even opponents. It is not the only danger: a Mr Francis in Ponty Pridd once gave a friend a giant pumpkin, only to discover later that it had been entered and had won first prize at a local show along the valley, under his 'friend's' name! Behaviour like this has a long history and, in 1924, stewards at one show were advised to mark any prize-winers so that they could not be exhibited at other meetings.[45]

Sanctuary

... we had some rabbits in a place on the allotments. We used to gather manure for a man, and he let us have half of his tool-house in the garden.

D.H. Lawrence,
'Lessford's Rabbits',
in Raymond and Joy Williams' (eds),
Lawrence on Education, 1973

It's magic to light the lamp.

Alan Todd, 1986

Jennifer Armstrong sensitively portrayed a child's-eye view of what the allotment means as a sanctuary in one grown-up-child's memory:

Each precious plot contained essentially the same parts, but assembled in an endless variety of ways. She recalled how the flowers were always grown in straight lines, like the vegetables. There was always a piece wired off for the hens and always a shed – nothing fancy, just a makeshift affair – for the pigeons. The evening visit to the pigeon house, straight after tea, had an almost religious significance in Mary's mind. She could see her grandfather now, pushing back his chair from the table, collecting his pipe from the mantelpiece and stretching out a great gnarled hand for hers. Together they would leave by the back door, Grandpa taking his battered cloth checked cap from its hook in the kitchen as they passed through. From the outhouse they would both scoop grain into their pockets for the birds. As far as she remembered all this took place in complete silence. And it was best of all on dry warm evenings when the dusky air was filled with the fragrance of sweet williams and low cooing of the pigeons. Then, as Grandpa offered mysterious words of encouragement to his beloved birds in queer melodic tones, such a peace descended on them that to Mary it was like being in Paradise...[46]

In the personal detail of the allotment shed the holder achieves a private sanctuary. Here, 'possessions are arranged in ways that show they are free from interference'.[47] The details can be sparse or comfortable: a stove, a kerosene lamp and one or two legchairs or old car seats. These sheds can form the focus of friendships, with the facility for brewing tea. After most holders had left for lunch one summer Sunday, the Cockney stage-whispers from one open door floated across a site in Newham, giving an impression that one was eavesdropping upon a hallowed conversation. As well as providing shelter from the elements, sheds can also offer a cherished respite from working the ground.

Ray Garner felt that the shed could express an individuality otherwise absent in the lives of many working people. To the plot-holder, the shed signifies a sense of control, a reflection of his own culture. The holders have been derided as enclosers, those who jealously fence in everything that can conceivably be fenced; the builders, thwarted architects whose huts seem sometimes more important than their plots.'[48] But perhaps they are not 'thwarted': 'the shed builder has become a master of constructional understatement; it will do, it's all right, it's good enough. There seems to be a conscious feeling that the work should be performed properly but equally the time and effort involved is given contemptuously ... It is easier and cheaper to use secondhand doors and windows, even if they are tatty. Brickwork is rarely used for it is too close to traditional building craftsmanship, it is time-consuming, it needs to be thought out and performed with skill. Brickwork is relatively permanent too and why should a tenant put time and money into permanent structures ...'[49] It is in the shed, home-designed and home-made, that the 'rebellious spirit' finds best expression. More than anything, the allotment shed of this type gives the impression of being rooted in the ground. Constructed on site, it has not been turned out of a factory many miles distant.

Alan Todd is no creator of the makeshift, and prides himself on his workmanship. He likes the brick and slate sheds that have been built on an allotment alongside the railway between Oxford and Coventry. He does not work artistically – rather, he is interested in solid, workmanlike structures. His father made grottoes in the garden at home, 'like pearly kings and queens'. A perfectionist who wanted natural stone, he was surprised when people wished to take photographs of his garden. Fascinated by his father's structures, Alan endlessly dug holes in the ground, just to look. He has always found fun in building in his garden, and experiences a letdown when the work is done: 'the interest is in the doing; then it is "just there"'. Perhaps this was part of the enjoyment he found in replacing the three sheds he accidentally set fire to when fighting the mare's-tail. He used secondhand materials, surplus corrugated iron, shop-window display units, and timber from floor joists thrown out in a factory renovation nearby. The end product is impressive. For a comfortably placed businessman, these ways of using materials point to a deeper form of attachment and meaning.[50]

Plot-holders in Wolverton, now part of Milton Keynes, continue to use the old railway carriages cast in the nearby works. They look more like summerhouses, and provide the nearest thing to the scene depicted in Eric Ravilious' *Train Landscape* painting, a view from a third-class railway carriage looking out across rural England – but at Wolverton the people actually make the landscape.[51]

Some sheds fulfil the great needs of housing tools and storing crops. The shed, with all its expression of individuality, can take pride of place on the plot. This is epitomized in one plot near Colchester in Essex. At the far side of his plot, Peter Mayhew has let a short stretch go to grass, self-seeded, with the help of the birds, into a lawn. This he keeps neatly trimmed through the year. Two morello cherries, planted long before he came, are heavily laden with fruit in late summer. The original two have run suckers to give half a dozen fruiting trees. These are behind the shed, itself in a sheltered island. Inside hang weighty onions, plaited carefully around strings that hang from the ceiling. Tools are placed with an equal care. Behind the shed and around the bases of the gently bending trees are rolls of wire netting, a bottomless bucket neatly placed, and a square of polythene wrapped in twine. On top of the shed is a metal pot with narrow neck, where blue tits take turns with the starlings and blackbirds to nest. Peter calls himself a big softy. The shed roof fills the waterbutts to save the trek from the water tap the other side of the site. In this setting of perfect tranquility, Peter feels himself to be in 'a real garden'. He has one at home (a 'garden' that is); the allotment is for potatoes, beans and root crops, all meticulously tended. He loves to sit out by his shed on the plot lawn, enjoying lunch with his wife and daughter – the deckchairs they keep in the shed, of course.[52]

In this way the shed operates as the means of 'access' both

to toil and to recreation whether it be by housing the deck-chairs for sitting outside on in fair weather, or by providing shelter from a shower – or by acting as the source of heat to set seeds or in which to recover from rheumatism. It extends a private world to the more public domain of the allotment plots themselves. Even those holders who don't crop their land contribute to the community of the site. For example, in the 1970s in Newham, east London, there was a man who spent time most weekends in the security of his shed discussing the world between bouts of shooting rats with his friends.

In Oxford in the 1970s, a match was made in an allotment shed, lamp-lit and furnished with a sumptuous car seat. Amongst the prize onions and bird scarers on an allotment in North Finchley: 'One man moved into his shed with his fancy woman. ". . . lived there with 'is young lady, they had a stove in there. It weren't a very big shed neither . . . The committee threw him out. I was agin' it. He used to chase people away. But they throwed 'im out.''[53]

It may be hard to imply the deliberately makeshift, and certainly there is good reason to save outlay if you are poor; but we were repeatedly told, by the most committed holders, of the meanness of the allotment fraternity. This is borne not of a cold and disinterested view of the world, but of a necessity to save materials and seed. Indeed, the allotment-holder is by no means tight on the amount of effort and ingenuity put in to the plot, and into the crop. This is displayed in the loving care in evidence on nearly every site. Moreover, despite an almost untamed individuality there is a sophisticated co-operation in getting work done, clearing sites and in sharing seeds and produce.

'All the delight, all the significance of these little houses lies in their diversity, in the informality of their haphazard compositions, so often exaggerated by a huddle of lean-tos, outshots and projections, in the unsophisticated crafts-manship which has given each one of them its own singu-larity, above all in the way they are absorbed into the landscape, setting into it as naturally as a yellowhammer's nest into a hedgebank.'[54] This is not to romanticize badly built, badly serving structures, but to identify attachments and relationships that people have expressed in their use of place. Actually serviceable, these have suffered, rather, from elite views that appear as paternalism, saving people from what they want to construct. Buildings are not the only sanctuary on allotment sites. Innumerable little gardens are created by their 'owners', surrounded by trees, shrubs and homemade trellises, often with a tiny lawn in the middle. The working environment of the cropped ground may be shut out, making withdrawal and rest a reality. This is part of the experience of being close to the earth.

The ecologists

Crouched beneath the rusted oil drum
the toad turns full circle
alarmed in my lifting
the lid off its hiding place.

Plunging the watering can
into the trough
I flush out a family of frogs
from inside the cistern.

Turning the soil we unearth
a pocket of sleeping newts
their bodies presed like fossils
into the clay.

Keith Spencer,
'Reptiles',
from *The Allotment*, 1985

On some sites, there used to be an open battle between those who poisoned everything on sight and those who spent a long time finding alternative methods; on some, there still is. The organicists complain that their crops are polluted by the neighbouring sprays; the inorganics blame the others for the survival of weed seeds and insect eggs that blow over their plot.[55]

At Newham, the loss of sites, local concern about vacant land, and the lavishness of an alien redevelopment brought together the allotment and wildlife interests as a 'green' grouping which, during the 1980s, shared a council sub-commitee. Both want green spaces left alone; the plot-holders realize the predatory value of birds (and their colleagues realize the nuisance of rats), but there is also the view that 'they don't see it like we do; we don't want rabbits running all over the place'. In one Essex town there are joint meetings between the wildlife and allotment groups. On one site in East Anglia there is a badger set. Like hedgehogs, badgers are insect-eaters and an asset to the allotment.

All this can be a source of much interest, exasperation or amusement for holders using more 'ordinary' methods. 'We started the slow, labourious task of clearing the land by our eccentric organic methods, which aroused all our fellow allotment-holders to dire prognostication and much head-shaking. We dig up the sods and shake out all the surplus soil; turn them over and leave for wind and weather to work on, then shake out more soil and pick out the matted roots. The clumps of (by then) dried grass are piled on the compost heaps and the roots left to dry out still further. They too are then composted. We can only hope that time and our better results will convince our neighbours that it should not be sent up in wasteful smoke.[56]

On one south London site a group of committed organic gardeners who cultivate a once vacant piece of ground in a residential suburban neighbourhood at Sunny Hill in Streatham took careful steps to retain trees to create an attractive setting that was also useful for wildlife, ecologically. This was part of an aim to grow food organically. This sylvan, south-facing site occupies land that was a back garden decades ago. Its alternative use is limited because it is above a piece of underground railway. One of the holders, in his twenties and a member of the Friends of the Earth, has a deep commitment to gardening. He had actually been working as a gardener until he began a professional course in landscape design. One aspect of the scheme is to provide a scrub area, neat but uninterrupted, for butterflies and ground animals. The local council, glad of the allotments scheme and the busy efforts of the holders who have improved the site, is discouraging this for fear that neighbours along the road may find it scruffy.[57]

The compost heap provides a reserve for wildlife. The interests of cultivation, wildlife and organic methods are mutually supportive. Michael Hyde identified the usefulness of 'wildlife' to allotment-holders in a passage where he describes an encounter with six young hedgehogs on his plot. His friend deftly deposited them among the crops and did his best to make them feel welcome. 'The soil being dry he sank a small trough of water in the ground to satisfy their thirst in case they failed to capture enough juicy slugs for this purpose ... We hope that they will become anti-slug benefactors to the allotments. The least (we) can do is to take along milk and show them we care, leaving it regularly in a sunken carton outside our hut.'[58]

Eric Simms called allotments valuable wildlife habitats. They provide resting places for many migrant birds. Oases of green land in towns and cities, with a variety of bushes, grassland, trees and other structures, allotments act as shelter for shy species of birds like the tawny owl, jay, wren and, perhaps less welcome for the fruit grower, the bullfinch. Kestrel, whitethroat, tree sparrow, willow warbler and pied wagtail have also been recorded on urban allotments. And whilst the bullfinch may be attracted to fruit buds, its main diet consists of softer thistles and groundsels. The linnet specializes in farmland weeds like fat hen, mugwort and persicaria, while other finches share dandelions, teasels and chickweed, and tits can clear a tree of aphids. Whereas the racing pigeon is revered, locally, the feral pigeon is an unwelcome visitor, attracted by brassicas, though it does

also eat weed seeds.[59] Simms identified the distinctive
nature of the allotment as habitat:

> A particularly interesting habitat in outer suburbia is
> that formed by plots of allotments where patches of
> cultivated earth are set among strips of grass and weeds
> rather like the squares on a chess board. Cover for birds
> often exists in nearby hedgerows, bramble brakes and
> small planted fruit trees. There is often a small belt of
> forest trees growing alongside the allotments and per-
> haps separating them from roads, houses and factories;
> these rows of trees often mark the old field lines. Water
> is usually available perhaps from a pond or stream or
> more probably from tanks fed by stand-pipes for local
> irrigation. There is nothing in nature quite like this
> habitat which forms an ecotone, or tension belt,
> between the environments of farmland and suburban
> house and garden; it may well contain elements from
> both bird communities.[60]

In the few years that an allotment was left uncultivated in
readiness for development, twenty-three flower species were
recorded, among them field rose, black bryony and teasel;
there were larger skipper butterflies and meadow browns
were abundant. Hedgehogs and woodmice balanced the
benefit and loss, probably in the allotment-holder's favour.
A site in northwest London was described as 'a mosaic of
small holdings with a considerable variety of crops that
provided a rich habitat for birds, with twenty-one species on
twenty-nine acres of the sites'.[61] During the war the
extension of allotments was welcomed by ecologists for the
reintroduction of numerous field species to the cities. 'A
white wagtail that was seen on the allotments near the
Albert Memorial in March 1944 was the second record of
that sub-species in Inner London.'[62]

A rare plant (or weed) figured in a campaign to save an
allotment from development. The Nature Conservancy
became involved, and both sides discovered a close mutual

interest. The species involved was a fumitory, Martin's fumitory (*Fumaria martinii*), which is extinct in Britain except for on an allotment on the Isle of Wight. A combination of persistent cultivation and much organic growing, shunning herbicides, had provided its sanctuary. The Nature Conservancy proposed that the allotment be made a Site of Special Scientific Interest, not stopping the plot-holders' work, because it was their cultivation that had created the right conditions for its survival and, being easily pulled, it is not a nuisance. Indeed, efforts to cultivate it at Cambridge Botanic Garden had failed.[63]

It is possible to buy a packet of frozen peas, even a whole meal, one minute – and cook it instantly the next, without knowing where or how or by whom it was produced. And this can be less expensive than seeding, nurturing and harvesting the food yourself, and a lot less 'trouble'. Like the allotment: 'The digging-up of suburban lawns to plant potatoes and cabbages is, perhaps, more significant as a declaration of independence than as a contribution to the world food problem.'[64] The experience of being Close to the Earth, *and* on the allotment, is clearly even more than that.

10
The allotment aesthetic

'... not merely
that there were a hundred plots or so, but all
The ways in which it had become a rooted place.
Sixty years of growth had changed the access tracks
To country lanes, with chest-high privet
Rose- and bramble-trimmed, secluding favoured plots.
A stranger looking at them, I thought
Of cottage gardens without cottages:
All else was there – in dilapidated sheds;
A pigeon loft (against the rules perhaps);
The old pot, gnome, and weather-vane; and rows
And rows of vegetables, green enfilades
Against the surrounding town, miraculously
Stopped short there ...'

Peter Walton,
'The Allotment' in The Green Book,
Vol. 2, No. 2, 1986

The development of recreation in Britain brought new pressures to bear on the allotment. It was argued that the traditional anarchic image of a diverse jumble of buildings and lack of presentation to the outside world were an impediment to the allotment's 'leisurely' potential. That people had loved being a part of such places for many years was ignored ... So we can see the disparity between the demands and expectations that surround the allotment landscape and the deep sense of affinity it evokes from its practitioners. The way that people create structures and use the ground in the allotment represents something of their own culture – and, thereby, what that piece of land, and the activities on it, mean to them. The allotment is a collective undertaking, conceived through shared labour, and containing many idiosyncratic elements. The plot-holders thus create their *own* landscape.

One particular view of the allotment is caught in this impression: There [is] a multitude of allotment sites whose individual sheds are a disgraceful eyesore. They are constructed of anything from soap boxes to old doors and windows: where they have rusted or rotted away many have been patched with strips of tarpaulin, linoleum, or even pieces of canvas. They have been built with little thought for siting with the result that the whole area often appears a confused jumble of squalid and unsightly sheds . . . Rows of rusting enamel buckets or disused oil and tar drums stretching across the plot are commonplace and do little to enhance the appearance of either plot or site. Scarecrows and other bird-scaring devices, pieces of tinfoil which are blinding in the sun and rattle continually in the wind, old tubes and boxes strewn around the plot, and sections of ancient bedsteads used as fencing further contribute to this sorry picture . . . a horticultural slum.[1]

There are no doubt allotments ill-provided by their landlords and neglected by their holders, but the Government Report presented images like these as typical.

Some allotment sites encapsulate, like Charles Tomlinson's, something of a visual paradise. At Bladon allotments, near Woodstock in Oxfordshire, only the cracking of the wheat and the occasional hallowed observation by visitors at the nearby monument punctuate the calm. Poppies stray over the edges of the cornfield that has missed treatment, to bloom amongst the french beans. A footpath skirts the length of the site, but an enterprising holder on a very well-tended plot has created a splendid scarecrow. Opposite the wheatfield the backs of council cottages and some larger houses from the eighteenth century contain the site. Only a matter of yards away an early church completes the landscape. This is a different way of seeing: here, it is possible to experience a positive, vigorous landscape and enjoy the visual product of people's labours.

Interestingly, a third way of looking combines the viewpoint of the critical voyeur with an expression of attachment that is felt at a different level. 'The site is virtually flat and markedly two-dimensional except for a motley collection of ramshackle sheds, greenhouses or other such shanties and the plots are laid out on a rectilinear grid-iron pattern, the detailed relationship of one plot with its neighbour is most unsatisfactory ... an untidy no-man's land fringed with grass and weeds ... the general appearance of the site is certainly all the better for the fact that gardeners not only work hard to produce edible crops but also enjoy and take pride in the aesthetic quality of the plot.'[2]

These observations of the allotment landscape demonstrate both the variety that is available and the variation in the measure of its aesthetic. The involvement of people in a landscape in the way allotment-holders are is a completely different way of experiencing landscape. The view that *we* see is little more than a clue to this, but at a deeper level it is a cultural representation. What is the aesthetic and what does it represent?

The construction of the allotment aesthetic

In Pontypridd, there is a sizeable allotment site along the flat bottom of the valley just ten metres above the raging Taff river. Largely disused factories of white painted brick stand the other side of the valley, almost shielded from view by thick trees. The river floods frequently, washing away soil – especially from up-valley plots – with some benefit to those lower down, and dislodging sheds. Behind the allotments can be glimpsed a dramatic view of miners' cottages, set in a long terrace against the cliffside. There is an excellent view from the cliff of the site below, of the patterns of cropping and the rich variety of texture discernible in the handmade structures.

The predominant landscape of the allotment today and

through most of its twentieth-century history was not formed through any conscious design. It did not have to comply with a particular way of seeing the landscape and its surroundings. Not surprisingly, allotments assume a whole range of visual identities, and here we explore and express this immense diversity up and down the country in different contexts, both contemporary and historical. The landscape that allotment-holders created was, as we have said, a collective result, and produced via particular conditions and pressures. Essentially, it remains a working-class landscape, a productive landscape, conforming to no 'style' and, with the exception of ventures like the Guinea Gardens, found in conditions of need and poverty. The landscape is thereby rooted in its history, through particular circumstances pertaining at different stages of its evolution.

The formative period of the allotment landscape was the turn of this century and the immediate decades thereafter. The tenants did not have land of their own. Landlords had not wanted to allot very much land, and councils provided plots for domestic use. The space was used thriftily. Cultivation was carried out when the holders had time, and with simple tools. The strict layout of the plot was part of a moral landscape that accompanied the broader attitude of many landlords to the holder; and how they sought to organize the land more strictly in order to regulate behaviour. Moral and religious education followed the landlord's instruction on the management of the plot. Good performance was encouraged by the staging of shows and the judging of plots, and prizes were awarded for 'good behaviour at evening classes'.[3]

The patterns and pressures of the land market and land ownership constrained the space available and the locations chosen. Not given high priority, allotments were often located in awkward corners, unattractive areas or steep land, or sites vulnerable to flooding – places where it was impossible to achieve a profitable rent from other uses. There were exceptions like the philanthropic colliery owners who put allotment sites in their model villages and extracted a return of good maintenance for them, whilst other sites ended up on subsiding land. Today, there are sites on roundabouts, along railway lines and in triangles adjacent to factories, on land not earmarked for other uses. An important part of their appearance derives from these settings. Around landed estates there still survive some plots granted to the farm labourers, just beyond the estate wall rather than inside it. 'Gas Works Lane' typifies the poor locations in which allotment sites were found. Dictated by practicality, sites were often near the tenants' homes, and so frequently abut high-density houses with short rear yards, approached through narrow alleyways in the cramped quarters of the city. Some of these have become hemmed in by later development, others bisected by roads and otherwise fragmented.

The formative conditions of so many allotments influenced their internal landscape too. All the available land had to be used at a maximum level, and plots were laid out to the perimeter, usually meaning an uninterrupted rectilinear layout. A fairly level plot was valued for reasons of moisture, drainage and ease of cultivation. The only necessity was an individual shed, where age and distance made storage on the site important, and a shelter from the weather was welcome. Landlords rarely invested in the sites, and so they were usually flat and open. The Allotment Act of 1922 required people to grow vegetables or fruit, and not flowers. They were not allowed to use allotments commercially (save some specifically let on that basis) and farm landlords did not want their labourers distracted by too much of their own land, so plots were small. This had a further impression on the appearance of the site.

There were no intended aesthetics, and so there were no rules of appearance to which to conform. However, the formative conditions provided their own aesthetic. The plot layout was reminiscent of the parallel patterns of the deeply hedged bulb fields of Scilly and, like earlier open-strip fields, presents a distinctive appearance that contrasts with the familiar large scale of contemporary rural agriculture. Often

191

loosely hedged at the boundaries, with internal paths that are not quite straight, such allotments are called 'country sites'. This was a collective landscape where the holders invested their time and energy in cultivation, construction and care, producing the distinctive internal diversity of the allotment landscape. It is an intensive and an inventive landscape, free from everyday outside controls and forced by necessity towards initiative and invention. Exemplified in the allotment shed, the whole plot represents a valuable opportunity for 'unselfconscious and relatively unhindered formal expression', with 'an unrestrained simplicity which is part of its delight ... design with room to breath ... the quality of the unfinished work lies in its understatement'.[4]

It was also a landscape of production, and became the annexe to the kitchen. As part of everyday life, an essential and ordinary part of community activity, the shared experience of the allotment constituted part of the 'take us as you find us' tradition of working-class neighbourhoods. There is a seasonal dynamic to the landscape, added to by the variation in human activity and impact. At times of greater prosperity improvements are made to the structures in this landscape; when tenants get too old this regular level of cultivation is impaired. It was just this 'kitchen annexe' tradition that came to disturb the landlords, who were drawn largely from the municipal-garden tradition.

Municipal improvement

The layout and design of the kitchen garden never threw off the yoke of formality. Within the protecting outer walls, fences or hedges, beds were generally laid out symmetrically ... one's social status determined the size of one's kitchen garden.

Joy Larcom,
'Kitchen and Vegetable Gardens' in *The Garden*,
Mitchell Beazley, 1979

The separate 'kitchen garden' emerged from the landed estate and the homes of the wealthy, a pedigree which provided for lavish expense on paths, boundaries and irrigation. The garden provided a model for the layout of the allotment when the latter became the concern of the municipal improvers during the twentieth century – though circumstances were very different, with wealth seeming to be in inverse proportion to the allotment land *needed*.

There were other influences on what may be called the municipal aesthetic. Municipal gardens had acquired a decorative style of elaborate flower-beds of a geometrical character created by 'carpet bedding'. The overall layout was derived from the landscape gardeners, complete with lakes, and with paths both curving and straight.[5] Whilst such gardens represent more than one tradition, there was an agreed feeling of the need for order in the 'urban' environment. This may have been influenced by the Victorian awareness of health and crime that necessitated clear visibility, neatness, tidiness, access and demarcation of space. Although flowers were seen to have no place in allotments, a structure could be imposed to create a recognizably 'urban' landscape. A limited budget and staff and a straightforward and uncomplicated routine of management was necessary for the maintenance of the allotment. Of course, there was a greater need for a serviced site in an allotment than in a park; one was for working, the other for contemplation.

The untamed collective individualism of the allotment-landscape 'back door' tradition contradicted what municipal designers wanted, and a fresh challenge to it was mounted in the years after the last war. In the wider community people became enthused with a growing awareness of design and the 'look' of towns. Damage done in the preceding years and the postponement of tackling earlier legacies concentrated effort in cleaning the environment and improving the landscape, and liberated the idea of starting afresh. Moreover, 'new' was in vogue, and numerous building forms and materials, many for ready self-assembly, became available to a wider market. This presented the opportunity to 'improve' the facilities on the allotment, with fencing, water, better access and communal buildings.

The 'rehabilitation' of the large site at Allensbank in Cardiff is a famous case. Originally established in 1916, it was well used with a warren of paths between plots: a uniform honeycomb, undifferentiated except for individual home-constructed sheds, greenhouses and, at a more intimate level, cold frames and stakes, water barrels and composting bins. These were swept away in the early 1950s in a programme of conversion to what has become known as a 'model' site. This meant the provision of a sound water supply, secure fencing and a communal store, with individual lockers and sturdy concreted pathways for easy access and management.[6] The combination of greens, corrugated iron and merging footpaths was replaced by a more visible structuring along formal lines. This happened to confirm the rectilinear pattern. The negative dimension of this change of landscape was the introduction of a regimentation that was made much more visible, and the loss of informality and the individuality of the personal structures. The site became serviced and accessible. A shed block was constructed, secure and weatherproof, a long concrete block that bisects and encloses the site. Order had been imposed on the apparent chaos of sheds.

However, it was precisely the sort of construction that was being replaced at Allensbank that had produced the distinctive landscape. A booklet published by the Ministry of Agriculture in 1936 suggested that allotments ought to be beautiful places. Although the author, John Stoney, a local council horticultural manager, recognized that they were essentially for food production, he saw no reason why they should be 'cheerless places' for most of the year.[7] Sheds needed proper designs, along with pavilions and summerhouses. Those local councils that prohibited the growing of flowers would need to change.

In the 1940s the allotment aesthetic was criticized from an architectural point of view rather than from the perspective of the municipal garden. In a report produced through the national Society, the architect Richard Suddell broached the issue of layout design and amenities.[8] This booklet has a 'New Age' cover in the style of documents used to promote reconstruction and the new towns. It includes a sketch of a Pavilion, dramatically in advance of what has yet happened in this country and reminiscent of the Bauhaus. The idea was to redesign allotments on architectural principles, making them more clearly structured with neat lines and not dissimilar to the styles of the holiday camps that were to follow.[9] There was to be landscaped planting, with special features like 'impressive entrances that would grace the finest park'.[10] This was in reaction to the belief that a lot of sites were bare and had 'ramshackle' huts. Suddell proposed 'amenity development'; shrubs and trees would divide the space and structure the view. Designed buildings would provide a visual focus, whilst the actual plot layout was unquestioned. Recognition was given to the continued importance of the proximity of sites to the tenants.

This concern to realize a conscious design for allotments was joined by the National Society in a booklet by W.G. Gibson.[11] Under the broader title of *The Right to Dig*, it discribed the benefits for the movement in a 'model' layout of sites. The three contributing authors, Stoney, Suddell and Gibson, from different traditions, brought together the sensitive horticulturalist, the professional designer and the enthusiast. They promulgated a shared view that landscape mattered; that it was an issue that had been overlooked, and was of significance in the defensive battle for allotments.

The landscape school and the gentrification of the landscape

The landscaped open spaces and walkways form a pedestrian network which gives the layout a feeling of visual unity and form, as well as incorporating features, such as the course of the stream, which might otherwise have deteriorated into neglected eyesores. Its tree and shrub-lined course has been cleaned up and incorporated into a turfed area; it is bridged in two places ... shrub and tree planting has been concentrated, as around the pavilion building, to create a strong and effective ornamental environment in a particularly important area of the site.

Elizabeth Galloway,
Design for Leisure Gardens,
University of Birmingham, 1977

The most comprehensive presentation of this landscape was the government report of the 1960s.[12] Reinforcing the earlier attitudes, it stressed good facilities and a well-serviced site, but also 'neatness, conformity and design, purposeful structure and layout'. Structure, control and naturalism were the key elements. The pre-Thorpe ideology was essentially towards a landscape that would enhance the experience of growing food. Thorpe acknowledged that this would continue, but emphasized the leisure interest, irrespective of financial need. A new landscape was needed that would express this shift of purpose.

The attitude of Thorpe was part of the redevelopment ideology of the 1960s, replacing old structures with inevitably better new ones, through a planned, professionally directed programme. Most expressive in its sections on the individual end of the landscape, the report denounced most allotment sites for their bad appearance, and sheds that were 'squalid ... disgraceful ... eyesores ... derelict ... ramshackle ... a motley range of materials ... and sordid'.

A view of the failure in the improvised structure of the landscape is unsympathetically if clearly stated: 'There is no limit to improvisation on many allotment sites. Here an Anderson shelter has been *pressed into* post-war service as a tool shed, with a crate-like annexe. Alongside, a length of corrugated-iron sheeting "screens" a compost heap.'[13]

In recommending a way out of this state of affairs, the report proposed that 'the plot shall be cultivated properly and assiduously, and shall at no time be neglected ... the tenant shall not bring onto his plot any contrivance of unsightly appearance'. Whilst any allotment-holder may reasonably be expected to look after his plot, this seems to place an unrealistic condition (do people get thrown off after a fortnight's holiday or illness?) that has probably never been relevant. The assertion of the 'unsightly' is even more difficult to realize. The report went on to outline what has become the rule, if not the practice, in many local councils: 'the tenant shall not, without the written consent of the local authority, erect any building on his plot (many other landlords do not allow buildings because of the added complications should they want to develop the site): if consent is given he shall, in constructing the building, observe any conditions as to the function, siting, size, design materials and colour which may be imposed ... He will no longer be able to cover his rhubarb with rusty old enamel buckets or protect his cucumbers with an old window frame propped up on a heap of bricks.'[14]

The allotments that the Thorpe committee envisaged were called Leisure Gardens. Based on a layout of curving roads and paths within the site, the area structured by mass planting of shrubs or trees, apart from the minimum provision needed on any allotment site, these had communal buildings where meetings, toilets and shop facilities could be housed. Regulations would be relaxed on the growing of crops, but tightened on the erection of sheds that individual tenants might require. In their place, communal blocks or weather-, vandal- and fire-proof lockers would be provided.

Communal buildings were not new, and places like Ponders
End in Enfield, north Londoin, have had a licensed bar for
decades – while Cardiff's Allensbank was one of the first
sites to provide a locker block.[15]

The idea of leisure gardens was taken up most enthusiastically by Birmingham City Council, who had several large
older sites and a waning market.[16] People we talked to liked
their new gardens. They were happy to have access to a
communal building in which to shelter and meet friends,
and were prepared to overlook their own shed for this,
enjoying the security of the lockers. Their plots are near the
main building, and the site has all the services of fencing,
car parking, water and clear access. The landscape that has
been created *is* more parklike, and walking round gives an
impression of plots for viewing, as the path takes you on an
ambling tour of the site.[17] The view certainly is simplified,
with all the vertical structures common to allotments stripped away. The big main buildings create a *sense* of community, although actual events and participation vary
immensely betweeen sites. However great the community's
determination to design places for people to meet each other,
the limitations – in an age when lives have become ever
more atomized, with different time schedules – are clear and
the success of such leisure gardens rests rather on the initiative and hard work of a few individuals. The plainness of the
landscape of the various Birmingham sites has been offset
by the hilly ground. In Bordesley Green, the largest site in
Birmingham – and indeed in Europe – the number of plots is
half the wartime figure as a result of changing local
demand, and this has enabled big blocks of ground to be
used flexibly. There are open greens and mass-planted trees
and shrubs, the latter taking the place of the close hedge
pattern, which was stripped away when the site was
developed for open-plan leisure use. The local Association
now wants the council to replant hedges to tame the strong,
drying surface winds.[18]

These sites have to be large to accommodate communal

planting and buildings, otherwise the land lost from cropping would be unacceptably high, and require maintenance
out of proportion to the rent income from the site. In Birmingham, the maintenance of communal areas is the
responsibility of the council. Because the site at Bordesley
Green is so huge, it is difficult to manage, and the Association is negotiating to divide it up, using the planted areas as
ready-made barriers. In contrast, there is a widespread shift
across the country towards smaller sites, which are easier to
manage, and where one can get to know people – as well as
keep an eye on the whole property to discourage vandals.
This shift is especially notable in the new town of Milton
Keynes. Not two decades after its building began, the council is changing to small sites of about twenty-five plots each,
influenced too by the high price of land and the greater ease
of allocating small areas.[19]

In the 1970s, Bristol transformed one of its sites into a
mirror image of another of Thorpe's proposals: the Chalet
Garden. 'Bristol pioneered the Leisure Garden Concept and
opened its Chalet Garden Site at The Park, Brislington, in
1970. The site is well-fenced, attractively landscaped, provided with toilets, a car park and a good road. Each tenant
has a 6 foot x 8 foot 6 inches cedarwood chalet and may cultivate his/her plot as he/she wishes [so] long as he/she leaves
the grass area around the chalet. Tenants are encouraged to
grow herbaceous plants, flowering shrubs and perhaps construct a rock garden and pool as well as grow vegetables.
There is no restriction on how the plot is set out or on the
proportion of flowers or vegetables.'[20] Chalet gardens are a
further extension of leisure gardens; typically, they have a
lawn, a chalet building (which is more for use as a summerhouse than a tool shed) and a kerosene lamp. Cardiff created
eight such plots in the 1970s. These are across a track from
the larger allotment site, and are fringed with overhanging
willows. They border a park and most people use the site for
a lawn, with some planted areas. On other sites, Bristol has
traditional allotments, but with a full range of services and

'standard huts are provided to escape the "Shanty Town" appearance so often associated with allotment sites'.[21]

Sunderland has expressed its commitment to improve the servicing and landscape of its allotment sites.[22] It has identified three categories: leisure-garden quality, near-leisure-garden standard – and sites that will continue to have pigeons and other things considered unsuitable for the leisure garden; the second, on the evidence of demand, will be upgraded. Having three categories means that a range of activities and uses is possible, and this will not prevent the provision of basic facilities in the third group.

By contrast, the London Borough of Hackney has implemented the other dimension of Thorpe's landscaping ideas, as the inner-city leisure garden. The Thorpe report called these Communal Gardens, small plots in a designed layout, typically using a 'cartwheel' layout where the plots are the spokes. These were intended particularly for flat-dwellers with only a limited amount of spare time or else for elderly or disabled people. They would be for people unable to reach the large out-of-town leisure gardens that Thorpe wanted gradually to replace ordinary allotments. Short of land and under pressure to provide local sites, Hackney Council landscaped small areas with paving flags, a shared shed, and raised beds made of old tyres, encouraging the growing of flowers. This is the 'urban', or 'inner city', landscape, as distinct from what Thorpe considered appropriate in suburban areas.[23] Not many other councils in Britain have considered leisure gardens, but there is a broad range of sites where facilities have been improved to the level of those existing in such places as Birmingham, where particular landscaping schemes have been used. However, numerous unmodernized sites remain.

Thorpe's 'Leisure Landscape' was formed from those allotments observed in mainland Europe that are laid out with 'weekending' in mind. Whilst the allotment has always been a productive landscape, the leisure garden is more for contemplation. Defending a proposal to remove allotments close to the centre of an Essex town, a council argued that 'the allotments occupy a prime location very near the town centre and [their] untidy appearance is incompatible with the status of the adjoining conservation area'.[24] Since the proposal was publicized, the allotment site *has* become neglected.

On the edge of a Hertfordshire town in the Green Belt, an Inspector found disfavour with allotments in a *countryside* location. 'The establishment of allotments on the fields ... would have a significant adverse effect on the visual qualities of this part of the green Belt, with sheds, greenhouses and more intensive activity, it seems to me that the site would have a semi-urban appearance instead of the pleasing aspect of a stretch of grassland linking the large areas of open countryside to the east and west.'[25] Elsewhere, the authors were told by plot-holders that their allotments were 'not a pretty sight'; the holders we talked to on one site referred to the allotments as 'Soweto', whereas we found them to encompass a landscape of great variety and attraction, with considerable human interest. This site was that at Pontypridd described in the early part of this chapter. There is an expectation of 'correct' and 'appropriate' landscape.[26]

The rediscovery of the organic landscape

Really a semi-rural dream the semi-rural villa couldn't give up, of a land John Clare knew and Dickens mourned: they're in no sense real country ... well, not in fact ... When I first saw it three years ago my allotment was bare and looked vast. Unlike the odd corners of my garden that I then used, this long, straight plot would have everything in one place. But it was the hawthorn hedges, elderberries, great trees and muddy lanes that said it to me. This was country and at last I could grow food. I could almost see the rows of beans and lettuces. I pictured myself sitting under a huge oak nearby before gathering my tomatoes.

Angela Harding,
'Grounds for Hope', *New Statesman*,
13 September 1985

The makers of the film *On Allotments* were first attracted to the subject by the landscape of one large and, as they put it, 'old school' site in east London.[27] 'Our first interest in the allotment site arose from the visual contrasts that it contained; the rural and wild surrounded by the intensely industrial.' This emerges strongly in the film, with cultivated land and land workers seen at human height against the backdrop of massive and extensive power, chemical and warehouse buildings, and slightly more distant tower blocks. This was initially viewed as the familiar incongruity and anachronism. As the film unfolds we see close-ups of allotmentholders, plants, people digging, dazzling creations to frighten birds; sheds made by hand; individual efforts to reclaim and cultivate; images of carefully planted rows, of harvesting, and of the change of landscape through the seasons. The film-makers went beyond the limited view of landscape to get into focus the actual activity taking place: the people themselves and the rich texture of that landscape, especially within the site. The film gets close to recording the high level of diversity in the crafted individual landscape and the determination to maintain it, and in doing so recognizes a wholly different aesthetic. Familiar images are removed from the realities of working the land, of seeing and expressing the landscape as being a worked one, and with people in it, along with the products of their labour.

The Inspector who spurned the allotment for being inappropriate in the country not only applied a modern concept of what 'country' should be like – unpeopled, cosmetic – but failed to appreciate what it is that many people like about their allotment landscape, and that it is the very evidence of human activity on the land that makes the allotment so interesting, visually. Numerous holders have expressed to us how they identify their allotment landscape as rural, even though it is in the town. People working their plots at Herne Hill, near Crystal Palace in south London, expressed it thus: 'It is so rural up here; you can see for miles', while one woman in Oxford told us: 'I just like being there . . . the birds . . . it's very rural.' The identification with 'rural' is part of the escape. The peopled landscape is not to be talked down in favour of an agricultural emptiness or the well-built urban form. Charles Tomlinson's poem was set in Stoke above Etruria in the 1950s, and shows that from this perspective the allotment does not spoil the view.

The landscape is undoubtedly another part of the escape, as Angela Harding indicates. It marks a complete break, so long as you are on the allotment, from the experience of late-twentieth-century life, the mental associations with an earlier countryside transporting the allotment-holder away.[28] It is a place where people feel free to let their hair down and express their personality, not only by what they build and grow, but in their dress, in their bonfires, even in their special mixtures . . .

The allotment represents a once more leafy city. There are numerous smaller sites, intimate landscapes in the squares created by the backs of terraced houses. Furthermore, there is the contrast between the landscape of the cultivated garden of ordinary people and the municipal and landscaped gardens that are extreme cases of gentrification. The contemporary cottage garden provides a telling illustration: 'For those sophisticated flowery little plots, the work of retired ladies and urban invaders of the countryside inspired by the cultivation of the cottage garden by Miss Jekyll and William Robinson, enchanting though they often are, do not belong to the tradition of the true cottager. The first essential characteristic of the genuine cottage garden is that it is not primarily ornamental: its charm is wholly unselfconscious and fortuitous. The cottager's garden was originally his family's larder and the vegetables and flowers mingle together in happy proximity.'[29]

Percy Grainger, who wrote *The English Country Garden*, said that 'the average English country garden is less a flower garden than a vegetable plot. Think of turnips when it is played.' The organic growth and the dynamism of the seasons and human structures provide relief and variety to the regularity of row cultivation. Along with the vegetables themselves, these provide a rich and varied texture in the landscape. The shed is an important feature of this texture. 'Whilst giving special attention to particular needs, the shed remained essentially simple. The self-built allotment garden shed has retained this intrinsic simplicity, which is a part of its delight ... in contrast to the often dull efficiency of proper architecture, the shed-bodger's artistry favours more colourful and spirited works.'[30] There is a considerable individual art that comes from the craft and care of construction, and the use of materials, in many improvised allotment sheds. Corrugated iron itself has been similarly recognized: '... although totally alien to any landscape, the pictorial effect, unlike that of concrete, could be amusing and folly-like. The little house on the smallholding at Bawdsley, Suffolk, one of the many created to help rural labourers during the depression, artlessly assumes the traditional design of a central block with cross-wings, the corrugated-iron walls painted viridian, the corrugated-iron roof and lean-to porch vermilion, the incredible colours and wavy surfaces vibrating to the harmonies of the shingle beach and the marshes between which it stands.'[31]

This is a dramatic case, as the contrasts in colour demonstrate. However, in close relationship to the diversity of natural greens, painted 'regulation' green never works. It creates some visual order, but inevitably contradicts with awkward semi-tonal conjuncture. Partly rusted, the slightly aged corrugated-iron sheeting blends into the cooler and textured earth in an irregular and unselfconscious way.

A further richness and diversity derives from the overall plot layout. In the case of the shed there is a design relationship between it and the saved material stacked beside or above it; for the plot layout there is the grass-softened rigidity of the path system and the seasonally varied plant geometry. This contrasts with the opinion that: '*Clematis montana* should replace old man's beard to achieve a cosmetic treatment to a less attractive fencing material.'[32] Values applied by outside observers to allotment landscapes are not based on the active use of the land, on those who labour on it, who enjoy its rhythms and making their own structures on it. The reviled rectilinear landscape has been misunderstood, and has proven a source of artistic inspiration, as the woodcut by Iles on page 63 illustrates.

The individuality of cultivation and construction within this organic and loose landscape represents organized chaos – words used to us by an enthusiastic allotment officer. The organization is in the overall site boundary, the facilities and the communal buildings. However, the individuality is not 'a mistake', a 'make do' culture that does not realize its surroundings. It is your *own* place, landscape, where the oppression of Style has no significance. 'Once clear of the signfields of the publicly presented fronts [of houses] which are the carriers of the new values, the signs of the allotment, and backs [gardens], which are the significant forms of the established attitude, take over. The signs are no longer to do with affluence, but are connected with a more relaxed attitude of apparently not thinking and not caring.'[33] Style is replaced by use, presentation by enjoyment.

In Newham, allotment-holders resisted regulation sheds, feeling that they would inhibit the individuality of their own constructions.[34] The more authoritarian efforts prevail in many parts of the country, but allotments escaped from their wider influences after the Thorpe Report through the revived interest in simply growing things. The self-promotion of this new wave re-established the authenticity of the well-worked old allotment without the imposition of new forms.

Frequently viewed from the train or at a distance from the road, the landscape of the allotment may be poorly represented. The view presents miniature, densely packed 'dinky' plots of ground with multifarious detail that can barely be appreciated. There is an appearance of 'other people's plots', akin to the massed view of suburban homes seen from the railway viaduct,[35] a collective but out-of-focus individuality. The allotment landscape contains a deeply involved human activity and attachment, much more than in the grand concourses of the commercial centre or grand house on the landed estate, where the collective but individual contribution is disguised in a presentation of the individual owner. Whereas the changing agricultural land-scape is best viewed from the train or the motorcar, the allotment is appreciated at a different scale which we would confront only in a private garden. Although a collective landscape, the allotment is also a private one. The critical scale is close up. It reaches the extreme in the secret, hedged plots in Birmingham's surviving Guinea Gardens that resemble the internal spaces of the Scillies' bulb fields, pro-tected by Pittosporum and Escallonia against the wind.

There *are* many allotment sites set within an agricultural landscape, as the observation at Bladon shows. There in Oxfordshire is an open site adjacent to fields – just next to it is a church and the graveyard where Churchill is buried. Coachloads of tourists, especially Americans, call by at the site after they have seen the church. The allotment is a spectacle for inquiry, and many people take photographs.[36] Roy Lacey saw his allotment site (authentically called Cowpasture, after its parent farm) 'set with jewel-like pre-cision in the landscape ... a charm that never fails, what-ever the season or the time of day, to enrapture ...'[37] many other sites melt away into the surrounding fields.

The broad allotment aesthetic has frequently fascinated the narrower aesthetic of two-dimensional art. The attrac-tion is the peopled landscape and the results of intimate human labour that it presents – witness the work of Pis-sarro. Gwynneth Leech has painted allotments full of people in Tuscany, and half a century earlier Harry Allen depicted a whole village out on its allotment.[38] These populous places have been painted by Emma Lindsey in Newcastle, and somewhat more whimsically by Miriam McGregor.[39] In a more expressionistic form, Edward Burra provided a painting of an allotment where only one person is present almost by defiance. This 'shadowy landscape with a large bird watching the man digging is one of Burra's most mysterious'.[40] The man seems to be struggling on a difficult site, with many plots around him empty; nature is ready to reclaim it.

The allotment landscape provides an escape in a way that the town park or other open space, for all its greenery, cannot. However designed for informality, the municipal park remains for recreation and is not a productive landscape where people can grow, create and adapt their own ground. The relationship enjoyed in the cultivation of the landscape is fundamentally different, and remains misunderstood by urban designers.[41] The pleasures of being close to the earth deny the lack of sensual and aesthetic experience and appreciation, however sub-conscious that may be. In contrast, the contrived, imposed *landscape* provides an artificial image for those who *use* the place that opposes so much of what it means to them.

The official landscape of the allotment has been consciously formed over half a century. In those places where local councils have provided sheds, or prevented tenants from erecting their own, they have created a symbol of interference that ignores the meaning of these structures to the individual. However, there is considerable common ground in the concern for decent, adequate services and for careful, consistent cultivation. The allotment landscape is a product of the actions and attitudes of the landlords and the plot-holders themselves. Their actions both affect, and are affected by, the wider public perceptions of the allotment as landscape and its place in contemporary society. In most cases, the landlords are represented by the allotments officer, usually sympathetic and often within

Shed interior. Drawing by John Grahn

the horticultural and municipal-park traditions. They have found the Thorpe landscape supportive of their efforts to improve sites, their image and security. Landscape has proven to be a significant factor in the survival of the allotment. An essentially peopled landscape, the allotment fits unfamiliarly in contemporary cultural expectations, somewhere between the city and the country and yet representing neither contemporary projected landscape. It falls between being a public and private landscape in a way that few others do. Its visibility is accompanied by the fact that it is not used or presented for display.

The allotment's position in contemporary culture is like the landscape of the plotlands, public-housing estates and bungalows, seen to display 'unsightliness, a disorder and vagueness ... a violent individualism'.[42] It does not fit into acceptable categories and the official landscape, nor does it possess the criteria of recognized design and position in culture that would make it respectable. Richard Hoggart captured this when he wrote that allotments were found 'behind the hoardings in the main street or on the edge of the permanent way'.[43]

Meanwhile, inside the landscape allotment-holders have appropriated the provided space for their purposes and uses in representation of their own culture. There is a notable variation in the allotment landscape that is still affected by local materials and soil, and the people who are involved. There is, of course, also the distinctive surroundings of each site. Together, these elements create numerous unique landscapes.

11
Cultures and places

'If I shut my eyes and think of Lower Binfield any time before I was, say, eight, it's always in summer that I remember it ... it's a hot afternoon in the great green juicy meadows round the town, or it's about dusk in the lane behind the allotments, and there's a smell of pipe tobacco and night-stocks floating through the hedge.'

George Orwell,
Coming up for Air,
Gollancz, 1939

There are many different local patterns in the culture and landscape that surround allotment activity. Their distinctiveness is a product of the continuing ways in which strands of older cultures affect and flow with the new structures of people's lives and how they relate and find value. The way that this relating of old and new happens depends on which strands survive, and which don't, and how they are transformed in the process. This picture is heavily influenced by the wider world of employment and educational opportunity, and the availability of individual rights and investment in land, in the same way that these helped produce the allotment over a century ago. In work on the land, this is obviously affected further by the immediate, local detail like the lie of the land, the climate and the condition of the ground. These are not independent variables, and the way that people use and modify these things means that they themselves will be another cause of variation. The product is the local landscape, which in turn influences the attachment people feel for their surroundings. Just as the landscape is enclosed or exposed, this reflects the way that the people involved in working land see each other, and the connection this has with other aspects of their lives. Places vary as a result, and so do the people living there, and the society to which they contribute.

The rural tradition in the Fens

In both Holland and Kesteven a few hired men were observed
to give up their positions (at piece-work rates) and become
ordinary labourers for the increased chance of cultivating a
bit of land.

Newlyn Russell Smith,
Land for the Small Man,
New York, 1946

It was Spalding that returned an 'allotments' candidate to
Parliament in 1887, the same year that would later
bequeath the Allotments Act that obliged local councils to
provide plots on demand. The Act increased the number of
plots around Spalding from 130 to 1252 in six years.[1] The
local agricultural workers of Spalding had been neither
acquiescent nor deferential, and they won. Conditions in
agricultural labour in the Fens were notorious,[2] although
the wages were not as low as in the more southern counties.[3]
The excellent condition of the heavy, rich soil made cultivation – on one's own terms – attractive.[4] Gangs did irregular
work, as a group employed for temporary labour and
insecure wages.[5] The attraction of allotment work and its
financial supplement was considerable. Ordinary allotments, up to five acres in extent, provided the door to at
least a wages supplement. It became known as the lowest
rung on the farming ladder, as other plots were accumulated
into a smallholding.[6]

There is still, in the last years of the twentieth century, a
close link between the allotment, smallholdings and the
farming ladder, and gang labour in Sutton Bridge.[7] Many
young people of small means, unable to obtain land owing to
the large-scale ownership of land locally, begin with an
allotment – often working it part-time, perhaps until they
can acquire enough land to work full-time. Several manage
to progress, almost of necessity, to land vacated on death.[8]
Many men working the gangs rely on the money they make
through selling allotment produce to offset against time

when they have no work in the gangs. These are large allotments, between $\frac{1}{4}$ and $\frac{1}{2}$ of an acre and 5 acres. There are still $\frac{1}{8}$th- and even $\frac{1}{16}$th-acre plots, but the demand is limited. The waiting list is dominated by those looking for larger amalgamations. In the 1950s there was such a need for plots amongst agricultural workers that the issue was discussed at meetings of the Spalding area of the National Union of Agricultural Workers, who passed a resolution to campaign for the government to make more plots available.[9] The allotments in Sutton Bridge, still a community not yet separated by a generation from working the land, were owned by the Ministry of Agriculture until the early 1980s. They had been bought in 1910. In the 1970s there were 243 plots on 83 acres, with a further 149 acres let through the Parish Council.[10] Although this area has diminished by about 30 acres, there remain around 130 plots, of varied size. The Government Report on Smallholdings recognized the potential flexibility of use between allotments and smallholdings, but the local Parish realizes, as did Thorpe, the difficulty of returning these to allotments – once their use as smallholdings is established – should that be in demand.[11] Elsewhere in the Fens land is owned by parish councils, and a variety of charities and private landowners. In most areas, the plots are on average large, and include land worked commercially.[12]

Allotments were one of the centres of local community culture, and a good example of this was the Pig Club. 'Every cottager had one pig or more. They were his most important possessions ... pigs were always a big topic of conversation in the village, and after the usual greeting, it was quite normal to ask how the pigs were doing ... The most important club in the village was the Pig Club ...'[13] The club met in local pubs, and provided a means of sharing experience and problems, as well as a way to save money for feed and buying pigs. Pig clubs survived in the Fens until at least the 1950s,[14] and the creatures themselves are still kept on allotments around Wisbech.[15]

The Fens have always been an isolated area, physically and socially.[16] This enabled the development of a distinctive culture, of which the allotment is a contributor and a focus. It is part of the close contact in work, recreation and the family. Women have long had an integral role in land labour in the Fens that typifies such an isolation.[17] The society is inherently conservative, and today most allotment-holders are men, but this is changing – although women do not usually enter as farmers. The community remains close-knit to a degree, and there is a network of people aware of allotment land, able to help those on the farming ladder to obtain their first land. There is still work for the gangs, on sugar beet, or strawberries, although there is an overall reduction in agricultural labour that has been immense in some areas; the surplus labour being taken up by the opening of local branches of firms whose base is elsewhere.[18] As a result of this there is an increasingly varied population taking allotments, but this does not keep pace with the changing employment pattern, and in many parishes the 'smallholding' remains the dominant form.[19] The huge scale of these plots is shown by there being more than seven acres per thousand of population in the Fenland areas in 1965, but on average only three plots to the acre.[20]

This farming community, where cultivation is more by the tractor, plough and rotavator than the spade, produces its own landscape. The sites are, of course, overwhelmingly and beautifully flat, sometimes without trees in the near views, and the land is dark in colour. Over short distances, you can move from earth that drains well to places where it remains a sticky mud. The tenants sometimes store a tractor at the site, and they will have a large wooden shed for the purpose, although many prefer to keep it nearer their home, or in old barns if they have them, for security and convenience. Where the plots are large, these make little impact on the landscape. Smaller plots on other sites do not have many buildings. The sites appear readily as fields, and blend, with their few constructions, rather like East

Anglian Wool Churches, into the open fields that charac-
terize so much of this large-scale farming country.

The tradition of large-scale allotments in farming communities extends away from the Fens to northern Norfolk
and Bedfordshire, where many areas have formed part of
the market-gardening hinterland of London.[21] Lorries from
the allotment villages around Flitwick took produce to the
markets at Luton and Bedfordshire and even to London
every day during the years between the wars. Now there are
occasional collections. Several parishes find that they have
to let plots to local smallholders or risk the loss of plots that
may later be in demand.

In Flitton the soil is light and dries rapidly, and ordinary
holders experience an uphill battle keeping the plots going
through the summer – although the oldest tenant, who died
in 1980, told of seeing 'up to forty tenants in one field on a
weekend, digging these large plots ($\frac{1}{4}$, $\frac{1}{2}$ acre) by hand –
necessary to feed their families but also a strong social
occasion. The morning usually finished up at the local for a
pint.'[22] In one case, the allotment land is crucial to provide
enough feed for the holder's herd, which he keeps on other
land. There has been some recent house-building on the
outskirts of the village, but it is dominated by older, larger
properties that have survived whilst other dwellings have
been lost. The plots that change hands the most frequently
are those taken on by newcomers to the village, who find the
land too difficult.

Astonishingly, in the nearby village of Barton, there is a
flourishing Allotment Association of domestic plot-holders,
growing food and flowers. The ground is good and deep, and
much more easily worked. The village is situated close to
both the M1 and the electrified railway line to London; there
are several small new housing developments, and many of
the newcomers have keenly taken up plots. The plot-holders
bought the land in 1975 for £25 each and sell Sutton seeds to
cover their annual expenditure.[23] This contrast represents
much of the changing culture found in villages across

Britain, where there is a mix of old and new populations. The attitudes to allotments do not divide simply between old and young, in age or in local residence, or between housing situation or job, but vary in the way that villages themselves do in their local histories and contemporary cultures.[24] Large council-house gardens can make allotments appear superfluous, and many commuters do not have time for gardening, although others do and welcome the escape.

South Warwickshire is typical of the changing cultures in the villages of Britain. Comprised of eighteen parishes situated in 'Middle' England, it is an equal distance from Birmingham, Oxford, Milton Keynes and Cheltenham. In several villages, smaller villages that earlier this century had an agricultural population, like Tidmington, Idlicote and Little Wolford, no allotments remain. The surviving houses, including those on some council estates built in the 1920s, have large gardens. Where charity allotments have been indebted to the poor during the last century, they survive – although in a changing village they may not be tenanted to people seeking to rely on them financially. The village of Tysoe has an allotment site over the road from a council estate. By no means all the plot-holders come from that estate, although a number do. The allotment is near the original site mentioned in Margaret Ashby's book on the radical agricultural worker, Joseph Ashby of Tysoe (Cambridge University Press, 1961). There are allotments in the four villages that have somewhat larger populations: Tysoe, Brailes, Stourton and Long Compton.[25]

The older sites laid out with regular-sized plots, are often open plan, and some present archetypal landscapes. In Brailes, the perfectly tended plots hug the cottages in one part of the straggling village. The old cottages, not untypical of villages a century ago, have small gardens. The tracks between the plots are wide, and kept mown. Several plot-holders use cultivators. The tracks wind away to a path that leads to a hill fort, two fields from the village.

In nearby Hook Norton, just over the border into

Oxfordshire, an advertisement in the post office led to the revival of allotment-holding in the village, where six used plots increased to sixteen in two years in the mid-1980s. The tenants include a customs officer, a teacher, a man who works on an oil rig and two retired people. Most of them live in modern houses with small gardens.[26] There is a similar diversity of population in the allotments in Cumbrian villages on the Solway Plain, where the ground responds well to cultivation, in the farming areas of Durham, and in the villages on the side of the Peak District.[27] Fiona Shave found a considerable increase in demand for allotments in Surrey villages during the 1970s amongst families moving into new houses on small estates.[28]

In Bladon, surrounded by the Duke of Wellington's land, there are still allotments provided by the estate, worked by tenants with a lifetime of working there. It was allotments on this estate where the landlord, in the nineteenth century, handed over the sites along with their cottages to the tenant farmers so that he could readily evict any tenants who became union members to gain higher wages.[29] In Oxfordshire as a whole, in 1900, half of the allotments had been provided by local landowners, 163 of 321 in 212 parishes, and 91 by the clergy, institutions or charities under the Poor Laws.[30] Although some sites are still owned by local farmers, the predominant example is the local council site serving a diverse and changing village population.

Allotment suburbia in Birmingham

What is most notable in Birmingham is the encouragement of allotments by the Corporation; for nowhere does municipal socialism flourish more than in this Tory stronghold.

C.R. and H.C. Fay,
'The Allotment Movement in England and Wales',
Yearbook of Agricultural Co-operation, 1944

Through the early years of this century allotments in Birmingham had been rented by the working class, in areas typified by the Gasworks Lane site, the 'eyesore' surrounded by cheap terraced housing and factories, peopled from the adjacent terrace.[31] However, since the inter-war years there has been a consistently high provision of sites; the council had a large amount of farmland within its boundaries that became useful for allotments: the city was ready to purchase these for plots, in its tradition of public provision.[32] The political significance of allotments, locally, had brought allotments candidates into the local council. Through several decades this has secured many sites against redevelopment.

There continued to be a high demand for allotments between the wars, through the depression years, and that pressure led the council to arrange peacetime leases with landowners whose land had been taken for allotments in the First World War.[33] Many new sites were opened in the same period, as crowded housing inside the city was replaced at lower densities in the suburbs, along with new owner-occupied houses, and both sets of dwellers enjoyed the use of allotments, even where the gardens were of reasonable size by late-twentieth-century standards. Some sites were created further from the city centre, often being laid out on open land peripheral to the built-up area, later to serve new housing which extended to surround them after the last war.[34]

During the immediate post-war years, the city was distinguished in experiencing a dramatic growth in the manufacturing sector, and a considerable increase in living standards as 'the workshop of England'. With the relief of the absolute necessity to avoid paying for prepared food, the demand for allotments diminished. The end of the emergency in 1945 led to an immediate drop in plot use, with 3000 of the 22,000 sites used in wartime vacant. Over the next few years, the emergency plots were returned to the landowners, but the decline in use continued, albeit at a slower pace.[35]

Unlike the case in mining communities, employment in

Birmingham was dispersed in a variety of places and trades, and close traditions of leisure activities had less opportunity to be sustained. With growing incomes, diversification of employment, the extensive post-war redevelopment and relocation of housing all served to change the communities in many areas. Through the 1950s and 1960s allotment vacancies remained high: 1953, 1291 plots; 1958, 3058 plots; 1963, 2200 plots, all this despite a fall in the number of plots in those ten years from 16,600 to 11,200.[36] This loss of plots included several in the inner city that lost their local population or were engulfed in other, usually commercial, uses.[37] The city was committed to a high level of provision, at 1.6 acres per 1000 of the population.[38] Several of the sites were replaced in outer areas, sometimes under specific local pressure, but demand became very varied, given the diversity in garden size and also of income.[39]

During the next ten years, this level of vacancies provided the City council with an opportunity that brought together the changing population involved in allotment cultivation and people's attitudes to the sites themselves. Continuing its reputation for public works, the city turned from site provision to site improvement. This meant providing essential facilities. Poor facilities and lack of maintenance discouraged people from renting plots. The landscaping of sites began at this time. By 1976, water was provided on ninety per cent of statutory sites, and fencing on eighty per cent.[40] Harry Thorpe's arguments that the condition of sites did not comply with the 'post poverty era' of allotments, as he saw it, were developed in Birmingham. This is no surprise, as the population itself was being transformed by work and housing. The population was not discarding allotment-holding – over ten thousand families had participated throughout the 1960s, and the number of used plots remained the same through that decade – but the drop had been significant. The changing population was receptive to modern styles and activities; other recreations were becoming increasingly popular, and new designs and newness itself had become attractive as an indication of improvement. In these circumstances, the allotment-holders generally were receptive to new ways of using allotments, and the potential to change what they looked like, if this was not simply cosmetic but actually made working the land more enjoyable.

Many of the sites were laid out in new ways, landscaped with curving paths and irregular plots; individual sheds were replaced by individual lockers and communal pavilions. The pavilions were in 'modern' style, and the sheds had, for many people, come to be associated with a past culture and class of which they felt no longer a part. The serried ranks of plots were replaced. What took their place assumed the image of the natural environment that was then becoming popular, through TV and family holidays. 'Landscape' was enjoyed as a thing in itself; and the replacement, for many holders, of growing for money by growing for fun made this more realizable. In these circumstances, the communal provision of facilities resembles closely the way equipment and space are shared in many other leisure pursuits. It was wholly appropriate that the term 'leisure garden' should have been developed in Birmingham. By 1976, there were 10,000 plot-holders in the city, with ninety-eight per cent in possession of a plot, and a waiting list of several hundred.[41] It would seem that the allotment population had changed, as many had left in the 1950s to be replaced by others newly attracted by the fresh outlook of the 1970s.[42] The surviving population found the new style attractive too. Many people now travel long distances to reach their sites.

The communal buildings serve as meeting places, mainly for the allotment committees and shows, but also for casual getting together, especially while it rains. They represent something of social engineering, and with corporation lockers provide an ordered landscape. The plot-holders like them and, through negotiations with the council, many have been persuaded of their benefits. Whilst the old sheds are not seen as part of this new culture, it is, paradoxically, the older, working-class areas and the middle-class havens of very early allotment sites that cling to the sheds that had the chimneys and served as real hideaways. Tenants remark on the clumsy way in which many treasured sheds were bull-dozed in the early 1970s, and gates still get mangled when the well-meaning city attempts to rotavate sites for new tenants, occasionally getting the number of these hidden sanctuaries wrong. These plot-holders like the serried rows of highly hedged secret gardens, which are unsuited to open landscaping. In contrast, the error of over-enthusiastic hedge removal has been realized at Europe's biggest site, at Bordesley Green; a show-piece of reconstruction, it is an exposed, undulating site, and the hedges are being re-planted.[43]

A further development in the culture that surrounds the allotment in Birmingham has seen the increased participation of ethnic groups. The extent of Asian and West Indian involvement is significant, especially on sites that abut housing in the inner suburbs, and they bring with them a commitment to cultivation that involves the whole family. In Handsworth, it is estimated that sixty per cent of plots are rented by Asians, and fifteen per cent by West Indians, an increase of several times the figure in the 1970s.[44]

Birmingham's paternalism is mixed with an amount of self-determination. Although the city has a rule with some of the new sites that only ten per cent of holders may have sheds, and then only British Standard dark green (Middle Brunswick Green) may be used, there is extensive self-management within the city's 126 sites. The political influence of allotments in the city may have deferred to other problems, but the chair of the District Allotments Association, Mrs Pickering, was for a long time a member of the City Council. Interest has flourished into a new culture of the late twentieth century. In 1987, 7148 plots were rented out of a total of 8218.[45]

Surviving archetypes in the Northeast

On the strip of land running between the end of the terrace
and the railway cutting had been what everyone called The
Garden. It was in fact a huge expanse of allotments, a spec-
tacular patchwork of homemade shacks and meticulously cultivated plots separated from each other by an extraordinary
assortment of fences and hedges.

Jennifer Armstrong,
'Day Return',
BBC Radio 4, 1982

The strength of mining communities has been marked by
numerous features that express their distinctive culture,
stemming in part from their vulnerability at the workplace:
'miners who were sacked, and the widows of miners killed
had to vacate their homes'.[46] This powerlessness at work
'strengthened a resolve to build a defensive line around his
home to protect his family against the vagaries of wage
labour. It cultivated in him a feeling that too great a dependence on one source of income was risky. Encouraged by his
father, like many young men he learned quickly to appreciate the importance of the garden, the pigs and chickens, and
the need to grab at any casual work when the opportunity
arose. Without such protection the alternatives in Heddon
in difficult times were to receive charity, to work on the land
or to emigrate.'[47] Where colliery owners were philanthropic,
they laid out 'model towns' for their workers, and these
always included allotments for worthy honest exercise.[48]
Most of the Coal Board sites have been sold to the local
councils, following the withdrawal of their interest in local
community activity and pit closures.

For the most casual observer, allotments are synonymous
with the northeast, or at least the mining communities. 'The
peculiar form of the North-Eastern "cultural landscape" –
the hillside clothed with wooden-framed, colourful pigeon
lofts – is very distinctive. Similarly, the symbolic role of the
annual leek show.'[49] It was not only mining communities in

the northeast that held close to an allotment tradition; South Wales, Yorkshire, the coastal towns of the Lake District and some parts of Glasgow share much of this culture and landscape, in locally distinct ways.

In Northumberland and Durham the culture of the working class has centred on a limited number of occupations around which have developed very close social networks – mining, iron and steel, and shipbuilding being typical. The works were localized, and the workforce huddled closely around it. Local identity grew strongly where people were closely situated physically to the workplace and to each other, and relatively segregated from other communities, even working-class ones. The local and close nature of employment lent to the employers a dominant influence over their lives. The jobs were typified by difficult physical labour, often in extreme temperatures or confinement, and above all by low pay. This situation obtained for a century during which close ties and customs developed from the necessity of mutual support and in protective reaction to a hostile world.

Strong patterns of local culture emerged from this, in the use of leisure time, in relationships with other families and within the household, and in the way people constructed their environment around them. Pigs were ubiquitous amongst the colliers. Mr Morris of Pelton Fell recollects that 'nearly everybody had a pig', and Mr William Kelly of Mainsforth remembers two pigs being kept, 'one for pork and one for bacon'.[50] Pig-keeping shifted from the backyard to the allotment with the advent of the bye-laws requiring that: 'The occupier of any premises shall not keep any swine or deposit any swine's dung, within the distance of ninety feet from any dwelling house.'[51] But it lost its popularity amongst the miners of the northeast because of disastrous outbreaks of swine fever around the turn of the century. It was replaced by a different and less utilitarian identification, with feathers rather than skin. Peter Wright relates this preoccupation with the traditional working lives of

County Durham: 'If he works with coal or metal or any other hard unyielding matter, his hobby will probably be keeping some form of livestock. On a nearby allotment, or at the bottom of his back garden, he will spend hours by his crudely built homemade pigeon cree, rattling a tin of corn and waiting in breathless excitement for his racing pigeons to come down, so that he can receive their rings and clock them in, hoping to win a prize. Or perhaps it is rabbits, their wet noses twitching against the rough, wire-fronted hutches that he is studying, show schedule in hand, trying to out-point his rivals down the hill.'[52]

Of course, the allotment was the ideal means of enjoying such pursuits. Separated from the home, it provided for a greater isolation and concentration, supportive of the intense competition but also the comradeship that surrounds pigeon-keeping. It is frequently undertaken in pairs, two men sharing the experience, perhaps sharing the jobs on the allotment – one the vegetables, one the birds. Sometimes this is a purely pigeon partnership, and some have become renowned.[53] In many of the pit villages, the duality of the pigeons and the vegetables provides the daily activity for the redundant miners.[54]

Reaching at the psyche, Keith Armstrong's poem, inspired in the Easington villages, caught the escape, the release that the pigeons represent to the miner, confined by housing, workplace and work relations.[55] They gave, and give, the keeper a pride and a status, enabling him to make a positive and shared contribution to a community in which people may have little of material worth to give.

In 1980, one-fifth of the plot-holders in Sunderland kept pigeons; the national figure in the 1960s was three per cent.[56] Pigeon racing is intensely competitive, and is not confined to the northeastern Up North Combine; there are people subscribing to the *Racing Pigeon Gazette* living in Chelmsford, Essex. In Glasgow's strong working-class communities on the council estates, 'flying the doos' is a rarified but popular pastime. 'Its sole object is to "catch" other men's doos ... men will spend every waking hour "at the doos", neglecting wives and families (women are united in their total contempt for flying the doos).'[57] In the northeast it is much less aggressive. From Durham the animals are transported as far as Selby, Reading and Beaune in northern France. 'Bird prices can range from £40 upwards plus at least £100 for a loft and feeding bowls, £150 for a timing clock, and each bird will eat 1 lb of corn a week at £7 a hundredweight, and most pigeon-fanciers keep at least 30 birds.'[58] There is an elaborate ritual of time-keeping; and, while the cost of feed is astronomical, prize-winning birds fetch huge prices. For example, it was reported in 1987 that a pigeon changed hands for breeding purposes for £41,000 in Leicestershire.[59] And Japanese fanciers will make the long journey to Durham and Northumberland simply to secure a prize bird.[60] Atypically, in 1985, a 'top man' (a champion) had his eighty pigeons decapitated, contradicting the prevailing atmosphere of comradeship. The expense of the sport extends to the fanciful creation of the 'cree'. This is usually home-constructed, and over the years since the last war has adopted a regular style, a proud presentation of a culture. It is a shed, containing the coops or cages, and fronted by a façade, like something out of a Western; it is often brightly coloured, appearing to impress but also to attract the birds home. On top is a series of struts or crenellations of two-inch by one-inch timber, intended to stop a bird flying past.

At the same time and place there grew up an even more unlikely cult: that of the leek. It so happens that the cool damp climate of the northeast of England, like Wales, provides ideal growing conditions, and there they grow very big, particularly if you nurture them, preferably indoors, through the winter. There is a twelve-month (Ayr) cropping programme for leeks, which was devised at Ponteland.[61] Harry Bone converted his loft, decking it out with extensive staging lit by five tungsten bars that can be adjusted through the winter until the plants are ready to be placed on the allotment. He started his plot – and growing leeks –

when he retired from shipbuilding ten years ago, at fifty-five. In that time he developed his own strain – with such success that he became World Champion in 1985. 'Ten years – that's only ten tries. You don't get much of a chance to play around.'[62] The champion is known as the 'top man', in leeks as in pigeons. Some few manage to create the 'world-record super-leek'. In the early years of this century it was normal for vegetables in local shows to be judged in terms of size, and from this there grew the mystique of the particular strains and the methods of cultivation that would win the prizes.

'Leek-growing was organized from the public houses and, after the First World War, from working men's clubs. It was an exclusively male activity financed by weekly lotteries and it was deadly serious. Before 1914 the prizes were simple. In 1905, for example, the first prize at the Frenchmen's Arms, a show my grandfather attended, was a blanket. The prizes were, and still are, invariably something for the home; this was a sop to the wives which justified the amount of time the husband spent in the garden tending his leeks.'[63] Another observer reports that: 'Annual prizes at North-East shows total more than £200,000; Easington Lane Workingmen's Club for instance, offering £1300 worth of prizes ranging from bed linen to kitchen cabinets. Even the little Leeholme Club offers £300. Small wonder then, that secret formula fertilizers range from sour milk and stale beer to dried blood and Epsom salts, and the growers erect electric fences or sit up all night, shotgun in hand, to stop the hated leek slashers from ruining their prize-winning entries.'[64] In 1986 it was reported that: 'World pot leek champion Joe Jones is retiring from the show scene after his entire stock was stolen during a night raid on his allotment.'[65] His allotment, where he teams up with his brother who does the pigeons, is an idyll near his terraced railway cottage surrounded by hills and fields, woodland, and the river where he washed his leeks ready for the show.

The social role the allotment played in the separation of men and women in mining communities was acutely observed by Norman Dennis, the men spending long hours away from the family sitting either on the park bench or on their allotment.[66] The landscape that is created is often very masculine, and certain plots – sometimes every plot on a site – are enclosed by corrugated-iron boards over six feet high, supplemented by doors saved from the refurbishing of nearby council houses. There is an atmosphere in the site at St Peters, Newcastle, at Hordon and Boldon, of hidden activity and preparation. It is difficult not to feel a latent aggression in the stacked walls, but they seems to represent security rather than secrecy.

With limited space at home, with rented accommodation and only a yard outside, Glasgow pigeon men have built 'doo huts'. These are tall, stark towers of corrugated iron and scrap wood, tarred felt cloth and black paint. They stand in the bleak spaces around the tenement blocks like Possilpark, 'as anarchic mimics of the impersonal blocks of flats'.[67] In 1986, however, Glasgow City Council agreed to the idea of an allotment for pigeon lofts.[68]

Caught up in the modernist fervour for the replacement of the old as though it represented the outworn, Easington Rural District Council, now sympathetic to holders, found itself in the 1940s arguing vigorously against this local sub-culture. 'The allotments have generally become ugly expanses of patched up fences and garden huts or crees ... due entirely to lack of any form of control. It must be a feature of any new planning proposal that strict control over erections including fencing be exercised on allotments when they are provided.'[69] The council did not know that this very lack of control had been a lifeline for mining families in the days of private colliery ownership when, if the breadwinner was sacked from the mine, the family had to move into the cree or the hut, rented for 2s 6d from the local council and thus not subject to the colliery owner's rule.

In one area in the 1930s, thirty-two families were living like this on the allotments at Hordon, Easington Colliery and Blackhall. One retired miner recalls the instance when a single family [was] evicted three times in two days ... sacked from one pit [the miner] was taken on at another belonging to the same company, sacked again when this was discovered, and sacked from a third when his dismissal from the other became known. His unfortunate family shunted its belongings on a handcart from one village after another, ending in the allotment gardens. Boys who lost their job at the mine would be obliged to leave their parental colliery-owned housing and move into a hut on the allotments, returning at weekends for a bath. One family at Hordon Colliery, resigned to living on the allotments, bought with their savings a hut from the mail-order firm of J. Thorn, and contrived a kitchen and other amenities.[70]

At least one man was living in a caravan on one allotment in the northeast in 1987. Unemployed and separated from his wife, he had offered to help the holder, who soon found the caravan cleaned and tidied. He agreed to let him live there, from which base he provides support, cleaning crees and trenching leeks on several plots.[71] Moreover, rather than the need being for strict controls, the tenants in the colliery villages are trying to get facilities provided on their sites, such is their commitment.[72]

Thorpe spoke moralistically about the pigeon-fanciers '... not in the least interested in cultivating their allotments, and ... the tasks of caring for the birds, preparing them for competitions, and their ancillary activities, leave them little time to make more than a token gesture of observance to the cultivation rule imposed by the authority'. There is no shortage of effort put into the crees, and pigeons epitomize the leisure ideal of the allotment, but it is of a distinctively local kind. Of course, it is the landscape that this particular culture produces that adversely affects the observer: '...the confused jumble of structures that can arise when an area of land is devoted almost exclusively to the rearing of pigeons'. Suspicion accompanies the judgement: '...it was hinted to us that their [the crees'] dirty and unkempt appearance is conducive to their use for a number of dubious purposes'.[73] Indeed, in the village of Boldon Colliery, it is the holders who complain of the state of some of the plots where horses are kept and no cultivation takes place; lively dogs angrily defend the plots behind large corrugated-iron panels.[74]

In Newcastle, a combination of the close, localized oversight of allotment associations – known in the neighbourhood as 'mafias' – a 'responsive' local council (practising what is termed 'benign neglect'), and intense activity on the sites, has meant that older sites with the traditional landscape have not been cleared. Some holders might indeed welcome an improvement in facilities, however, and the council has an active programme in hand to provide these. The larger-scale and derelict sites in the city that result from industrial decay attract greater attention, although the environmental improvements financed with Urban Aid have included some allotment facelifts.[75] Traditional sites like St Peters Allotments, sloping above the Tyne, were saved from redevelopment in the great Byker scheme; presumably their gradient helped in this. The chair of the recreation committee in the city in 1987 was an allotment-holder, and so was the Mayor of Durham for the same year. There remains a political influence – not only in the site level of management and the allocation of plots, which is often tribal, but also in the official structure of local power – which influences this landscape.

There has sometimes been a gulf between the 'official' perception of this particular local culture and the enthusiastic talk of quiet, peaceful satisfaction that the Fancy gives, just as there has been a gulf between the municipal urge to tidy everything up and the perception of photographer Dave Thomas who sees allotments as 'havens of individuality and vigour, and if you look closely enough, a visual extravagance of form and colour'.[76]

In Newcastle, sites like Heaton Allotments form part of a green strip that cuts deeply into the city's eastern side. In the mining towns and villages of South Wales, the allotments either straggle, hugging the sides of the valleys just above the houses, or else enjoy the level land in the valley bottom, hemmed in between industrial plant and sidings. Pigeons never caught on in the valleys, but leeks did, and many plot-holders keep chickens. The steep slopes can be a real problem, not only for shifting materials and manure, but also for water. Above Ystrad, tenants have tapped the main council supply of water from the spring line coming from the mountain side, their home-constructed pipes reaching direct to their plots. Over recent years, mining jobs have gone but new people have joined the allotment community, and there is a broadening social base. The Rhondda Show is the third most important show in Wales. Although the council at Ystrad would like to save money by relocating the dispersed plots centrally, the tenants have defended their ready access to the sites where they are; the settlements lie for miles along the valley.[77]

The allotment survived: whereas Birmingham lost a third of its allotments in the decade to 1963, Newcastle lost only fifteen per cent. Throughout this time, twenty-five per cent of plots in Birmingham went unused, but only one per cent in Newcastle. Redevelopment did eventually come to Newcastle, peaking in the late 1960s, but recent figures show little change: 1948, 5298 plots; 1963, 3319 plots; 1987, 3100 plots.[78] Curiously, although the vast majority of these are temporary, they are closely protected by the city, and are replaced where development is unavoidable. Almost every site has piped water.

Whilst the intensive husbandry and perfecting competition of pigeon-keeping have contributed to the sexual division within the household as well as the distancing of the community from the outside world, there are now signs of change. There is 'a good cross-section of the public and not confined as they used to be to the mining communities and the working classes. Pigeon clubs are mostly male-dominated with a lot of younger men taking an interest, especially if their father keeps pigeons. Various social functions take place during the year to raise prize money and to get families out for a night, usually at the local working men's club for a pie and pea supper and dance.'[79] But there are women's pigeon clubs, and women members of hitherto men's clubs, and several women are hallowed as 'champions' in men's conversation. At Hordon, the women will join their husbands on the allotment to survey the scene. The men wait for them to return home from work with their 'pocket money', as most of them lost their own jobs when the pit closed in 1985. Mr Bone claims that his wife played a crucial role in their partnership when he won the World Leek Cup. She logs the measurements as they assess the progress their plants have made. In fact, women are now entering these competitions themselves, *and* winning prizes . . .[80]

The allotment culture in the northeast extends beyond the cities and mining villages, and another champion, for leeks and pigeons, dahlias and chrysanthemums, Tommy Taylor, lives in the farming village of Hutton Henry. Retiring early from his career as a lorry driver, he has extended his allotment to the size of four.[81] Carol Youngson, a biologist in her thirties, lives outside Durham, and to her the allotment is part of an ecological lifestyle.[82] As in so many other parts of Britain, the social profile of the allotment has broadened, and in areas away from the more traditional it is as representative as anywhere. Holders on Little Moor, a site on the far side of Newcastle's Town Moor, as neatly set out as a model site, regard St Peters as 'another world'.[83] It is true that St Peters is no longer typical of the sites in the city. However, there are thriving allotments across Newcastle, including the sites around the Town Moor, and in most of the settlements in County Durham and, save on sites of very poor land, there are waiting lists and no empty plots.[84] Eight per cent of the plots in Sunderland are uncultivated, but half of these are in one small area.[85] The council report proposed the improvement of many sites, some to leisure-garden status.

Unemployment has been a stimulant and a constraint on allotment cultivation in the northeast. The redundant miners in Hordon have found respite and encouragement in their plots, and in South Tyneside the council has found hundreds of unemployed people keen to get allotments where they are offered reduced rates.[86] There is a similar interest in many of the outlying parishes in the area, where help is obtained locally to reduce costs for manure and seeds. There are districts of Newcastle with so many people without jobs on the same estate that there is a prevailing negative feeling that taking an allotment admits permanent unemployment; the allotment is justified not in its own right, but as recreation from a job.

Cultivating the inner city

... a piece of land protected by history and structured by the whims and traditions of people working there.

On Allotments,
Four Corner Films, 1976

The inner city does not have much room for allotments, but many people there relish the opportunity of having one. Places like Newcastle retain expansive allotments on the 'moors' inside the city, but these are unusual. *The* distinctive feature of allotments in the inner city is that they represent, in the last decades of the twentieth century, a revival of interest in cultivation. The activists include professional people and managers, the old and the deprived, as well as the surviving traditional growers who have maintained old plots amidst redevelopment, or have obtained newly fenced and landscaped ones following local campaigns.

In London, twelve inner boroughs have allotments: Hackney, Camden, Lambeth, Wandsworth, Tower Hamlets, Southwark, Islington, Hammersmith and Fulham, Haringey, Newham, Greenwich and Brent. These are all surrounded by built-up areas, and some, like Camden, are particularly densely developed. Newham, for example, has been incorporated in the built-up area for a century, but retained open areas, partly because of its proximity to London's Docklands, until these were developed in the 1980s. In 1977, these boroughs had 7303 plots on 593 acres of land.[87] Since then, Camden, Tower Hamlets and Islington have become allotment councils, some councils never having had sites, others having lost theirs early in the century, as their open areas were built upon.

In the ten years up to 1979, Haringey lost nearly two hundred plots through road building.[88] This loss has been concentrated in the parts of the borough where most lower-income people live; however, the council is committed to increasing site provision in these areas. It is in the inner city that poor people have been trapped by the housing, land and job markets, and these forces present the same challenges for allotment availability. They also create concentrations of these same people, living in high-density and often high-rise housing, and clearly in need of garden space.[89] Another contemporary group of people living in the inner city and wanting allotments are the new arrivals, often young professionals seeking places of character and influenced by ecological ideas, disenchanted with commercially produced food and the prevalent attitudes to the environment.

These two populations do not always share the same feeling about what to *do* with the inner city, as the experience of Hackney demonstrates: 'Middle-class incomers value Abney Park cemetery because it is overgrown and four-fifths wild – a good place for a Gothic stroll. A very different view is taken by some working-class people (far more likely to have relatives buried in the place) who find the unknown

and neglected appearance of this nineteenth-century
cemetery a mark of decay, and argue that it should be
definitely tidied up.'[90] Whilst there do seem to be differences, determined by age and sex, between these two groups as
they are represented on allotments, nevertheless there has
been an immense coming together over the matter of allotment cultivation and securing sites, and the newcomers
were eventually accepted. Because so much of the inner
areas has been built on, allotments are found in awkward
corners difficult to develop for other uses, because of underground structures or steep gradients, or difficult road access.
Otherwise, they are relic sites in areas that managed to
avoid development earlier on. In both of these cases there is
a growing track record of effort to protect or obtain a site.

In 1984, Haringey Council agreed explicitly to use allotments as one way to compensate for some of the consequences of borough residents 'being brought up in a built-
up inner-city area'.[91] There were about a thousand plots in
the borough in 1985, a provision of 0.3 acres per thousand
people. The council's aim is to improve this to 0.5 acres, at
the same time balancing the availability of plots between
areas, and especially in higher-density areas such as Tottenham and Green Lanes. Haringey's allotment population
reflects the right mixture of the people who live in the
borough, although ethnic minorities are underrepresented,
and this is an influence on the policy to even up the distribution and accessibility of sites, and provide more information
to the public. Another is to provide crèches and toilets to
enable women, especially in the poorer districts, to work a
plot. In Tottenham, eight per cent of plot-holders are
women; on the other, western side of the borough, the figure
is twenty-five per cent, high by any comparative standards.[92]

This is typical of the other side of inner-city culture, the
middle-class gentrifying community that loves gardening.
Stimulated by small or steep gardens, unconstrained by
attitudes towards women doing allotment work, and

233

actively involved in the community, these women have become champions of the allotment movement locally. It was in Highgate, betwen Crouch End and the Archway Road, that Dr Schwitzer campaigned to get a neglected railway allotment into use, which she achieved.[93] Several women activists are involved in the local committee which repeated its initial success in Highgate with another case where there were proposals to lose a site to parkland, and then the original site to road widening. Locations like these, in the inner city, are vulnerable on many fronts.

Faced with constraints on space and the deterioration of many pieces of land through economic decline, groups of people have got together all over the inner cities to create allotments. Through local councils and voluntary pressure groups alliances have been formed between new and old residents. In Tower Hamlets five sites have been created in places including Bow and Bethnal Green, on small areas between buildings. The Bethnal Green site was the result of interest by the Globe Town Tenants' Association, long-time residents.[94] Tenants living in the tenements of an inner area of Glasgow have shown a similar enthusiasm in taking part in making allotments in their back courts, and have shared the council's desire to spread the benefit of the city's International Garden Festival to the local people – the festival itself will see the introduction of several extra allotment schemes to mark the event.[95] Amongst Manchester's nineteenth-century terraced houses an allotment has been produced as part of a scheme for revitalizing the area's homes and surroundings.[96]

Enthusiasts and, often, newcomers to the inner city were responsible for the many schemes that Friends of the Earth stimulated across Britain in the 1970s. The inner city was the focus of the campaign because it combined a high local population, a lack of allotments – often as a result of redevelopment – and land left over from developers' schemes. The land was often in awkward places, by railways and roundabouts or next to tall blocks. This did not dampen enthusiasms, but rather provided an opportunity for local residents to effect a radical change in their landscape. One site was by the Cut, next to Waterloo station in London, right beside a busy road junction and hoardings.[97] These sites are today used by both local families and young single people who have only recently moved into the areas.

Allotments were part of another incursion into an unsuspecting area of inner London, this time by a group called Inter-Action, which gets involved with local projects, with the community, on a voluntary basis, with some paid full-time staff. They persuaded British Rail, with the local council, Camden, to use derelict railway land, right next to the Euston–Birmingham line. Gillian Tindall saw it was 'a symbol for the new urban peasantry, as a focus for the idea of the village that lurks disguised in city streets and as a means of creating a sense of the revival of the lost past, it could not be bettered ... people were eager to believe that it was an actual fragment of farmland overlooked for a hundred years. Originally feared to be Maoists, "nearly everyone was pleased when, in 1974, they succeeded in opening a riding stable, allotments, and a miniature 'farm' on a segment of railway land".'[98] The allotments are only for retired people living nearby, except for model school plots. The experience has been repeated with sites on the unsympathetic land of London's Docklands, at Mudchute and other romantically sounding places. They have been able to create a close involvement with the local, often deprived, communities in these areas. With the support of the Manpower Services Commission, these schemes become much more than fancy ways of using time and develop into an integral part of the local culture. The Kentish Town City Farm has provided an opportunity for longstanding allotment holders to continue having a small plot near their retirement flat, and others on retirement to take up cultivation. One man who had never grown anything before has made an attractive plot with an interplanting of cabbages and roses that would have delighted Edward Hyams *and* Harry Thorpe!

Although Inner London boroughs are not obliged to provide any allotments,[99] they nevertheless have. Camden uses allotments as part of local community development. Based outside the Recreation Department, this initiative relates directly to the local area and the local population. Over twenty people have plots on numerous small sites that were hitherto unused waste spaces.[100] The inner cities have a concentration of retired, unemployed and disabled people, and several boroughs provide free or reduced rates for them. Hackney had one private allotment site for many years. In the late-1970s Jon Fuller, a local doctor (but then a student), worked with the council to obtain the first new site for years. When this was secured, he found the local people keen to take up the plots. This success was followed by several others and there has been throughout an involvement of people who have lived in the area for decades and generations of ethnic cultivators and those, like Jon Fuller, who have chosen to live and work in the area only recently as one of the new inner-city dwellers. The landscape of these sites is typical of the street to street contrast in the inner cities. One site at Springhill is adjacent to a sports field, a street that is being 'gentrified', and a densely inhabited terrace. The space was unused, at the end of a driveway to the sports club's hall. This 'space', only handicapped by the presence of overhanging trees enjoyed by the residents in the improved terrace opposite, is now well-cultivated, with a fine display of compost heaps and sunflowers. Another site is fenced in by seven-foot-high iron railings but internally has a strong conscious landscape content of paving, shed, seats and tyre-raised beds. This creates a protected feeling within. It is surrounded by tower blocks only yards away and by a cross-roads, and litter blows easily to the fringes of the site. Landscaped with the help of the council's architect, the small plots are arranged in staggered pattern across the paved area, providing a haven where flowers grow alongside a variety of vegetables.[101]

Allotments in Newham are either on Water Board land or

on property owned by the council. Situated near the docks in east London, Newham contains some of the main drainage conduits of the city. Next to these have been secure allotment sites for generations, and they are enjoyed by the traditional East End population that lives in the many rows of terraced housing that, despite many tower blocks, still accommodates most of the borough's population. The council sites are mainly in the east of the borough, closer to the docks, and were part of the provision for dock workers and the vast Beckton gasworks adjacent to them. The allotment population is again traditional to an area that changed little until the 1960s. The changing face of the East End saw the loss of the docks and the jobs they once offered, with little to take their place. The gasworks closed in the 1970s, and the borough today has a high population living in council accommodation and without work; though much bad housing has been eliminated, it has been replaced with nearly two hundred tower blocks. The vast allotments provide a surviving link with the Dockland community and provide a source of food that is increasingly needed. The sites are surrounded by a large-scale urban landscape of chemical works, tower blocks and warehouses. On them the tenants had erected sheds and a variety of other structures. In fact, the Beckton area is one relic of a local tradition of smallholdings that, in the nineteenth and early twentieth century, served London's growing population. A few of these holdings survive, near the allotments. New arrivals are trying to recreate this tradition, working with local people and local schools.

The need to redevelop the decaying land of the Docklands led to pressures to use the allotment sites that were in the line of chosen locations for roads and lorry parking areas. The allotment-holders showed their resentment and local solidarity to those proposals in a march and demonstration in the 1970s, reminiscent of the Peak District Trespass to create public access to the hills. People who had recently moved into the area, like Sheila Beskin, supported this action. Whilst many felt that the street action was the culmination, Sheila and local people like Bill Gladwell knew that years of negotiation would follow. She helped to establish Allotments for the Future, a campaign body that has worked with the more traditionally representative local federation of allotment associations to champion the interests of the tenants. The transformation of the docks was masterminded by the London Docklands Development Corporation, appointed by central government in the face of local opposition. The redevelopment of the district for a wider market typified inner-city policy in the Britain of the 1980s, the new upmarket housing attracting a whole new population – though many newcomers are taking allotments. The Corporation's objective is satisfied through intensive world marketing, but it has also sought to respond to local agitation – partly through the creation of a new allotments site within the Docklands boundary. Situated alongside a major relief road, the plots are provided with serried rows of regulation sheds – in marked contrast to those on the old sites that, in small proportion, they replace. Thus the old and new cultures of the inner city and local council have come together to continue the campaign for secure allotments and their cultural identity.[103]

12
Holding your ground

'An old man is setting a row of broad beans. So small a row, so shakily, dibbling a hole for each by jiggling a twig in the ground until it has made a space large enough. His allotment runs to the narrow verge between the cliff of chalk and the sunk road; right on the edge of an arm of the cove where the lorries enter. Balanced up there he sets his broad beans, while many shovels eat away at the ground below him. In three months they have taken this huge bite out of the hill: it will take three months from now for his beans just to be in bloom. Once he was a ploughman driving a team over a hill. Now, shakily on this little remnant of allotment, he sets a few beans. Because it is the time of year: it is time to sow beans.'

Adrian Bell,
Men of the Fields,
Collins, 1936,
Alan Sutton, 1984

One in forty households in Britain has an allotment. This has been the result of the extension of power in land through local councils to ordinary people. There are few other examples where land is available on such an equitable basis. What was originally envisaged as a gesture to the poor, alienated from any rights to land through the enclosures and then the factory system over a century ago, has been partaken of by everybody. We can call this an 'entitlement' in the sense that Amartya Sen used the term – as a way of linking the *availability* of allotments with political, economic and cultural practice, rather than by some fixed inevitable and *physical* limitation on their supply. To quote Sen, entitlement is a '"semi-legal concept" focusing on the bundles of goods and services that a person (or a family) can legitimately establish command over using the laws, regulations, conventions, opportunities and rights, ruling in the

society in question'.[1] In market economies, these entitlements reflect ownership; in socialist ones, they are contained in rights in relation to the state. Allotments have
gradually become part of that 'bundle of goods' that have
been recognized by government as legal rights. Political
claims made by common people during the nineteenth century were legitimated and translated into entitlements by
the legislation of 1908. The Allotments Act of 1887 had
provided equity of access to land to grow things, mainly for
food. But it was predicated in the failure to obtain land
through private agreement. Then councils had to provide
allotments if four or more people demanded them.

The 1908 Act removed the private proviso and, ever since,
local councils have had to provide allotments 'on demand'.[2]
The allotment had failed to become a commercial proposition, with most of them 'let at rates higher than workmen
could afford'. Already, in the middle years of the nineteenth
century: 'The bulk of the workmen's gardens . . . have since
been covered by buildings.'[3] When the majority of those who
rented expensive 'Guinea Gardens' in the early nineteenth
century obtained their own gardens in houses they bought
or rented there was not a sufficient market to sustain them.
The landowners frequently found alternative uses for their
sites, although one or two of these early sites were leased to
local councils and remain allotments, let now at rents of a
few pounds a year from the local council (as in the case of
Westbourne Road, Birmingham). Otherwise allotments in
the nineteenth century had relied on the kind-heartedness
of the landlords and employees, although in many cases this
was seen as an alternative to alcohol and political protest, a
path to a more respectable life – 'the objective of making
these allotments is moral rather than economic; the cultivation of a few flowers is a pleasing occupation and has a
tendency to keep a man at home and from the ale house . . .',[4]
and in many cases this was less charity than the reaction to
strong political campaigns.

It was only through the public ownership, or leasing, of

land that strips could be made available to the working class for use as allotments. This invention broke the impasse of land ownership – allotments still provide one of the few means of access to land for a livelihood in the Fens and Bedfordshire. It secured access in ways that are still not available to any other land, providing people with direct rights in relation to land over which they have considerable, if not complete, freedom of use. Campaigners today, as they did over a century ago, see the allotment as one of the individual's rights, a means of reclaiming rights to land, its attendant culture and economy – which had been lost before the enclosures.[5]

However, their becoming public provision did not reduce the political quality of allotments, and there has been a continuous struggle to secure these rights, especially when councils, or other landowners, want to develop allotment sites. District councils (then urban districts, boroughs and parishes) were responsible for allocation.[6] The acceptance by the public sector meant that allotments became involved in public accountability and, as the century progressed, with professionals. Local councils were required to provide allotments 'in reasonable number' to meet the local demand, i.e. where people came forward to ask for them. After eighty years this remains the main way to get an allotment. Since the 1908 Act this has to be provided on land that the council owns, possibly through compulsory purchase if none other is available, or by lease.[7] The land may then be leased to local Allotment Associations, many of which have the power to allocate plots.

The right to land

The ordinary landless man or woman's right to rent about an eighth of an acre of their own country for the purpose of growing some food . . .

Irene Evans,
'Allotment Provision in Scotland',
The Land for the People,
Scottish Socialist Society, 1985

Land was allocated to people who would use it to grow food, although, until 1919, this was restricted to the 'labouring population'. Commercial use of allotments was constrained, if not prohibited, by the 1922 Allotments Act, so that it would be 'wholly or mainly cultivated by the occupier for the production of vegetables or fruit crops for consumption by *him*self and his family'. (Commercial allotments do remain the most direct survivals of the enclosures.)[8] The entitlement for the poor was extended by the 1922 Act to universal status, thereby acknowledging the right to cultivate one's own food. In later years the emphasis on food was relaxed, too, as the wider 'recreational' value of and demand for, allotments were recognized in the creation of a 'right to recreate'. Irene Evans expressed reservations, not on the recreational value of allotments, but on the loss of the right to land that she fears would come if, in law, allotments were only regarded as a 'recreation' – an area of policy often regarded as 'soft'.[9] However, it was in *defence* of allotments that Thorpe, the London Association of Recreational Gardeners and the supporters of Lord Wallace of Coslany, as well as the National Society, championed the cause of allotments as recreations.[10] Their concern is the antagonistic feeling towards the single occupation of ground for the growing of food at a time when few people actually *have* to rely on their plot for sustenance.

When local councils became involved with allotment provision, it was realized that demand considerably exceeded supply; not only that, councils also faced other pressures regarding the use of sites. The inevitable result was the introduction of further regulations, designed to ration the use of existing plots and to maximize their use. The issues, specifically, were: *who* should obtain a plot; *what* could be considered a reasonable provision for a town; and, related to this, what rules were needed to ensure maintenance of the land? Given the limited supply, it was necessary to repossess plots that were not being well-cultivated so that others could use them. Also to be taken into account was the growing professional concern about the rationalization of recreation – in particular, with the cost of land and the efficiency of its use. Although the 1922 Act made eligibility equitable (the 1919 Act had increased legitimacy to ex-servicemen), at times selection criteria have been applied. In the Depression of the 1930s, special measures were introduced to ease access for the unemployed;[11] locally, the Quakers worked to expand supply to provide more allotments for people living in the most depressed areas.[12]

In similar conditions in the 1980s some local authorities in places where allotment demand is especially high have discriminated in favour of the unemployed, giving priority through a separate waiting list in which every third vacancy goes to someone who is out of work.[13] The rent in such cases is halved. Other councils work a link support system to cut the cost of materials, whilst certain authorities offer plots rent-free for six months out of twelve. The pressure of allotments in the mid-1970s led commentators to argue for the selection of tenants on the basis of greatest need, although they acknowledged the difficulties involved in making a fair assessment.[14] In a different way, some allotment sites are available only to pensioners, others for school use. The example has been followed in the case of several city farms, where the authorities are not bound by the need to provide equal access.[15]

Many councils realize that allotments are not for the public presentation of civic pride, unlike municipal gardens. The overriding objective has always been to provide a piece of ground, rather than the facilities. There are some notable exceptions, like Birmingham, Cardiff, Coventry and Bristol – where practically every site has available water. However, many compare poorly with the wrought-iron fencing, the water and the greenhouses provided in the municipal parks. The charitable attitude prevailed. Change occurred with a wider, growing interest in leisure amongst people who may be considered less prepared to put up with the conditions on the poorer sites.[16]

One question that faced the providers was 'how much land?' From 1925 local councils were required to work out the number of allotments needed to meet local demand.[17] This was to be calculated when preparing town plans, so that any land could be safeguarded from other development. Unfortunately there was no obvious way to estimate the requirement, and no ready way to assess demand. Councils relied on the people who had come forward to ask for a plot, who were on the waiting list until one became vacant or a new one was provided. This approach, though, depended on people knowing their rights and also how to exercise them.

A solution was worked out for a later generation of town planners by the government-appointed Allotments Advisory Committee in 1949. This Committee was set up in response to the new circumstances existing after the war, when it was evident that things were likely to change: land was needed for building, there was an increase in vacant plots, and there remained a need for cheap food in an age of rationing. The Committee proposed that there should be made available four acres (1.6 hectares) of allotments per 1000 people (*not* households), about one for every twenty-five people; this was duly backed up by legislation in 1950,[18] but was given scant regard in the plans that followed it.

By the time that an effective measure was introduced, allotments were considered under the broader heading of 'recreation' rather than as a separate entity. The later Thorpe report recommended one acre of allotment land – about ten plots – for every 1000 people, and the Middlesex Development Plan had recommended 0.55 acres on that basis. In 1987 Enfield, once part of Middlesex, provided 0.8 acres per 1000 people; only Hounslow was higher in Greater London, with 0.96 acres per 1000. Newham, in east London, provided 0.5 acres, and Glasgow 0.1, in the same year. Harlow in Essex has a standard 1:1000, but actually reached 0.6:1000 in 1987. Milton Keynes policy was to provide 1.7 acres per 1000 people in the 1970s (interestingly in contrast to Thorpe's fears that new towns would ignore allotments –

indeed Wolverton had the highest provision of any council in the 1960s, but by the 1980s this had fallen to 0.86 acres, close to the figure actually available). Sunderland had one of the highest rates of *provision*, with 1.05 acres for every 1000 people. In the county of Essex the range available in the mid-1980s was from 0.3 to 3 acres for every 1000 people. Glasgow changed its use of what it considered to be an 'unrealistic' (overgenerous) standard in terms of resources and likely provision, to relating provision to the actual demand recorded.[19]

The variation of allotment popularity across the country suggests that there is no 'magic' national figure that will be appropriate to all councils. The figures recorded represent a mixture of previous practice, local (expressed) allotment interest, growing conditions and local traditions, and a knowledge amongst the local people of their council's attitude to provision. Whilst it may be attractive to use a simple, inalienable and quantifiable measure, this is elusive; the measure itself is an amalgam of experience, knowledge and attitudes. The issue is really about the appeal of sites, the publicity and track record of the council *and* of the local allotment movement. At best, a measure can only be used as a guide, so long as local councils are able to ascertain local demand by means more efficient than passively awaiting people to sign on. The subsequent spread of the devolution of control to local Associations, combined with the improved quality of some councils' leaflets, makes this possible.

The increased pressure on land for house-building use during the 1950s, amidst growing concern about the loss of farmland, meant that allotments again came to be seen as prime candidates for development. However, in what became known as the 'garden controversy', it was claimed that allotments and back gardens had not only provided ten per cent of the country's food during the last war, but that their productivity had challenged commercial agriculture's at that time[20] – thus, it was said, there could be no

Cartoon by Mallet from the *Countryman*

justification for building on allotments. Commenting on this, Thorpe suggested that productivity may have been overstated, given the variable efficiency of the plot-holders and the variation of soil quality on allotments.[21] He emphasized the cost of the urban land occupied by many allotments as compared with that of agricultural land, and argued that the allotment case was not necessarily cost-effective. He did not consider the saving in transport costs, or in the lower investment in machinery that characterized allotments, even more so in the 1980s. However, it was precisely the increase in residential density and the reduction in garden size that swelled the demand for allotments in many parts of the country.[22]

Food was again the claim for allotments made by the new activists in the broader allotment movement in the 1970s. Although 'provision' has become the bureaucratic response to this demand, in some areas of the country there was a shortage of plots, and an enhanced awareness of the land. People everywhere joined waiting lists for allotments, but in the inner cities, as well as some more rural areas, they joined a new campaign to release more land for allotments. This was fequently land that was caught up in the problems of the inner urban areas and was not being used. Friends of the Earth helped to co-ordinate local campaigns to increase access to allotments and utilize this land. They introduced a revived urgency, as well as new skills of publicity and negotiation, into the claim for allotment land. They used petitions, lobbied politicians and generally made the local people more aware of the issue. In many places they were successful. They combined these styles with sound research on site availability, ownership and quality,[23] adding a new dimension to the allotment movement.

The campaigns and the subsequent experience brought a mixed response from the more experienced holders and from professionals in local authorities. It awakened council officers to the issue of allotments in a new way, and many councils found very attractive the idea of utilizing eyesores for productive purposes for which there was a local demand and ready help in clearance and preparing the sites. In Redbridge, east London, three lorry-loads of waste material, including old bedsteads, were cleared from a site of 1½ acres to make ten plots. The plots were then marked out, and half were taken by people living next to the site, half from the council waiting list: 'There was a shared satisfaction in what had been achieved. It is nice to see tangible results; from an eyesore into something nice to look at.'[24] In Cardiff, a scheme was launched in association with the Council for the Elderly,[25] whereby plots were shared. These and other similar developments brought allotments to the attention of local councils, and money from the government's Urban Programme has subsequently been used to provide allotments on unused land.

Another approach to gaining access was used in Hackney. The council had no allotment sites at all in the 1970s,[26] so Jon Fuller approached the Planning Department on the matter with the decade nearing its end. Keen to get a plot near his home, Fuller received a positive response, and set to work with the support of many local people – including a neighbourhood allotment society. Together, they found land that was both suitable for cultivation and acceptable to the council. The largest site now has twenty-nine plots, the smallest just one. There are about seventy plots in all, and negotiations for new sites are continuing with demand unceasing; some sites have been set aside, with the assistance of local housing associations, for the old and the disabled. Despite considerable success, however, the Allotment Society is aware of the particular frustrations experienced in the battle for land reclamation at this humble though highly committed level: 'Many potential sites have been held up for inspection and then disappeared from view. We have had to learn to hold back our enthusiasms until we are actually on site.'[27]

Throughout the last twenty years or so, a campaign has been waged to persuade central government to acknowledge the allotment as a legitimate recreational facility, and to extend entitlement to leisure.[28] A headline in *The Times* in 1975 summed up the situation: 'Growing Shortage of Allotment Plots'.[29] Councils held divergent attitudes on the subject: 'The London Borough of Westminster has 80 acres of Public Open Space (excluding over 1000 acres of Crown Lands) and has no allotments, and refused to create any when asked. Neighbouring Hammersmith has only 200 acres of Open Space, but 400 5-pole allotments.'[30] 'In 1981 the National ... argued the failure of the government to expand allotments in a situation of lengthening waiting lists and high unemployment, with the products of boredom and poverty, and called for a national campaign to extend provision.'[31] Some novel forms of the latter surfaced, among them one that revived a century of allotment history: 'The rector of a Cheshire Parish Church offered his parishioners the use of the Rectory orchard as allotments to save the trouble and expense of keeping the undergrowth under control.'[32] In Stowmarket, employees asked their company if they could use a vacant triangle of land next to the factory for allotments, and ten plots were established.[33]

The episode of Friends of the Earth (see Chapter 11) called into question the adequacy of the local allotment movement, and of local councils to make allotments an active issue, attractive to a wider world. Some Associations were embarrassed by the Friends' success; a few councils were upset that Friends of the Earth had talked directly to local people about it.[34] In most cases of local difficulty it was the lack of procedures for dealing with vacant land rather than council intransigence that was the problem.[35] It may be of more concern to the allotment movement that Friends of the Earth campaigned for the use of vacant sites, even though they were often earmarked for development 'at a later date'. But though the result might have been to shift attention away from permanent sites, it did nevertheless achieve more plots.

Negotiations

The bourgeoisie, whether conscious or not, has preserved
those marginal zones of autonomy formed by tiny allotments
or backyards of workers' houses...

André Gorz,
Farewell to the Working Class
Pluto Press, 1982

However, with legislation legalizing the claims to allotment
land, providing universal access as of right – at least, in
theory – the issue that has dominated the allotment movement over the last half century is how to hold on to sites.
Redevelopment and new building, and the vulnerability of
allotments in the land market, made this inevitable at a
time when, as the country progressed, the anticipated fall in
numbers of aspiring plot-holders did not occur. In fact, the
widening of the movement in the 1970s to include recreation
and environment interests – and the increased political
awareness that this brought – produced a more vigorous
defence of sites under threat than had existed for decades. In
certain parts of the country the movement remained a significant political interest, notably in the northeast. The
representation of allotment-holders on local councils *as of
right* had ensured some consultation if changes were proposed.[36] Released from the difficulty of being seen as the
deserving poor, the movement challenged schemes to
remove sites with a new fervour. After years of statutory
provision and bureaucratized organization, people with
renewed radical attitudes became involved. However, this
had a historical precedent in the allotment-holders of the
1930s, who spoke out strongly at public inquiries against
proposals to relocate sites.[37]

In west London, Dick Grant occupied four plots on different sites in twenty years of being a plot-holder. Though at
no time did he *want* to move, he had spent only two years on
one site before being forced to leave; while, at another site

he was first asked to vacate – only to return later when the plot was overgrown, and after local plans had been changed.

Glasgow University owns several allotment sites. One of these it repossessed in 1973 for building. However, when old mine workings, typical of many parts of the city, were discovered, the site was reinstated as an allotment through a lease to the City Corporation, four years after the holders had quit. Six sites in Glasgow, all in the local area of one Allotment Association, experienced a similar history.[39] Tom Hume, a veteran campaigner to safeguard allotments from this fate, has experience of three of his own sites being closed.[40]

The chances of saving a site from development can be dependent on its legal status – that is, whether it is 'statutory' or 'temporary'; in practice, though, the vast majority of temporary sites are unlikely ever to be built upon, and hundreds of sites never made statutory are well-kept and productive. The attitudes of tenant and landlord are crucial in such matters. Statutory sites have some protection in law. If a council wants to dispose of a site that it owns it must first obtain approval from the Secretary of State.[41] There has to be a public inquiry at which the government appoints an Inspector, through the Department of the Environment, who considers the proposal in the light of any opposing arguments presented by the allotment-holders and their supporters. The government sought to repeal this safeguard in 1980, in section 8 of the Local Government, Planning and Land Bill, but withdrew the measure in the face of vigorous opposition.[43] None of the legislation applies to private sites, but statutory sites leased from a local council to an Association enjoy the same protection. There are safeguards on some private sites, in the form of covenants, and many charitable sites are similarly secured.

If a council decides to apply for the disposal of a site it must convince the Minister's Inspector that there are no tenants still working the plots. If there are, it must show that other land is available for them. The alternative site must be equal in size, meet local demand, be suitable for 'spade cultivation', and be within reasonable distance of plot-holders' homes. Any money made by the sale of a site must be used in ensuring the adequate replacement of the site.[44] If the council does not wish to replace the land, it has to demonstrate that there is no longer any demand for the plots that are to be cleared. Some councils have gone in the other direction and replaced temporary sites with permanent ones and sites without facilities with those that have them.[45]

Decisions by the Department of the Environment Inspectorate frequently go against a local council that does not have a sufficient case and where the local allotment-holders make a good claim to the land. When permission is given to develop on allotment sites, councils may be required to undertake particular site preparations. In one case, thirteen of these 'conditions' were placed on the council if it wished to proceed with the development. These included rabbit-proof fencing, toilets, water, removal of sheds, a rent-free year, liming and rotavating.[46]

In 1985 the council at Potters Bar, Hertfordshire, was required to spend three years preparing a new site if it wished to use it to replace another it wanted for housing. As this was a decision given at an Inquiry into a Local Plan, the council had the right to reject the Inspector's advice on the Town Planning issue. However, the next stage was the permission for disposal under the allotment legislation. (The allotment-holders have more chance of being heard at this stage and have the right to go to the High Court if the council's action does not comply with the decision given.)[47] The holders petitioned both the council and the government,[48] and in 1986 the Allotment Association won the case. The council's argument was rejected because of the unacceptable time lapse between disposal and site preparation; the potential pollution from a motorway adjacent to the new site; the site's exposed position; and the unsuitability of part of the site for spade cultivation.[49]

In another case, even though one piece of a site proposed for disposal had never been cultivated, the council was not allowed to develop it. The section was only 708 square metres but there was a waiting list of eighteen for the site. The Inspector said that: 'It is only in exceptional circumstances that consent would be granted ... the criteria apply ... particularly in urban areas. Your council does not propose to provide alternative land although clearly a demand exists.'[50] A similar decision was reached in another case at Boldon Colliery where allotment plots were to be made shorter to accommodate a drainage scheme. With six people on the waiting list, the land 'could not be considered surplus to requirements'.[51] In contrast, Leamington Spa council was unable to sustain its refusal to permit development of a site. The council argued that there was a growing demand locally, and more houses were being built with small gardens. In this case, the Inspector argued that there were idle plots, large gardens, and available land elsewhere.[52]

Councils have to get planning permission to develop temporary sites or use them for other purposes. One safeguard is that there is still an obligation on local authorities to provide sites, even in the 1980 Local Government, Planning and Land Act. Local people can campaign to gain local and political support for these sites, just as they can for statutory sites. They can also fight to have new sites provided and old ones replaced, whatever the status of the sites – indeed, tenants have had the right to be consulted over such matters since the 1925 Act,[53] which required councils to include allotment-holders as representatives on council sub-committees. However, the 1980 Local Government Act rescinded this right.

The strength of the statutory protection is clearly discernible from the table below, which records the provision of sites – and the total acreage involved – for the period 1935 to 1978.[54] The private and temporary sites have clearly been lost in greatest number, although the data are perplexingly inaccurate.[55] Furthermore, there have been many switches of status between temporary and statutory that are obscured in the available statistics. In Leeds between 1948 and 1958 the number of plots on temporary sites fell from 3523 to 1006, from 301 to 92 acres. During the same period statutory plots rose from 1486 to 2184, 122 to 149 acres. The situation in Birmingham is more dramatic. 8968 statutory plots (on 860 acres) in 1948 grew to 9305 (915 acres) in 1958, whilst temporary plots fell from 8881 (712 acres) to 3765 (357 acres) over the same period.[56]

Allotments Provision in England and Wales[57]

Year	Statutory	Temporary	Private	Total Acreage
35	27802	7264	24337	59403
50	49808	18412	37061	105281 (reflects wartime increase)
55	51115	11810	35470	98395
60	45934	10044	29191	85169
70	28531	12969*	17015	58242 (peak development decade)
75	26402	9406	10823	47455 (main loss private sites)
78	26739	11223	11143	49105 (1970s campaigns)

*This may be simply a result of corrections to categories following the Thorpe report.

In 1965, 192 statutory sites were disposed of by local councils in England and Wales. This meant a total loss of nearly 400 acres, or 4000 plots.[58] During the 1970s, the rate of disposal declined by more than half, this level being maintained in the 1980s.[59] In every case in 1965 holders could be accommodated on alternative sites (through vacancy); in a further 5 cases on 26 acres there were no vacancies on suitable alternative sites.[60]

Statutory and temporary sites are still vulnerable to development pressure where local provision seems to exceed demand. With 10 per cent of their plots vacant in 1987, the London Borough of Enfield undertook a review of allotment land. Fifteen years previously 16 per cent had been vacant, and a further 8 per cent left uncultivated by their holders. The council then proposed that 50 of its 225 acres be disposed of, but within five years the waiting list had reached 1000 and the action was shelved.[61] By 1977 there was a demand for one-third more plots than the borough had. During the 1970s the Department of the Environment came up with a ready measure of the degree to which provision satisfied demand for each county. This was to be ascertained by taking the ratio of the number of plots available against the number let plus the number of people on waiting lists; the result, translated into a percentage, provided the measure. In those boom years, 18 counties met less than two-thirds of their demand, and one, Warwickshire, only half. Cambridgeshire was highest and provided over 80 per cent with plots.[62] In London, Hounslow supplied 87 per cent of its demand, Richmond-on-Thames 52 per cent.[63] However, as Irene Evans has argued, there is a tendency for people to be more aware of plots being available where there *are* more plots and local promotion of them is greatest.

Crucial legislation for holding on to allotments[64]

1887, 1892. Councils required to provide allotments when four or more local people request them – as long as they can show they have been unable to obtain any privately; for the labouring poor.

1908. Councils obliged to provide plots to meet demand, i.e. at least four local people requesting them, and to a 'sufficient number'; by compulsory purchase if necessary.

1919. Everybody eligible for allotments.

1922. Security of tenure introduced plus consultation, notice-to-quit periods, and compensation on termination of the tenancy.

1925. Statutory sites given protection, requiring government permission before they can be developed or sold.

1980. The right to consultation ceased to be official.

Security outside the council sector

There are other landlords that, between them, have a considerable acreage of allotments. In 1978 British Rail still owned 670 acres, in the form of 8885 plots.[65] This was two-thirds the number of plots in its possession in 1976, and half the 1970 acreage. Whilst BR's policy is to treat each site on its merits, it no longer has a great interest in keeping them. Administration is expensive and fewer railwaymen live close to their tracks. A widespread section of society uses the plots now and, where they are not unguarded and close to the tracks, local councils negotiate with BR for control.[66]

In a similar way, British Coal has ceased to have a landlord's relationship with the local workforce, and the National Union of Mineworkers has no interest in allotments as an issue. Miners, whilst they almost created the allotments tradition in some districts, live further from the pitheads. Though some interest survives in the newer mining areas, the old association of the plot with low wages – the latter being the *raison d'être* of the former – is hard to lose. The Board's policy is to sell off all their sites, and again, many are bought by local councils for continued use as allotments.[67]

The British Waterways Board had 800 plots on 47 acres in 1969. One tenth of these survived its rationalization of assets by 1987, 'Allotment Gardens would not normally be considered a very good investment'.[68] About 11 acres remain, some 95 plots, but one third of these are vacant. The vacancies are concentrated on one site, near Rickmansworth, that contains half of the total number. One one site near Nuneaton, run by the Canal Allotment Association, there are few vacancies.

The Charity Commissioners remain responsible for many thousands of allotments in Britain. However, a great number of their sites have been transferred to the ownership and control of local parishes, subject to the same conditions as had bound the former trustees.[69] Land allocated for allotments under the Inclosure Acts also became transferrable to the parishes.[70] Land set aside for allotment use under the Inclosure Awards requires the passing of an Act of Parliament for its disposal.[71] It was this safeguard that protected plot-holders in their successful opposition to the local council plans to dispose of pieces of allotment land at sites in Windsor Forest, Clewer and on Cardigan Common, Cardigan. Any land remaining in the control of the Charity Commissioners can be dealt with as the Commission decides, within reasonable interpretation of the trustees' purpose.[73] The Commissioners are required to act as near as possible to orginal trusts that endowed the land for allotments. 'It is the policy of the Commissioners to make changes ... readily and sympathetically, particularly where the original trust is for the relief of the poor and it is clear that such benefit can ... be better conferred in some way other than the provision of allotments.'[74]

Inherited from the Bishops and the Deans and Chapters, allotment land is still in the hands of the Church Commissioners. Their policy is to hold on to it for four reasons: the sites are considered to preserve amenities of the See Houses; they are a worthwhile facility for the local community; they raise a reasonable income; and most of them are unlikely to be saleable, being unattractively situated for development purposes (in the long term, however, Commissioners consider there *is* development potential if the sites are part of a larger estate being sold).[75] In addition, the Church possesses glebe land, containing allotments for which the individual chapters and dioceses express a similar policy.

Planning and the quality of sites available

The successful defence of a statutory site at an inquiry may hinge on whether there is sufficient demand for the plots. This is also another measure used when planning for local demand, through an analysis of waiting lists *and* vacant plots. The vacancies are supposed to suggest local disinterest, especially when this is balanced by a short waiting list. At a time when planning was reaching an increased level of sophistication, measuring everything to achieve ultimate precision, allotments presented a problem. The factors that caused plots to be neglected, making many hopeful plot-holders give up, were not quantifiable, and the knowledge of poor sites keeps people from the waiting list.[76]

It would be foolish to infer that there is an *inevitable* connection between the quality of plots and the length of a waiting list; in Bristol, for example, though every site has water and the city is renowned for good servicing, one-seventh of the city's plots were empty in 1987. However, those lying vacant were mainly on large sites – reflecting a countrywide trend towards smaller sites, which tend to be more successful, being more easily managed, and where people know each other, thus helping to reduce the incidence of vandalism (strangers are noticed), and there is a greater community feeling and commitment. There are some striking exceptions to this pattern, however. Bordesley Green is a 'model' site in Birmingham, and the largest in Europe; it was laid out under the inspiration of Thorpe, and possesses a committed management group. Despite the vulnerability of the site to vandalism (several entries/exits and an extensive boundary), it is well and fully cultivated. Ponders End in Enfield boasts a strong Allotment Association, as well as a sizeable clubhouse and bar, where members regularly play shove ha'penny. This is indeed a large site with 279 plots, all of them let.[77] These cases illustrate the importance of holders' involvement in the activities of their site as one of the best ways of ensuring that they hold on to it.

Some sites are just badly located, on poor ground or in other ways unattractive to cultivation. Exposed positions; poor or stony ground (some bear the name 'stoneyfields' and 'stoneyflint'); broken fences adjacent to thoroughfares; a lack of water, especially on light soil – any of these may lead to empty plots and almost discarded sites. In other places there are simply too many plots, provided for a local need that has passed. They may also have been neglected, perhaps because they lacked facilities, and have become untidy in appearance. Sunderland Borough Council, together with Harlow and Braintree District Councils, undertook surveys of their sites in the 1980s. They proposed the improvement of some sites and that others be grassed, or developed, depending on local demand, in an effort to retain some land in the event of rising local demand later on. This course avoids the deterioration of sites and retains some flexibility.[78] Hounslow, the London borough with the second-highest provision, has found one solution to surplus plots in the creation of larger, chalet gardens requiring less work and providing more space in which to sit.[79]

Three out of four new holders may not survive one season, over-burdened by the unfamiliar effort and lacking the skills of cultivation. Over a hundred people a year moving to Milton Keynes become plot-holders, but of these many give up. Ron MacParlen feels that the newcomers are not alone in this, and that substantial numbers of those who have been holders for years use long-tried but imperfect methods, unwilling to absorb improvements. Some eventually leave their plot in a 'sick' state for the next holder – scarcely an encouragement.[80] Good cultivation is thus another strength in the battle to hold onto your ground.

Holding on

The Corporation, having. . . purchased the private interests in the. . . field, intend to lay it out as a public park and garden, so that it can no longer be used as allotments, which the allottees consider a very severe loss to them.

G.W. Johnson (ed.)
*The Cottage Gardener and Country
Gentleman's Companion*, 1853

There is frequently a need for a much more political attitude to ensure that a site is not lost. This means a demonstration of the political significance of allotments within the community and in the local culture. Publicity is a key to this, and the members of many local Associations and other groups of holders have shown that, whatever their age, they are a far from spent force. Petitions, debate, political lobbying and marches remain, after a hundred years, the stock in trade of allotment-holders in defence of their right to land. 'In Berlin in 1973, 12,500 holders staged a protest demonstration to try to put a stop to takeovers of their gardens.'[81] Referring to the vulnerability of non-statutory sites in the early 1970s, a town clerk said that 'a little more militancy, a little more tub-thumping and self-thumping and self-advertisement could help'.[82] When the British government tried to abolish the safeguards on statutory sites, allotment-holders visited parliament with a petition and banners.[83] Lord Wallace of Coslany led the Lords debate, and the opposition in both Houses led to its withdrawal.[84] In 1975 hundreds of allotment-holders and their families in Newham joined in a mass meeting on a site proposed for closure and marched through the main High Street to greet the Prime Minister who was there for an official opening that day.[85] Like the mass trespasses and marches on the hills in the 1930s, this drew attention to the issue, albeit at a local level, but continued lobbying and negotiation by a committed core were still necessary thereafter.

Three times during the 1970s the Railway Allotments Group (RAG) in Haringey was forced to fight for the retention of allotment land,[86] and each time it won. In the first instance, British Rail wanted to develop a derelict railway allotment site for use as a car park. The local council had just won a case to build an estate on a larger site at Broadwater Farm, in the face of protests from the holders, arguing that there were sufficient plots elsewhere. However, the railway case was the first of many where a new wave of holders was campaigning, and the RAG duly won the day, subsequently letting all the plots. The second instance occurred a year later and concerned a strip site situated alongside an old railway line. The plan was to turn it into a park, but the council welcomed the RAG's idea of creating a model site and an urban farm on the land. The snag was a lack of funds. The site lay dormant until a few years later, when it was proposed to build a slip road on it for the north London Archway Road. The RAG's eighteen plot-holders obtained 600 signatures, stirred up press interest, produced papers for the public inquiry on the Road Scheme, and put forward an alternative route for the sliproad. The council then took up the argument on behalf of the RAG in the second phase of the inquiry, and the site was saved.

In achieving all this, the RAG had shown itself a coherent, well-organized force wielding substantial political clout on the home front. It continues to be represented on the council's Environment Committee and retains its network of contracts should they be needed in any future campaign. Its work is practical in other ways, and the group has collected money, laid pipes, and planted hedges as a shield against vehicle fumes emanating from the street.[87]

Sympathetic local councillors and active Allotment Associations will often work together to secure good land for allotments, possibly better than that it replaces. It may be in the plot-holders' interest to find new sites to replace old ones, where they are nearer the holders' homes, where the land is better, where improved servicing can be provided, and where the plots are removed from the threat of vandalism. In such circumstances plots become more attractive and waiting lists lengthen. Local councils are able to use the old sites for development, with considerable profit that can be used for equipping the replacement sites. This process is called rationalization, and is usually undertaken by the Planning and Recreation departments of local councils. The idea behind this process is to provide a 'system' of allotment sites that are located where the need is, and to coordinate them with other recreation land.[88] The relocation of sites provides an opportunity to reassess supply, layout and servicing in relation to demand. For example, Cardiff has found that, while demand has diminished for the oldest inner allotments, it has increased in the newer suburban estates;[89] and Sunderland and Birmingham have both implemented notable rationalization schemes for their sites.[90] Change leading to the creation of smaller plots can be of benefit to the holders where full-sized plots are found to be too much of a handful; it can also provide the space for the addition of vital services. But a proposed introduction of smaller plots can mask an attempt to reduce the overall provision of allotment land where demand might indicate a need to increase it...

Plot-holders and landlords do not always agree on how rationalization should be achieved, and sometimes the holders feel that it is not in their interests at all. In the Rhondda Valley at Ystraad the council would like to consolidate the many small sites distributed about the mining town. This would make council maintenances more efficient and the plot-holders might get a better service. However, it is not welcome amongst holders because many would have further to travel to reach their sites. Strung along and up the narrow valleys, the places where the sites developed are close by the homes of those who work on them.[91]

A local council's proposal to rationalize a large allotment site in the middle of an Essex town has provided its tenants with direct experience of how to hold on to their ground. The council wishes to redevelop part of the site, and use the rest as an open green. It recognizes the existence of local demand, however, and plans to replace the redeveloped site with others situated elsewhere in the town. The allotment-holders, for their part, argue that the central site is well-located for their members, and that, as a statutory site, it requires special consideration and treatment. But the council disputes the validity of this 'statutory' status, based as it is on ambiguous records. It further asserts that, whilst the site has maintained the open character vital to its location next to the old town wall, it is untidy and incompatible with the conservation area next to it. During the three years that the isssue has been debated many plot-holders have lost confidence in the future and abandoned the site, adding weight to the council's case that the site is not popular and that fewer plots are needed to replace it. The proposed scheme is part of a local plan for the area and, as such, the council is not obliged to follow the advice of the Inspector in this case. The Inspector has advised that the council and the plot-holders should agree on the destiny of the site; if it is proven not to have statutory status, there is no need for an allotment inquiry. The campaign is the unfortunate culmination of several years' joint management by the holders and the council, during which time both vandalism and vacancies were reduced.[92]

The best laid plans may founder. When Haringey tried to even out provision across the borough area, the Greater London Council approved the building of a road line directly through one of the sites in an area of least provision. The nearest alternative location was in an area already well served.[93]

Seven Allotment Associations grouped together as a Federation to campaign for allotments when major redevelopment proposals were made for the London Docklands in Newham. They joined another active group, Allotments for the Future, formed to spearhead action against closure proposals two years earlier. One large site became involved with major redevelopment plans for an old gas works. The site, known by its shape as the Triangle site, with 400 plots, was proposed for a lorry park in 1975. That hot summer hundreds of people took to the streets in a protest march. During the next four years the allotment groups joined a community forum and argued for an alternative proposal. They found their scheme to be widely supported, and became part of a broader movement to conserve land resources. Eventually, however, the site was disposed of with the Inspector's permission but being a statutory site several replacement sites were secured elsewhere. One remaining concern is that some of this replacement land is 'vested' in the London Docklands Development Corporation and cannot therefore acquire statutory status as the Corporation is not an Allotments Authority.[94] At a later Inquiry the Inspector endorsed the Federation's view of the importance of allotments in an expanding built-up area and recognized the authenticity of the evidence of a continued demand for plots. A decade of negotiation has produced a report from the council that is very positive about the allotments case.[95]

Rents provide another focus around which allotment-holders have found themselves battling to hold their ground. Increasing rents may be used as a tool by some landlords to release sites for development and other uses. One private landlord in Oxfordshire does not even consult his tenants on their allotments. The latter were originally provided for workers on the estate. In the 1980s the agent issued demands for a fivefold increase in rents to £10 per annum. The site has no water, fencing, hut or path provision, and no structures are allowed to be built on it. The holders campaigned against the rise and the local press took up the issue. The rate was finally resolved at £7, with self-management introduced to reduce the landlord's overheads.[96] Allotment-holders in Reigate made legal history when they opposed the council's proposal to increase their rents by a similar margin. They fought the proposal on the ground of the recreational status of allotments, and argued the case for the financial equity of allotment rents with charges raised on other leisure facilities in the town. The case was won in the High Court, and the equity principle confirmed in case law.[97] Reference was also made to the obligation on councils to behave with 'reasonableness' when setting rents.[98]

The Thorpe report argued that 'A system geared to economic need must adapt itself to the new concept of allotment gardening as a recreation.' However, 'if the present allotment-holder continues to profess that society has an obligation to provide him with a vegetable plot without asking anything in return' except rent, there would be difficulties in maintaining that hold on the land. But if a plot of ground is a right, an entitlement, the position is very different, whatever purpose the holder chooses for that land. 'Growing food is a productive occupation, significant to the economy as well as to the health and well-being of the allotment-holder. To deprive people finally of their right to an allotment would be the last step on the way to cutting people off from the land.'[99] This may be an argument made with an especial force in Scotland, with its experience of the Highland Clearances, but the majority of people in England too are cut off from land, not only the flat-dweller but the increasing number of people living at high densities.

The struggle to hold on to that ground did not end with the achievement of legal safeguards nearly a century ago, but continues with a need for increasing sophistication, as the cases show. There is a crucial relationship between the holders as a group, the landlord, and the public. During the twentieth century the dramatic realignment of plots from private to public ownership emphasizes the need for the political case, where officers and councillors form the triangle with the plot-holders. There are still, however, many private plots and it is there that the greatest effort may be needed.

13
Allotment futures

'Landowners, faced with prohibitive prices for fuel and fertilizer, realized that the most logical extension of "Pay-and-pick" crops was "Pay-and-grow", and began leasing out their land in strips along lines that were scarcely distinguishable from the medieval open-field system. The most eager tenants were health-food enthusiasts from north London and the Stour Valley, many of whom gave up the dole to tend their vast new allotments. As a result, the vegetable fields of central Norfolk, garlanded with the flowers of Jerusalem artichokes, asparagus-peas and pumpkins, have become as great a tourist attraction in blossom time as the fruit orchards of Kent.'

Richard Mabey,
'The Promised Landscape',
from *In a Green Shade*,
Hutchinson, 1983

There is no typical allotment-holder or allotment site. The diversity of allotments has been shown in the variety of experiences in different parts of the country that we have described. We could generalize and say that the allotment-holder is likely to be aged over thirty, although we met several who aren't; male, although in places many are women; skilled, unskilled or semi-skilled, retired, redundant, professional or owning her or his own business. He/she is unlikely to have a large garden at home, unless it is steeply sloping, has poor soil, or unless the holder so loves cultivation that more land or an extra area for growing is needed. It is less easy to generalize about the site, which can be anything from a solitary plot in size to over 500 plots; next to a tower block or surrounded by fields – but more likely to be somewhere in between, although, as a result of British Rail policy, the traditional site alongside the railway lines is less and less in evidence. The site is most likely to be owned by a local council, and probably has some protection in law.

The main aim of this book has been to present the rich history and culture of the allotment and the way in which that culture has produced very distinctive landscapes. Other countries have evolved their own gardening culture and, through migration, their people have contributed to the diversity of our own. At one time the struggle for allotments was the focus of a necessarily collective approach to political rights, including the most basic of all human rights: that of a household to feed itself from its own small share of the earth. Nowadays allotments provide one of the ways in which people relate to each other, free from material pressures and indications of status. 'On the plot you're just another gardener.'

At the turn of the century the culture of the allotment was embedded in the material conditions of life. Just as employers feared that allotment gardens would be 'taking their workers away' so political activists came to feel that the right to dig was not part of the argument over rights in an industrial society. Today, people happy on their plot, like those involved in other deeply seated pursuits, may indeed be distracted from the wider political issues connected with their workplace or the nature and future of work. Popular consciousness and people's individual goals have shifted away from production, what they produce either at work or as individuals, to consumption. They accept that fulfillment and satisfaction are likely to lie elsewhere. We prefer a home-centred life-style.

The irony is that the allotment is now seen as an escape from the pressures of life and competitive human relationships. For some it represents a sought-after privacy, for others a co-operative form of social behaviour and shared activity. There is a further paradox in that the mutual helpfulness that plot-holders say is one of the great rewards on the site is all too infrequently reflected in the collective politics of the allotment movement. Its voice in national politics is far less influential than it was a century ago. The survival of the allotment amidst a social context changed out of all recognition from the background of its own history, strangely mirrors the experience of the household economy in the Soviet Union and in the countries of Eastern Europe which are described as 'people's democracies'. There, activities like carpentry, gardening and maintaining 'the personal subsidiary farm plot' leave 'an imprint on the whole tenor of life; the values created are qualitative, since the products are consumed by the household and not sold'. Theirs may be an extension of 'habits, traditions and patterns formed in a previous, recent, semi-subsistence economy ... but these survive on urban soil'. The experience of many of the plot-holders we spoke to in Britain affirms the same sort of revival of older values. These relationships (and there is a certain piquancy in the fact that we are quoting from a Soviet source) help to turn 'the daily routine into a sphere for the development of personality ... One must keep in mind the growing importance of this tendency in urban life.'[1]

The discovery of a revival ignores the *survival* of many of these traditional relationships in what we have called 'local allotment cultures' in an area that stretches half-way across the country. The uneven consequences, geographically and socially, of the replacement of an industrial and self-provisioning economy by a service economy has meant that people with low incomes are in the same relationship to allotment gardening as their grandparents were at the beginning of the century, in terms both of the plot's contribution to the household economy and to individual well-being. In places with large-scale redundancies in the same work-force people can be rocketed from relative affluence into a world where activities like allotment gardening are crucial in maintaining identity. These areas are not homogeneous, and nor is the rest of the country caught up in a new wave that has extinguished the allotment gardening urge among low-income people living in affluent neighbourhoods. It has been the more affluent, moving into houses inside cities and in villages too, who have turned to allotments. Some have found their garden too small, but all of them have found the attraction of a non-competitive and non-commercial way of living.

On those depressing outer estates on the edges of our big cities, once remodelled and made more tolerable, there will be demands for individual space to grow things. Acres of their 'open' space will be easily adapted to allotments. The high density of our housing stock is unlikely to be swept away within generations, and the availability of allotments will be the only alternative. The small gardens that typify old cottages and new houses in villages permit only the most limited cultivation.

There is a common identity that goes beyond class and income barriers, based on old local cultures, among people with a shared interest, whether it is football, pigeons or leeks, and has to do with a shared relationship with growing things and with the culture, folklore and paraphernalia of efficient kitchen gardening. The allotment extends beyond the mechanistic participation in a 'hobby' or the material maintenance of the household. For although many recreations fulfil deep-seated personal and social needs, 'the right to grow some of your own food is fundamentally different from any right you might have to score a goal or sink a putt'.[2]

Our exploration of the allotment has pursued questions about the way we relate to places around us, to land and to landscape, and how that is essentially a human, cultural and social experience, as John Berger argued in his portrayal of peasant life in the Jura.[3] Popular images of allotments are acquired from those fleeting train-window or motorway glimpses or from the media, and in both cases we are isolated from what is actually going on. Given their prominent, very visible locations, it is inevitable that the landscape is a crucial element in the way that we imagine

them. Outside that landscape we are unable to realize the
nature of the relationships, experiences and rewards found
there. This particular means of escape seems an eccentricity. It conflicts with our society's dominant image of landscape: empty countryside, a place to visit rather than use,
where ordinary people are held back in awe of the grandeur
of machine cultivation, a commodity considered on buying a
house, on deciding about a holiday location. Space in the city
has to conform to an organized appearance, with the equally
organized municipal park that is non-productive and is used
for display. There is an 'inability to contain within the
landscape idea a collective sense of the meaning of their
land and place to those actively engaged in and experiencing it'.[4]

Inside the allotment, the experience of the surroundings
is very different. People have individual interests in their
plots of ground, there is a close and continued involvement
with that space, there is a chance to achieve personal
expression outside the conventional rules. This use of the
ground takes place alongside other people equally liberated
from those constraints. Together they produce a shared culture: their own landscape, made out of *their* use of space,
materials and crops. They share in these continuities, pressures and rhythms.

Allotments undoubtedly did, and do, extend popular
rights to land that would not have been achieved in any
other way than the demand for a small, productive plot.
They did not, in the 1890s any more than today, provide,
alone, much of a solution to the 'land problem' in the cities,
or in the country. This was realized by country people at a
time when they hoped to remain rural dwellers, with a need
for land which would feed and clothe them. People who in
those days overstated the contribution that allotments could
make were influenced by the knowledge that this was as
much as they could expect to win, while the great bulk of the
land remained in the form of massive estates and large
farms. Then the allotment idea spread to the romantic

ruralism of the Back to the Land movement in the last decade of the nineteenth century. But allotments as they actually exist have been the result of municipal socialism, conservative paternalism and liberal civic pride. The problem for local authorities is that allotments contradict their ideas of urban and rural, being a mixture of the two. In their administrative conception of the landscape councils find it hard to categorize unofficial horticulture. The dilemma today remains whether allotments really are a means of enabling poor people to grow their own food or whether they are a location for family leisure. Twenty years after Thorpe urged that allotment gardening should be given the same consideration as other recreations, the professionals and administrators of the leisure world argue that allotments are in a separate category since *space* is not actually shared, unlike the space of a golf course or a swimming pool, because each piece of ground is privately *occupied*. The fact that it is nearly always productive is omitted from the calculation, or is actually held *against* the allotment.

The very fact that allotment gardening is a productive form of leisure implies that it is officially suspect. Jeff Bishop and Paul Hoggett comment pertinently in their study of mutual aid in leisure that:

> ... most communal leisure groups can be considered as organized forms of mutual aid – in this case, as vehicles through which people can help each other to pleasure. Strangely enough, one often encounters a viewpoint which suggests that such organizations, because of their self-interest, cannot also serve the community. The following extract from a memorandum circulating within a large state-controlled, grant-giving body illustrates our point. The memorandum outlines the various criteria to be used in judging when a community organization is suitable for grant aid: a key criterion refers to 'bodies which exist to service a membership without a direct public commitment but which may undertake

projects or events of wider public interest'. In other words, mutual-aid organizations are held to have no 'direct public commitment' and will only be eligible for grant aiding if some of their activities are of 'wider public interest'. But why on earth should it be thought that if the public combine together to service themselves, their activity somehow or other fails to express direct public commitment? Do we have two 'publics', a real one which does nothing and therefore needs servicing and a not quite legitimate one which presumes to organize in its own exclusive self-interest? How is the community 'best served'? By being helped to help itself as self-interest transforms itself without difficulty into a commitment to mutuality, or by being helped to remain helpless?[5]

The allotment fails to conform to the leisure industry's concept of passive leisure and, in the wider landscape, to the ideal of private, individualized space, provided, constructed and clearly demarcated in the form of the house-and-garden. In country and city people are encouraged to be anxious about the value of their property and to make judgements about the activities they want around them according to that valuation. The allotment is a different kind of place in which different values prevail. Some councils and their officers are coming to terms with the way in which plotholders appropriate the space provided, and are gradually accepting the individualism of ordinary people who want to create their own space. The task of the professionals is not to design environments but to enable people to create their own. The allotment began as a moral landscape with rules that promoted Useful Toil. Over many decades this was adapted and adopted to become a working-class landscape, as the holders, usually poor, added their own features and built their own structures. But whereas the back garden has been the symbol of home, the allotment has often, though not invariably, been a symbol both of separation and escape from the conditions surrounding the home, and of masculinity and productivity. But as it is increasingly sought after as a conscious alternative to contemporary 'real' life, so the symbolism changes. The implication of escape is still important, the allotment representing for many a haven where can be found solace in the midst of a more sophisticated, but ultimately alien, world. The allotment remains, with whatever new designs, layouts and improved services, the archetypal vernacular landscape, the curtain behind which a range of human activities, attachments and cultural encounters take place. At the close of the twentieth century, allotments, while never central in our history, remain as significant in contemporary society as they were when the century began, and part of the lives of a remarkably large segment of the population.

It would be easy to prophesy that the inflation of land prices in urban and suburban areas will continue to erode allotment provision. But all cities have their pockets, and in some cases, vast areas, of vacant and derelict land, and one of the pressure groups campaigning for the 'greening of the city' – represented by the new interest in 'city farms' and 'urban wildlife parks' – is the allotment lobby. People in high-density areas *do* want allotment land, as the experience of Hackney, to take just one example, shows. With young people becoming increasingly attracted to the allotment and the lifestyle it represents, demand for plots will correspondingly rise; in addition, a new, youthful voice will be added to that of a population more used to limitations than liberations in its access to urban space, in the battle for adequate land provision.

Outside the cities, Mabey's vision of the future rural landscape anticipated a new debate on the alleged crisis of agricultural land. A government report in 1987 argued that there will be a surplus of 700,000 acres of farmland by 1995. Large regional variations are expected, through what is called the 'shunting' effect and the uneven consequences of the way the market works. At a time of surplus the high-investment areas continue to increase yields as the 'marginal' or 'less-favoured' areas decline further.[6] The report assumes a continued diminution of the number of people working on the land (0.75 per cent of the full-time working population in 1986, a total of 150,000), but does not consider a diversification of ownership. The debate centres on an increased separation of land between agriculture and recreation.

One reaction to the growing awareness of the crisis in agriculture is the pressure to allocate more land for house building, but at lower densities than were current when land was considered 'precious'. Only a narrow, privileged section of the market is likely to be affected by this. The picture of the future conjured up points to an advanced leisure economy where food production is concentrated in the hands of an even smaller minority than at present, and where the rest of the country is divided between leisure on marginal land with ranch homes on selected areas where a rural idyll can be played out.

The environmental pressure groups have responded in interesting and suggestive ways. The Town and Country Planning Association urges that 'there may be scope in certain locations to encourage smallholdings of perhaps two to five acres, the income from which would supplement other home-based enterprises'.[7] And the director of the Council for the Protection of Rural England has suggested that the time has come for the Restoration of the Commons.[8] They bring us back to the issues discussed at the very beginnings of allotment history, when the question of access to land was dominant in the ideology of landscape.

Language as well as ideology shapes our attitudes. The word 'allotment' implies deference and allocation, qualities that indicate a relationship between the powerful and the powerless that seems unattractive now, and which has been challenged throughout history. Thorpe perceived this in the 1960s. Yet 'leisure gardening' is an inappropriate term for something that goes much deeper and has a history of its own, and which continues to play an economic role in the sense of self-provisioning and self-help. Allotment gardening is important in being a productive activity outside the dominant consumer society. The escape it offers from market relationships and from total reliance on buying and selling is vital, and it is of deep significance when the fundamental issue of people's rights in relation to land is considered.

The American term 'community gardens' comes close to encapsulating this set of meanings, and has already been adopted in Britain. In May 1987 the Culpeper Community Garden was opened, thanks to the work of a few dedicated individuals, in Islington in the heart of London, with the intention of providing 'local people who were without a garden, with an opportunity to work together collectively, or individually by way of having their own plots, to create a public garden under community management'.[9]

Probably the best surviving name, sanctified by history, would be 'common lands'. However, given the diverse results of the last effort to change the label, as well as the positive recognition of the continuing importance of allotments by both old and new plot-holders, it may be best to live with the traditional word, and to promote its positive image. Several allotment gardeners told us that, given the opportunity, they would rather have a large garden of their own. There are good reasons for this: the convenience of a garden on the doorstep, the security from vandalism and theft, the instant availability of normal facilities. Maybe everyone would prefer this, but it is not going to be a reality for millions of people in the foreseeable future. But many more people on allotment sites have spoken of quite different rewards: the immense enjoyment, the depth of meaning and struggle too, in working the earth. 'The allotment is fifty-one per cent hard work, and forty-nine per cent disappointment', one gardener said to us, but he went on digging.[10] Telling fellow gardeners of conquests and trials, asking for guidance, sharing seeds, creating structures, spending time over a beer and organizing the site, enjoying the sun, topless in a deck-chair, feeling a sense of consummate skill in harvesting and showing -- all these experiences acquired in shared surroundings cannot be measured on the same scale as the involvement of the individual in buying a packet of frozen peas at the supermarket. Allotments throw a distinct and disconcerting light on the way we live now.

Who would disagree with Richard Mabey's picture of the food-producing future? Not you as readers or us as writers, but simply those who appoint themselves as spokesmen for the multinational food-processing industry, mouthpieces of the market. The allotment is a humble part of the contemporary world but it enshrines values and priorities that everyone agrees with. It reasserts a whole range of human rights. It offers 'a form of human relationships within a physical world: in the full sense of a way of life ... co-operative relationships ... compatible with other major energies and interests'.[11] The man with a bunch of carrots over his handlebars has not survived *despite* the enormous changes in our culture, but because of them.

Appendix:
Allotment law and lore

The reader will have found that, unlike every other book about allotments that we have come across, ours is not a manual of hints and tips on vegetable cultivation. Nor does it seek to advise allotment gardeners, present or potential, of their rights and duties. We have simply explored the allotment as part of our landscape and culture, something very valuable and essential which has its equivalents all over the world. But we may have inspired some readers to put into effect the ambition they have had for years, to cultivate an allotment. How do they go about asserting their right as a citizen and their duty as a plot-holder?

Allotment law, built up through a century of agitation, is both vague and voluminous, and has been in urgent need of revision for decades. The guide for the local society secretary is Professor J.F. Garner's book, *The Law of Allotments*, 4th edition, available at the time of writing for £6.60 including postage from Shaw and Sons Ltd., Lower Sydenham, London SE26 5AE. Basic guidance is available to members from the National Society of Allotment and Leisure Gardeners (see page 281).

Local authorities (district and parish councils) have a duty to provide allotments for their resident citizens, provided for by Section 23 of the Small Holdings and Allotments Act of 1908. But the law does not say where, when or how soon the citizens can have their plots. Some have waiting lists, other have embarrassingly empty plots. Some would-be allotment holders telephone the local authority, ascertain which department they need (Leisure Services, Parks and Recreation, etc.), and demand their rights. Others are more circumspect, visit sites, talk to plot-holders, find the address of the secretary, and write with a stamped, addressed envelope. Politeness and perseverance help.

There is no very clear definition of what an allotment *is*, but Section 22 of the Allotments Act of 1922 says that an allotment garden is 'an allotment not exceeding forty poles in extent which is wholly or mainly cultivated by the occupier for the production of vegetables or fruit crops for consumption by himself or his family'. A pole is a little over 30 square yards. The standard size of an allotment plot is 10 rods or 300 square yards (250 square metres). It is thus perfectly legal for a plot-holder to have several plots. On the other hand local authorities with long waiting lists may divide a standard plot into two half-size plots, so as to accommodate more people. The tenant who stays the course may graduate to a full-size plot when it becomes available. This seems to us to be a good practice, as taking on an allotment is a bigger undertaking than many novices believe, requiring much more of a change in the family timetable than a back garden where the odd minute can always be spent. We have been assured by people with first-hand experience that, once established on a site with a half-size plot, the really keen gardener is in a good position to inherit the next full-size plot that falls vacant. Michael Hyde, the allotment correspondent of the *Guardian* (the only national newspaper to have one), is – as his readers know – happy to share a plot with his friend Nelson.

Council expenditure on allotments (their maintenance, or the leasing of land to provide more sites) is authorized to the extent of the product of a 0.8p rate, under Section 16 of the Allotments Act 1922, amended by Section 11 of the Allotments Act of 1950. Not many councils spend this much, however. Section 54 of the 1908 Act requires councils to keep an Allotments Revenue Account showing each year's expenditure on, and income from, allotments, and to make this account freely available to any ratepayer. The surplus from the sale of allotment land approved by the Secretary of State should be treated as income for this purpose. This brings us to the distinction between what is known as *statutory* and what is known as *temporary* allotment land. The Allotments Act of 1925 requires that: 'Where a local authority has purchased or appropriated land for use as allotments the local authority shall not sell, appropriate, use or dispose of the land for any purpose other than use for allotments, without the consent of ...', and the current Minister for this purpose is the Secretary of State for the Environment. Here we enter huge problems of definition and can only refer readers to the criticism of Professor Thorpe and the interpretation of Professor Garner.

On the question of local councils' Allotment Revenue Accounts, the National Society makes an important comment which is borne out by our conversations with local secretaries: 'There is a mass of evidence throughout the country that Allotment Revenue Accounts are being loaded with administrative costs which vastly exceed the amount of allotment rents collected. In one case central administration charges of £5 for each plot were proposed on a thousand plots. Electricity and water charges are being included in the accounts, even though neither of these services are "laid on" the allotment site.'

This brings us to the vexed question of allotment rents. Section 10 of the Allotments Act of 1950 requires that land let by a council for use as allotments 'shall be let at such rent as a tenant may reasonably be expected to pay', with a provision that it may be let at less rent 'if the council are satisfied that there exist special circumstances affecting that person which render it proper for them to let the land to him at a less rent'. Allotment tenancies are such that proposed rent increases create a new tenancy unless a rent review clause is part of the tenancy agreement. The National Society takes the view that in signing a tenancy agreement including such a clause, plot-holders are signing away their rights under the Allotments Acts of 1908 to 1950. But as an increase of rent creates a new tenancy, Section 1 of the Allotments Act of 1922 as amended by Section 1 of the Allotments Act of 1950 requires a minimum of twelve months' notice to quit on or before 6 April or on or after 29 September in any year, in order that a new tenancy agreement may be concluded between the parties. Some authorities have stepped outside the law in their efforts to increase allotment rents and some have been successfully resisted in the courts.

Thorpe's committee recommended (paras. 820 to 834) that rents should take notice of the amenities, personal and communal, provided on any particular site, and to the degree in which the site was council-managed or tenant-managed. Some authorities have accepted this principle; others have not, and have even ignored the model rules for allotment gardens issued by the Department of the Environment. The rent issue is not academic. We encountered one district where, in seeking to increase its revenue as directed by central government, a council proposed to increase allotment rents by 600 per cent. In court the London Association of Recreational Gardeners was able to show that *no* directions had been issued by the government on this matter, and that the proposed increase in rent was not legal. This, and the Reigate case mentioned in Chapter Seven, show the vital importance for allotment-holders of their local societies and regional federations, if they are to defend their hard-won rights, including that to compensation if they are displaced from their site.

Rents vary enormously. In one borough we found an old self-managed site rented on a nine-year lease from the Land Services Department of the local council, where plots were rented from the Association for £11.15 a year, with a half-rate for pensioners. Plots in the same borough rented from the Recreation Department of the same council and managed by them cost £22 a year in 1987. Some sites are still owned collectively by the members of a Friendly Society or a co-operative. The Bradford and Bingley Allotment Association in Yorkshire has owned its site at Beckfoot since 1923. Each tenant holds six shares in the Association and annual rents are £5. There are no vacant plots. Tenancies change hands at £6 for the six shares plus £200–250 depending on the state of the allotment, greenhouse, sheds, etc., all transfers being subject to approval by the Committee.

In our view, all allotment societies, whatever their mode of tenure, should affiliate to the National Society (National Society of Allotment and Leisure Gardeners Ltd., Hunters Road, Corby, Northants, NN17 1JE). The fee is ludicrously low and is instantly cancelled out by buying supplies through the Society's Seeds Scheme, but apart from that a minimum gesture towards providing an effective national voice for the allotment movement is long overdue. Anyone who for some reason is unable to join an affiliated body can join as an individual member for a few pounds.

There are other useful bodies, often sadly unconnected with the traditional allotment movement but which are still valuable contacts for new ventures in allotment gardening. One is the City Farms movement which has grown from nothing since the mid-1970s. Today there are between fifty and sixty such ventures, linked by a quarterly journal (*City Farmer*, from The Old Vicarage, 66 Fraser Street, Bedminster, Bristol BS3 4LY). The Urban Unit of the National Council for Voluntary Organizations, 26 Bedford Square, London WC1B 3HU, runs frequent conferences on such topics as 'Urban wasteland: its potential as a resource in the local community', and 'Vegetables from derelict land' (including advice on the question of soil pollution from heavy metals). In the north-east, VIVA (Voluntary Initiatives in Vacant Areas), 6 Higham Place, Newcastle-upon-Tyne, NE1 8AF, is involved in a variety of new allotment enterprises. A demonstration organic allotment is maintained by the National Centre for Organic Gardening, Ryton-on-Dunsmore, Coventry CV8 3LG.

Allotment gardeners need not, therefore, be isolated individuals on their plots. Rather, they can become part of a network of half-a-million fellow enthusiasts: a power in the land.

Notes

Chapter one

1. Beryl Bainbridge, *Forever England – North and South*, Duckworth, 1987
2. Sirkka-Liisa Konttinen, *Byker*, Jonathan Cape, 1983; John Grahn, 'The Wonderful World of Sheds', *Good Housekeeping Magazine*, July 1977; Peter Davies, 'Great Little Tin Sheds of Wales', Crafts Council Gallery , London, May 1986; Dave Thomas, 'Ramshackles', Darlington Arts Centre, December 1986; Alan Leggett, 'Secret Gardens', Nottingham Arts Centre, May 1987
3. Peter Walton, 'The Allotment', *The Green Book*, Vol. 2, No. 2, Bath, Spring 1986; Charles Tomlinson, 'John Maydew' or 'The Allotment' in *Collected Poems*, Oxford University Press, 1985
4. Inspector's Report on the Public Local Inquiry, Waltham Forest District Plan, November 1978
5. Report of the Departmental Committee of Inquiry into Allotments, Cmnd 4166, HMSO, 1969
6. Harry Thorpe, 'The Homely Allotment: From Rural Dole to Urban Amenity: A Neglected Aspect of Urban Land Use', *Geography*, No. 268, Vol. 60, Part 3, July 1975
7. Thorpe report, para. 455
8. *ibid.*
9. *ibid.*, para. 695
10. *ibid.*
11. Four Corner Films, project report in 'Film, Video', Greater London Arts Association, spring 1975
12. Arthur Marwick, *The Deluge: British Society and the First World War*, Penguin, 1967
13. Philip Jeffery, *Harvest of the Spade*, Longmans, for the British Council, 1944
14. Thorpe *op. cit.* para. 698
15. N.J. Habraken, *Supports: An Alternative to Mass Housing*, Architectural Press, 1972
16. Colin Buchanan, 'Why every man must have a shed', *The Countryman*, Vol. 80, No. 2, summer 1975

17. Ray Garner, 'After the Coal Rush: Attitudes and Aesthetics of the Allotment Garden Shed', unpublished dissertation, Hull School of Architecture, January 1984

18. 'The Allotments Movement', *The Recreational Gardener*, Journal of the London Association of Recreational Gardeners, No. 14, December 1977

19. Pete Riley, *Economic Growth: The Allotments Campaign Guide*, Friends of the Earth, 1979

Chapter two

1. Linda Nochlin, *Realism*, Penguin, 1971

2. Doreen Massey and Alejandra Catalono, *Capital and Land*, Edward Arnold, 1978; Marion Shoard, *The Lie of the Land*, Temple Smith, 1987

3. David Crouch, 'Words and the Cultural Meaning of Place', paper to the British Sociological Association Sociology and Environment Study Group, February 1987

4. John Clarke and Chas Crichter, *The Devil Makes Work: Leisure in Capitalist Britain*, Macmillan, 1985; Raymond Williams, *Culture*, Fontana, 1981

5. Denis Cosgrove, *Social Formation and Symbolic Landscape*, Croom Helm, 1984

6. David Crouch *op. cit.*

7. Patrick Wright, *On Living in an Old Country*, Verso, 1985

8. Raymond Williams *op. cit.*; Danny Miller, 'Modernism and Suburbia as Material History', in Danny Miller and Chris Tilley (eds.) *Ideology, Power and Prehistory*, Cambridge University Press, 1984

9. Patrick Wright *op. cit.*

10. Pierre Bourdieu, *Distinction: A Social Critique of the Judgement of Taste*, Routledge and Kegan Paul, 1984

11. Raymond Williams, *Marxism and Literature*, Oxford University Press, 1977

12. Danny Miller *op. cit.*

13. Dennis Hardy, *Alternative Communities in Nineteenth Century England*, Longman, 1973

14. Robert Blatchford, *Merrie England*, Clarion Office, 1893, new edition Journeyman Press, 1976

15. Roy Douglas, *Land, People and Politics: A History of the Land*

Question in the United Kingdom, 1878–1952, Allison and Busby, 1976

16. Roy Douglas *ibid.*
17. Ebenezer Howard, *Garden Cities of Tomorrow*, 1965
18. André Gorz, *Farewell to the Working Class*, Pluto Press, 1982
19. Dennis Hardy and Colin Ward, *Arcadia for All: The Legacy of a Makeshift Landscape*, Mansell, 1984
20. Marion Shoard, *The Theft of the Countryside*, Temple Smith, 1980
21. Ramblers' 'Forbidden Britain Campaign', Ramblers' Association, 1986
22. Marion Shoard 1987 *op. cit.*
23. The Tudor Walters, Dudley and Parker Morris Reports, discussed in Alison Ravetz, *The Government of Space: Town Planning in Modern Society*, Faber and Faber, 1986
24. John Clarke and Chas Crichter *op. cit.*
25. Ray Pahl, *Divisions of Labour*, Blackwell, 1984
26. Nicely illustrated in Frank Tilsley's novel *I'd Do it Again*, about the £2.50-a-week clerk whose life is transformed by the acquisition of a suburban bungalow and vegetable garden, Secker and Warburg, 1936
27. Raymond Williams, *Border Country*, Chatto and Windus, 1959
28. Elizabeth Roberts, 'Working wives and their families', in T. Barker and M. Drake (eds.), *Population and Society in Britain 1850–1880*, Batsford, 1982 quoted by Ray Pahl *op. cit.*
29. Bonnie Lloyd, 'Women, Home and Status', in J.S. Duncan (ed.), *Housing and Identity*, Croom Helm, 1981
30. Ray Pahl *op. cit.*
31. Alfred Williamson, *Life in a Railway Factory*, Duckworth, 1915, quoted by Ray Pahl *op. cit.*
32. Ray Pahl *op. cit.*
33. Dora Greenhill, 'Home', in *The Cornhill Magazine*, September 1863, quoted by Leonore Davidoff *et al.*, 'Landscape with Figures: Home and Community in English Society', in Anne Oakley and Juliet Mitchell (eds.), *The Rights and Wrongs of Women*, Penguin 1983
34. Leonore Davidoff *et al.*, *op. cit.*
35. Jeff Bishop and Paul Hoggett, *Organizing Around Enthusiasms: Mutual Aid in Leisure*, Comedia Publishing Group, 1986
36. Richard Titmuss, *The Gift Relationship: from Human Blood to*

Social Policy, Allen and Unwin, 1970

37. J.R. Kelly, *Leisure Identities and Interactions*, Allen and Unwin, 1983

38. Jeff Bishop and Paul Hoggett *op. cit.*

39. Paul Wild, 'Recreation in Rochdale 1900–1940', in J. Clarke *et al.* (eds.) *Working Class Culture*, Hutchinson, 1982

40. John McEwan, 'Cultural Forms and Social Processes: The Pub as a Social and Cultural Institution', in Alan Tomlinson (ed.), *Leisure and Popular Cultural Forms*, Brighton Polytechnic, 1983

41. Paul Wild *op. cit.*

42. John McEwan *op.cit.*

43. John Clarke *et al.*, 'Subcultures, Cultures and Class', in Tony Bennett *et al.* (eds.), *Culture, Ideology and Social Process*, Batsford, 1981

44. John Clarke and Chas Crichter *op. cit.*

45. Chris Hutt, *The Death of the English Pub*, Arrow, 1973

46. Raymond Williams 1981 *op. cit.*

47. John Clarke and Chas Crichter *op. cit.*

48. *ibid.*

49. Raymond Williams 1959 *op. cit.*

50. John Clarke and Chas Crichter *op. cit.*

51. Alan Tomlinson 1983 *op. cit.*

52. Geoffrey Crossick, *The Artisan in Victorian Society*, Croom Helm, 1978; M.J. Daunton, 'Public Place and Private Space: The Victorian city and the working-class household', in D. Fraser and A. Sutcliffe (eds.), *The Pursuit of Urban History*, Edward Arnold, 1983

55. Ray Pahl *op. cit.*

54. Quoted in Gillian Darley, 'Cottage and Suburban Gardens', in *The Garden*, Mitchell Beazley, 1979

55. John Clarke and Chas Crichter *op. cit.*

56. Fred Inglis, 'Nation and Community: a Landscape and its Morality', in *The New Universities Quarterly*, autumn 1976; Dennis Hardy and Colin Ward, *Arcadia for All: The Legacy of a Makeshift Landscape*, Mansell, 1984; Sirrka-Liisa Konttinen, *Byker*, Johnathan Cape, 1983

57. Martin Youngs, 'The English TV Landscape Documentary', in J. Burgess and J. Gold (eds.), *Geography of the Media and Popular Culture*, Croom Helm, 1985; 'Rural Myths', special

issue of the journal *Ten 8*, No. 12, 1983
58. Patrick Wright *op. cit.*
59. Raymond Williams, *The Country and the City*, Chatto and Windus, 1973
60. John Blunden and Nigel Curry (eds.), *The Changing Countryside*, Croom Helm, 1985
61. John Barrell, *The Dark Side of the Landscape: The Rural Poor in English Painting 1730–1840*, Cambridge University Press, 1980; M. Rosenthal, *English Landscape Painting*, Phaidon, 1982
62. Raymond Williams, *Keywords in Culture and Society*, Fontana, 1976
63. Herbert Read, 'The Empty Landscape', in *The Countryman*, Winter 1965–6
64. Herbert Read *op. cit.*
65. Quoted in E. Jussim *et al.*, *Landscape as Photograph*, Yale University Press, 1985
66. John Punter, 'Landscape Aesthetics: a synthesis and critique', in John Gold and Jaqueline Burgess, *Valued Environments*, Allen and Unwin, 1982; David Cosgrove *op. cit.*
67. Herbert Read (ed.), *Peter Kropotkin: Selections from his Writings*, Freedom Press, 1942
68. Peter Kropotkin, *Fields, Factories and Workshops*, 1899, new edition ed. Colin Ward, Freedom Press, 1985
69. C. Thacker, *The Wilderness Please*, Croom Helm, 1985
70. John Clare, *Selected Poems and Prose* ed. E. Robinson and G. Summerfield, Oxford University Press, 1966
71. Quoted in W.G. Hoskins and L. Dudley Stamp, *The Common Lands of England and Wales*, Collins, 1963
72. Vita Sackville-West, *The Land*, Heineman, 1926; 1970
73. Dennis Hardy and Colin Ward *op. cit.*
74. John Seymour, *The Fat of the Land*, Faber and Faber, 1976
75. John Berger, *About Looking*, Writers and Readers, 2nd edition 1984
76. Albert J. Lubin, *Stranger on the Earth, the Life of Vincent Van Gogh*, Paladin, 1972
77. John Berger *op. cit.*
78. Fred Inglis *op. cit.*
79. John Berger, 'The Field', in *About Looking*, *op. cit.*

Chapter three

1. Lewis H. Berens, *The Digger Movement in the Days of the Commonwealth*, 1906, Holland Press and Merlin Press 1961

2. Garrett Hardin, 'The tragedy of the commons', *Science*, Vol. 162, 1968

3. Richard Boston, Richard Holme and Richard North (eds.), *The Little Green Book*, Wildwood House, 1979

4. Michael Thompson, Michael Warburton and Tom Hatley, *Uncertainty on a Himalayan Scale*, Milton Ash Editions/Ethnographica, 1986

5. Mark Overton, 'Agricultural Revolution?: England, 1540–1850', *ReFRESH* (Recent Findings of Research in Economic and Social History), No. 3, autumn 1986

6. J.L. and Barbara Hammond, *The Village Labourer*, 1911, Guild Books 1949. The other important historical studies in the early twentieth century were G. Slater, *The English Peasantry and the Enclosure of the Common Fields*, 1907, and W. Hasbach, *A History of the English Agricultural Labourer*, 1908

7. Griffiths L. Cunningham, 'Early Allotment Garden History', unpublished paper, York University, Toronto

8. Notably J.D. Chambers, 'Enclosure and labour supply in the Industrial Revolution', reprinted in D.V. Glass and D.E.C. Eversley (eds.), *Population in History*, Edward Arnold, 1965; J.D. Chambers and G.E. Mingay, *The Agricultural Revolution, 1750–1880*, B.T. Batsford, 1966, and J.A. Yelling, *Common Field and Enclosure in England 1450–1850*, Macmillan, 1977

9. List of adjectives gathered by K.D.M. Snell from the writings of G.E. Mingay

10. Michael Turner, *Enclosures in Britain 1750–1830*, Macmillan, 1984

11. K.D.M. Snell, *Annals of the Labouring Poor: Social Change and Agrarian England 1660–1900*, Cambridge University Press, 1985

12. Arthur Young, *An Inquiry into the Propriety of Applying Wastes to the Better Maintenance and Support of the Poor*, 1801

13. M. Betham Edwards (ed.), *The Autobiography of Arthur Young*, 1898

14. 'Mentor', in the *Gentleman's Magazine*, 1800, quoted by Griffiths L. Cunningham 'Early Allotment Garden History' *op. cit.*

15. *ibid.*
16. Thorpe report, paras. 10 and 11
17. *ibid.*, para. 8
18. W. Hasbach, *A History of the English Agricultural Labourer*, 1908
19. *ibid*
20. E.J. Hobsbawm and George Rudé, *Captain Swing*, Penguin, 1973
21. J.L. and Barbara Hammond *op. cit.*
22. Quoted in Jean Russell-Gebbett, *Henslow of Hitcham*, Terence Dalton, 1977
23. Jean Russell-Gebbett cites a copy in the University Library, Cambridge
24. Jean Russell-Gebbett *op. cit.*
25. John Lindley, 'A Village Horticultural Show', *Gardeners' Chronicle*, 24 September 1859. Jean Russell-Gebbett explains that 'Professor Lindley, in conjunction with George Bentham, had organized the first flower shows of the Horticultural Society (later the Royal Horticultural Society) from 1830. With this successful experience behind him, Lindley's praise of the Hitcham shows could not be ignored.'
26. J.D. Chambers and G.E. Mingay, *The Agricultural Revolution 1750–1880 op. cit.*
27. J. Bennet Lawes, 'The Rothamsted Allotment Club', *Journal of the Royal Agricultural Society*, Vol. 13, 1877. Reprinted in *The Recreational Gardener: Journal of the London Association of Recreational Gardeners*, No. 17, December 1978
28. Richard Jefferies, 'The Allotment System', letter to *The Times*, 23 November 1872. Reprinted in Richard Jefferies, *The Toilers of the Field*, Longmans Green, 1892
29. J. Bennet Lawes *op. cit.*
30. Richard Jefferies *op. cit.*
31. Pamela Horn, *The Rural World 1780–1850: Social change in the English countryside*, Hutchinson, 1980, quoting James Obelkevich, *Religion and Rural Society: South Lindsey 1825–1875*, Clarendon Press, 1976
32. M.K. Ashby, *Joseph Ashby of Tysoe 1859–1919*, Cambridge University Press, 1961
33. *ibid.*
34. Pamela Horn, *The Changing Countryside in Victorian and*

Edwardian England and Wales, Athlone Press, 1984, quoting Mentmore Estate MSS at Buckinghamshire Record Office

35. Patrick Wright, *On Living in an Old Country: The National Past in Contemporary Britain*, Verso, 1985

36. E.N. Bennett, *Problems of Village Life*, Thornton Butterworth: Home University Library, 1913

37. Newlin Russell Smith, *Land for the Small Man*, King's Crown Press, Morningside Heights, New York, 1946

38. Marion Shoard, *This Land is Our Land*, Paladin, 1987

39. P.H. Mann, 'Life in an Agricultural Village in England', *Sociological Papers*, 1904

40. Special Commissioner of the *Daily News*, 'Life in our Villages', 1891

41. Quoted in Roy Douglas, *Land, People and Politics*, Allison and Busby, 1976

42. *An act to facilitate the provision of allotments for the labouring classes*, 50 and 51 Vict. Ch. 48

43. J. Frome Wilkinson, 'Pages in the History of Allotments', *The Contemporary Review*, Vol. 65, 1894

44. *ibid.*

Chapter four

1. Richard Jefferies, 'The Allotment System', letter to *The Times*, 23 November 1872. Reprinted in Richard Jefferies, *The Toilers of the Field*, Longmans Green, 1892

2. Ronald Webber, *Market Gardening*, David and Charles, 1972

3. Robert John Charleton, 'The Streets of Newcastle', articles from *Newcastle Weekly Chronicle*, 1885–6, Newcastle Central Library

4. R.J. Charleton, *Newcastle Town*, Walter Scott 1885, 4th edition Frank Graham 1978

5. *ibid.*

6. Annual Report for 1932, National Allotments Society Ltd.

7. Harry Thorpe, Elizabeth B. Galloway and Lynda M. Evans, *The Rationalisation of Urban Allotment Systems – A Case Study of Birmingham*, University of Birmingham, Dept. of Geography, 1977

8. J.A. Langford, *History of Birmingham 1741–1841*, Vol. 2, 1871, cited by Thorpe, Galloway and Evans *ibid.*

9. James Drake, *A Picture of Birmingham*, 1825, cited *ibid.*

10. Thorpe, Galloway and Evans *op. cit.*

11. Robert Mellors, *The Gardens, Parks and Walks of Nottingham and District*, J. and H. Bell, 1926

12. Colin Haynes, 'Nottingham's Hanging Gardens', *Nottingham City News and Calendar*, November 1971

13. Robert Mellors *op. cit.*

14. Colin Haynes *op. cit.*

15. Roy A. Church, *Economic and Social Change in a Midland Town: Victorian Nottingham 1815–1900*, Frank Cass, 1966

16. Roy A. Church, 'James Orange and the Allotment System in Nottingham', *Transactions of the Thoroton Society*, Vol. LXIV, 1960

17. 'Family Life and Work Experience before 1918', project, Essex University, Interview 217

18. Thorpe report, paras. 37–8

19. T.H. Middleton, *Food Production in War*, Oxford University Press, 1923

20. E.S. Turner, *Dear Old Blighty*, Michael Joseph, 1980

21. Frederick A. Talbot, 'Those Amazing Allotments', *The World's Work*, January 1919

22. James Bishop, *Illustrated London News Social History of the First World War*, Angus and Robertson, 1982

23. E.S. Turner *op. cit.*

24. Frederick A. Talbot *op. cit.*

25. *ibid.*

26. J.A. Venn, *Foundations of Agricultural Economics*, Longmans, 1933

27. F.E. Green, 'The Allotment Movement', *The Contemporary Review*, July 1918

28. R.L. Layton, 'Agriculture in Epping Forest during the Great War', *Essex Journal*, Vol. 21 No. 3, winter 1986

29. Thorpe report, para. 42

30. *ibid.*, paras. 48 and 131

31. C.R. and H.C. Fay, *The Allotment in England and Wales*, National Allotments Society n.d., 1944

32. Walter L. Creese (ed.), *The Legacy of Raymond Unwin: A Human Pattern for Planning*, MIT Press, 1967

33. C.R. and H.C. Fay *op. cit.*

34. K.J. McCready, *The Land Settlement Association: Its History*

and Present Form, Plunkett Foundation for Co-operative Studies, 1974

35. Thorpe, Galloway and Evans *op. cit.*
36. *Agriculture*, September 1941
37. Angus Calder, *The People's War: Britain 1939–45*, Jonathan Cape, 1969
38. Keith Murray, *Agriculture*, 'History of the Second World War', UK Civil Series, HMSO, 1955
39. Thorpe report, para. 50
40. *ibid.*, table 10
41. Department of the Environment statistics. The 1981 Local Government and Planning Act removed the obligation to collect statistics on allotments and waiting lists
42. Thorpe *op. cit.*, para. 134 and chapters 3 and 4
43. Elizabeth Galloway, *Design for Leisure Gardening*, Birmingham University, 1977
44. Thorpe *op. cit.*, table 11
45. *ibid.*, para. 162
46. *ibid.*, para. 169
47. Rachel Carson, *Silent Spring*, Penguin, 1965
48. Peter Riley, *Economic Growth: The allotment campaign guide*, Friends of the Earth, 1979
49. Department of the Environment statistics. (British Rail no longer makes available aggregated data at a national level.)
50. *ibid.*
51. Figures provided by the London Borough of Haringey, 1987
52. Figures provided by Newcastle City Council, 1987
53. Locally gathered statistics, 1987
54. *ibid.*
55. *ibid.*
56. Birmingham City Council minutes, 1987
57. Irene Evans, 'Allotment provision in Scotland 1985', in Irene Evans and Joy Hendry (eds.), *The Land for the People*, Scottish Socialist Society, 1985
58. Irene Evans, interview, 28 March 1987
59. Thorpe *op. cit.*, and Department of the Environment statistics

Chapter five

1. 'First Report of the Royal Commission on the Employment of Children, Young Persons and Women in Agriculture', 1967–8, XVII
2. Interview with Fred Tolley 1969–70 in Raphael Samuel, 'Quarry roughs: life and labour in Headington Quarry, 1860–1920', in Ralph Samuel (ed.), *Village Life and Labour*, Routledge and Kegan Paul, 1975
3. Interview with Mrs Gurl, 1969–70, in Raphael Samuel *ibid.*
4. Spike Mays, *Reuben's Corner*, Eyre and Spottiswoode, 1969
5. Ken Ausden, *Up the Crossing*, BBC Publications, 1981
6. *ibid.*
7. Interview 98 in 'Family Life and Work Experience Before 1918' project, transcripts in Dept. of Sociology, University of Essex
8. Interview 281
9. Interview 195
10. Interview 391
11. Interview 366
12. Interview 110
13. Interview 121
14. Interview 133
15. Interview 383
16. Interview 384
17. Interview 59
18. Interview 57
19. Interview 426
20. Interview 219
21. Interview 278
22. Interview 30
23. Interview 133
24. Interview 435
25. Interview 391
26. Interview 381
27. Letter from Phyllis Reichl, January 1987
28. 'Family Life and Work Experience' project. Interviewer's comment on Interview 102
29. Norman Dennis, Fernando Henriques and Clifford Slaughter, *Coal is our Life: an analysis of a Yorkshire mining community*, Eyre and Spottiswood, 1956

30. *ibid.*
31. Ray Garner, 'After the Coal Rush: Attitudes and Aesthetics of the Allotment Garden Shed', unpublished dissertation, Hull School of Architecture, January 1984
32. Interviews, October 1986
33. Interview, February 1987
34. Interviews, Februry 1987
35. 'Beating the Men at their Own Game', *Garden News*, 1 March 1986
36. Thorpe report, para. 381
37. *ibid.*, para. 350
38. *ibid.*, para. 348
39. *ibid.*
40. Harry Thorpe, 'The Homely Allotment: From Rural Dole to Urban Amenity: A Neglected Aspect of Urban Land Use', *Geography*, No. 268, Vol. 60, Part 3, July 1975
41. Interviews, 1986
42. Raphael Samuel *op. cit.*
43. Sheffield Allotments for Unemployed Scheme, Fifth Annual Report, 1934

Chapter six

1. Peter Kropotkin, *Mutual Aid: A Factor of Evolution*, Heinemann, 1902
2. Samuel Smiles, *Self-Help*, John Murray, 2nd edition 1866
3. D.A. Riesman, *Richard Titmuss: Welfare and Society*, Heinemann, 1977; Titmuss's formulation is in his *The Gift Relationship*, Allen and Unwin, 1970
4. 'Family Life and Work Experience before 1918', project, Essex University. Interview 384
5. *ibid.*, Interview 391
6. Ken Penney, 'Aspects of local economic self-sufficiency', paper read at The Other Economic Summit, 1984
7. Interview with Fred Tolley 1969–70 in Raphael Samuel, 'Quarry roughs: life and labour in Headington Quarry, 1860–1920', in Raphael Samuel (ed.), *Village Life and Labour*, Routledge and Kegan Paul, 1975
8. Joe Bee, 'Afternoon on the Allotment', *Allotment and Leisure Gardener*, Vol. 2, No. 8, spring/summer 1986

9. E.W. Brewster, letter to *Garden News*, 20 July 1985
10. John Benson, *The Penny Capitalists: A Study of Nineteenth-Century Working-Class Entrepreneurs*, Gill and Macmillan, 1983
11. Cited in John Benson *ibid.*
12. Helen M. Marshall, *Changes in the Function and Use of Leisure Gardens*, unpublished research project, Dept. of Geography, University of Southampton, January 1977
13. J.S. Mill, *Principles of Political Economy*, Vol. II, London, 1848
14. William Lazonick, 'Karl Marx and Enclosures in England', *The Review of Radical Political Economics*, Vol. VI, No. 2, summer 1974
15. 'Allotment of Land to the Poor', *The Hull Packet*, 16 November 1830, reproduced in John Whitehouse, *Cottingham's Care of its Poor to 1834*, Cottingham Local History Society, 1970
16. Pamela Horn, *The Changing Countryside in Victorian and Edwardian England and Wales*, Athlone Press, 1984
17. Walter Rose, *Good Neighbours*, Cambridge University Press, 1942
18. Pamela Horn *op. cit.*
19. F.E. Green, 'The Allotment Movement', *Contemporary Review*, July 1918
20. *ibid.*
21. H. Rider Haggard, 'The Unemployed and Waste City Lands', letter to *The Times*, 19 July 1906; 'Landgrabbing at Plaistow', letter to *The Times*, 5 September 1906
22. Ronnie Wharton, *The Girlington Klondyke*, Roar Projects, Bradford, 1978
23. Colin Ward, 'The Early Squatters', in Nick Wates (ed.), *Squatting: The Real Story*, Bay Leaf Books, 1980
24. Cited by Joan Mary Fry, *Friends Lend a Hand*, Friends Book Centre, 1947
25. John Farmer, 'The Growing Years – 1930 to 1980', in *The Gardener's Companion and Diary*, National Society of Leisure Gardeners, 1980
26. Joan Mary Fry *op. cit.*
27. John Farmer *op. cit.*
28. *ibid.*
29. Sheffield Allotments for Unemployed Scheme, Fifth Annual Report, 1934

30. Trevor Skeet MP, on *About Anglia*, Anglia TV, Norwich, 7 August 1986

31. J.T. Haworth, 'Meaningful activity and psychological models of non-employment', *Leisure Studies*, Vol. 5, No. 3, July 1986

32. Roger Ingham, 'Psychological contributions to the study of leisure, Part Two', *Leisure Studies*, Vol. 6, No. 1, September 1986

33. Interviews with Councillor Jon Gower Davies and others, February 1987

34. Interviews at Horden, Co. Durham, February 1987

Chapter seven

1. Thorpe report, para. 663

2. *ibid.*

3. *ibid.*, para. 419

4. Newlin Russell Smith, *Land for the Small Man*, King's Crown Press, Morningside Heights, New York, 1946

5. *ibid.*

6. *ibid.*

7. Montague Fordham, *The Rebuilding of Rural England*, Hutchinson, 1924

8. F.E. Green, 'The Allotment Movement', *Contemporary Review*, July 1918

9. C.R. and H.C. Fay, *The Allotment Movement in England and Wales*, National Allotment Society n.d., 1944

10. *ibid.*

11. *ibid.*

12. Mr John Souter, a member of the West Humberstone Allotment Society for 54 years, president of the Leicester Allotment and Gardens Council for 33 years, and a national executive member of the Society for 12 years, remarked that: 'During the war the government paid the National Allotments and Gardens Society £10,000 a year to push the dig for victory campaign. I'd like to see the Society get similar grant aid now.' *Garden*, autumn 1975

13. John Farmer, 'The Growing Years – 1930 to 1980', in *Gardeners' Companion and Diary*, National Society of Leisure Gardeners, 1980

14. W.J. Gibson, *The Right to Dig*, National Allotment Society, 1951

15. Vivian Price QC, Deputy Judge in the Chancery Division of the High Court, in the case of Howard *v.* Reigate and Banstead Borough Council, 13 November 1981
16. Bill France, secretary of National Allotment and Garden Society, in *Garden*, October 1966
17. Richard Sudell, *Future Planning of Allotments*, National Allotment Society, 1945
18. Thorpe *op. cit.*, caption to plate 29
19. *ibid.*, para. 417
20. *ibid.*, paras. 528, 529 and 608
21. *ibid.*, para. 607
22. Harry Thorpe, President's Address to Annual Conference of National Society of Leisure Gardeners, Plymouth, June 1974
23. Harry Thorpe, 'The Homely Allotment: From Rural Dole to Urban Amenity: A Neglected Aspect of Urban Land Use', *Geography*, No. 268, Vol. 60, Part 3, July 1975
24. Harry Thorpe, 'The Proud Status of Leisure Gardening in Britain Today', Annual Conference of National Society of Leisure Gardeners, Guildhall, Portsmouth, 4 June 1975
25. *Hansard*, House of Lords, 17 March 1976, Columns 226 to 263
26. Recreational Gardening Bill (to amend the law relating to allotment gardens and to confirm that allotment gardening has the status of a recreation). *Hansard*, House of Lords, 3 December 1984, Columns 1129 to 1138; 24 January 1985, Columns 433 to 438; 7 February 1985, Column 1275; 18 February 1985, Columns 433 and 434
27. Lord Wallace of Coslany, personal communication, 24 October 1985
28. Lord Skelmersdale, *Hansard*, House of Lords, 10 July 1985. Columns 187 and 188
29. Thorpe report, para. 536
30. Ted Smith, Chairman's Address, *Allotment and Leisure Gardener*, Vol. 2, No. 7, autumn/winter 1985
31. Thorpe report, para. 533
32. *ibid.*, para. 534
33. *ibid.*, para. 535
34. Lord Wallace of Coslany at the London Association of Recreational Gardeners (LARG) Symposium, Montague Hall, Hounslow, 19 April 1986
35. *Recreational Gardener*, No. 27, January 1983

36. 'Society urges mass walk-out', *Garden News*, 30 November 1973, which reported that: 'A vote of confidence was moved in Tom Hume as area representative, and some delegates told the meeting that their Societies had already decided to disaffiliate. Tom Hume said afterwards, however, that he was not happy with the decision to ask Societies to disaffiliate, despite the lengthy wrangle which had taken place. "I want to stay in and get things put straight", he said.'

37. *Garden*, spring 1976

38. *Garden*, Conference issue, 1982

39. Tom Hume at 55th Annual General Meeting and Conference of National Society of Allotment and Leisure Gardeners, Redcar, 5–7 June 1985

40. *Recreational Gardener*, No. 32, November 1974

41. *Recreational Gardener*, No. 34, September 1975

42. Ted Smith *op. cit.*

43. P.L. Greer, Treasurer's Report at 56th Annual General Meeting of National Society of Allotment and Leisure Gardeners, Southport, 4–6 June 1986

44. Jeff Bishop and Paul Hoggett, *Organizing Around Enthusiasms: Patterns of Mutual Aid in Leisure*, Comedia Publishing Group, 1986

45. Thorpe report, para. 603

46. Len Parnell, at 56th Annual General Meeting of National Society of Allotment and Leisure Gardeners, 4–6 June 1986

47. P.L. Greer, *op. cit.*

48. Jane Stoneham and Helena Williams, 'Why bother with landscape design?', *Community Care*, 21 August 1986

49. Thorpe report, para. 351

50. G.v.d. Pouw Kraan, speaking at 50th anniversary conference of National Society of Leisure Gardeners, Hastings, 10 June 1980

Chapter eight

1. Peter Kropotkin, *Campi, fabbriche, officine*, new Italian edition ed. Colin Ward and translated Franco Marano, Edizioni Antistato, Milan, 1975

2. Recollections kindly provided by Vernon Richards

3. Peter Kropotkin, *Fields, Factories and Workshops*, Hutchinson

1899; new edition, ed. Colin Ward, Allen and Unwin 1974, Freedom Press 1985

4. Interview with Henry Shuster, Washington, DC, 10 July 1979
5. Egon Johannes, *Entwicklung, Funktionswandel und Bedeutung städtlischer Kleingärten*, Kiel University Geographical Institute, 1955
6. *ibid.*
7. P. Brando, *Kleine Gärten einst und jetzt*, Verlag Christen, Hamburg, 1965
8. Letter from Andreas Kuehnpast, Düsseldorf, 26 February 1986
9. Hans Stephen, President of the Federal Society of German Garden Friends, reporting on allotment research in Germany, at 18th International Allotment Garden Conference, Vienna, 1972
10. Birgit Malmström and Carl-Magnus Wanbo, 'Allotment gardens and leisure villages in Stockholm', address given at International Leisure Gardeners Congress, Birmingham University, 8 September 1976
11. *ibid.*
12. *ibid.*
13. G.v.d. Pouw Kraan, speaking at the Syracuse University Centre, USA, 21 April 1977. See F. Zantkuijl, *Van Coelghaerde tot Vrijetijdstuin*, Algemeen Verbond van Volkstuinders Vereenigingen in Nederland, Amsterdam, 1978
14. G.v.d. Pouw Kraan, speaking at the 50th anniversary conference of National Society of Leisure Gardeners, Hastings, 10 June 1980
15. Thorpe report, para. 612
16. *ibid.*, para. 615
17. *ibid.*, para. 629
18. George Woodcock, *Pierre-Joseph Proudhon*, Routledge and Kegan Paul, 1956
19. Philip Mattera, *Off the Books: The rise of the underground economy*, Pluto Press, 1985
20. Information on Bilbao and San Sebastián kindly provided by Pilar Barry
21. Michel Bonneau, *Les jardins ouvriers et familiaux en France et dans le Nord*, Université de Lille/CNRS, 1981
22. Francoise Dubost, *Côté Jardins*, Scarabée et Cie, Paris, 1984

23. *ibid.*
24. *ibid.*
25. C. David, 'Les Jardiniers du Dimanche', *Cahiers de l'Institut d'Amenagement et d'Urbanisme*, December 1986
26. Mikhail Prishvin, *The Lake and the Woods*, Routledge and Kegan Paul, 1951
27. J.P. Cole, *A Geography of the USSR*, Penguin, 1967
28. Hugh Stretton, *Capitalism, Socialism and the Environment*, Cambridge University Press, 1976
29. Denis Shaw, 'Recreation and the Society city', in F.E. French and I. Hamilton (eds.), *The Socialist City*, John Wiley and Sons, 1979
30. Martin Walker, 'The Seeds of a Revolution', *Guardian*, 14 May 1985
31. Nigel Swain, *Collective Farms Which Work?*, Cambridge University Press, 1985
32. Ljubo Sirc, 'Peasants in their place', *The Times Literary Supplement*, 10 January 1986
33. Ian Hamilton, 'Spatial structure in East European cities', in F.E. French and I. Hamilton *op. cit.*
34. Jiri Musil, 'Housing, Domestic Economy and Locality', paper given at the Conference on Urban Change and Conflict, at Essex University, April 1985
35. *Community Garden Master Plan*, San Francisco League of Urban Gardeners, 1986, citing T.J. Bassett, *Vacant Lot Cultivation: Community Gardening in America 1893–1978*, thesis, Dept. of Geography, UC Berkeley, 1978
36. Peter J. Schmitt, *Back to Nature: the Arcadian myth in urban America*, New York, Oxford University Press, 1969
37. Studs Terkel, *Hard Times: An Oral History of the Great Depression*, Allen Lane, 1970
38. For example, the works of Ralph Borsodi, and of Helen and Scott Nearing. Borsodi's *Flight from the City*, Harper, 1933, and the Nearings' *Living the Good Life*, were both reprinted in the 1970s
39. *Subsistence Gardens*, US Department of Commerce, Washington, 1932
40. *Community Garden Master Plan, op. cit.*
41. Sara Levine, 'Interview with a Victory Gardener', *Journal of Community Gardening*, Vol. 5, No. 2, summer 1986
42. National Gardening Association, 180 Flynn Avenue, Burlington, Vermont 05401, USA

43. American Community Gardening Association, c/o Chicago Botanic Garden, PO Box 400, Glencoe, IL 60022, USA
44. Special Report on Community Gardening in the US, National Gardening Association, 1985. See also Sam Bass Warner *To Dwell is to Garden*, Boston, Northeastern University Press, 1987
45. City Farmer, 801–318 Homer Street, Vancouver BC, V6B 2V3
46. Information from Norio Tsuge, Agricultural Economics Research Institute, Tokyo

Chapter nine

1. Carol Youngson communication
2. Written for *Twentieth Century Authors*, W.W. Wilson, New York, 1942, reprinted in *The Collected Essays, Journalism and Letters of George Orwell*, Vol. 2, Secker and Warburg, 1968
3. John Burnett, *Plenty and Want: A social history of diet in England from 1815 to the present day*, Scolar Press, 1979
4. Newlin, R. Smith, *Land for the Small Man*, King's Crown Press, New York, 1946
5. Griffiths L. Cunningham, 'Allotment History', paper given at the Allotment Symposium, London Association of Recreational Gardeners, 19 April 1986
6. John Burnett *op. cit.*
7. Richard Jefferies, 'Wiltshire Labourers', letter to *The Times*, 14 November 1872, reprinted in Richard Jefferies, *The Toilers of the Field*, Longmans Green, 1892
8. The River Project, Amber Studios, Newcastle, 1983
9. P. Kemp, 'The Production of Fruit and Vegetables in Kitchen Gardens and Allotments', *Proceedings of the Nutrition Society*, 36, pp. 301–5, 1977
10. P. Kemp *op. cit.*; Peter Hammond, 'The Importance of Allotment Gardening in the Community' (with particular reference to County Durham), unpublished dissertation, Co-operative College, Loughborough, 1985
11. Charles Tomlinson, 'John Maydew Or The Allotment', *A Peopled Landscape*, Oxford, 1963
12. G. Payne and W. Williamson, 'Communal Leeks', *New Society* 14, No. 364, 1969
13. Interview with Ted Harwood, 1986

14. Interview with Dr Schwitzer, 1986
15. Communication from Hilary Scuffham, 1986
16. *Losing Ground*, Friend of the Earth, 1974
17. Michael Leapman, *One Man and his Plot*, John Murray, 1976
18. Jeremy Bugler, 'Grow it yourself', *New Society*, 12 August 1976
19. *Planning*, 12 September 1975
20. *Public Service and Local Government*, 25 March 1975
21. *Nottingham Evening Post*, 2 May 1975
22. Edward Hyams, *English Cottage Gardens*, Nelson, 1970
23. *ibid.*
24. *ibid.*
25. Flora Thompson, quoted in Edward Hyams *op. cit.*
26. Linda McCullough Thew, *The Pit Village and the Store* (p. 22), Pluto/Coop Union, 1985
27. Beryl Bainbridge, *Forever England – North and South*, Duckworth, 1987
28. Interview 1986
29. Interview 1986
30. Interview 1986
31. Edward Hyams *op. cit.*
32. *ibid.*
33. John Carey, *Sunday Times*, 24 February 1980
34. Interview with Allotment Officer, 1986
35. *Daily Mail*, 28 July 1981
36. Angela Harding, 'Grounds for Hope', *New Statesman*, 13 September 1985
37. Peter Watson, 'Growing Pains', *Vole*, Vol. 3, No. 6, pp. 12–4
38. John Carey *op. cit.*
39. Michael Hyde, 'Vegetables with a view', *Guardian*, 3 January 1987
40. Interview February 1987
41. Flora Thompson, quoted in Edward Hyams *op. cit.*
42. Interview 1987
43. Interview 1987
44. G. Payne and W. Williamson *op. cit.*
45. *The Florist's Gazette*, 1824, quoted in Gillian Darley, 'Cottage and Suburban Gardens', in *The Garden*, Mitchell Beazley, 1979
46. Jennifer Armstrong, *Day Return*, BBC Radio Four, 1982

47. Ray Garner, 'After the Coal Rush', unpublished dissertation, Hull School of Architecture, 1985
48. Miriam MacGregor, *On Allotments*, Whittington Press, 1985
49. Ray Garner *op. cit.*
50. Interview 1986
51. Visit 1986
52. Interview and visit 1986
53. Byron Rogers, *Sunday Telegraph*, 21 February 1975
54. Olive Cook, *English Cottages and Farmhouses*, Thames and Hudson, 1982
55. Thorpe report, para. 445
56. Lucy Gough, 'We are Urban Peasants', *Practical Self Sufficiency*, 1976
57. Interview 1986
58. Michael Hyde, 'A Harvest of Hedgehogs', *Guardian*, 9 August 1986
59. Eric Simms, *Birds of Town and Suburb*, William Collins, 1975
60. *ibid.*
61. *ibid.*
62. Richard Fitter, *London's Natural History*, Collins, 1945
63. *Garden News*, 6 June 1987
64. John Burnett *op. cit.*

Chapter ten

1. Thorpe report, para. 462
2. Elizabeth Galloway, *Design for Leisure Gardens*, University of Birmingham, 1977
3. Gillian Darley, 'Cottage and Suburban Gardens', in John Harris (ed.), *The Garden, the Guide to the Exhibition at the Victoria and Albert Museum*, Mitchell Beazley, 1979
4. Ray Garner, 'After the Coal Rush', unpublished dissertation, Hull School of Architecture, 1985
5. Clive Wainwright, 'Municipal Parks and Gardens', in John Harris *op. cit.*
6. Thorpe *op. cit.*, para. 470
7. John Stoney, *Allotments: Their Acquisition and Cultivation*, Ministry of Agriculture Advisory Bulletin No. 90, 1936
8. Richard Suddell, *The Future Planning of Allotments*, National Allotment and Gardens Society, 1944

9. Colin Ward and Denis Hardy, *Goodnight Campers!*, Mansell, 1986

10. Thorpe *op. cit.*, para. 178

11. W.G. Gibson, *The Right to Dig*, National Allotment and Gardens Society, 1950

12. Thorpe *op. cit.*; considerable advice, most of it very positive, is given in paras. 693–715 and Appendix X

13. *ibid.*, caption to plate 11

14. *ibid.*

15. Visits to Cardiff 1986 and Ponders End 1987

16. Described in detail in Chapter 11 of this book, 'Cultures and Places'

17. Visit to Birmingham Leisure Garden and Model Sites, notably Meadow Road

18. Interview with Clive Birch, 1987

19. Communication from Milton Keynes Development Corporation, 1986

20. Bristol Corporation leaflet, 'Grow your own', 1986

21. Thorpe *op. cit.*

22. Sunderland Borough Council, Report on Allotments, 1980

23. Thorpe *op. cit.*, paras. 684, 685, Fig. 26; Jon Fuller visit and interview 1986

24. Maldon Borough Council Evidence to Local Plan Public Inquiry, 1986

25. Inspector's Decision on Chauncy Avenue allotment site, Potters Bar, Hertsmere, *Recreational Gardener*, No. 26, August 1982

26. Visit 1982

27. Four Corner Films, project report in 'Film, Video', Greater London Arts Association, spring 1975

28. Raymond Williams, *The Country and the City*, Chatto and Windus, 1973

29. Edward Hyams, *English Cottage Gardens*, Nelson, 1970

30. Ray Garner *op. cit.*

31. Olive Cook, *English Cottages and Farmhouses*, Thames and Hudson, 1982

32. Thorpe *op. cit.*

33. Ray Garner *op. cit.*

34. Communication from Bill Gladwell, 1986

35. Michael Frayn made this observation on the view of suburban

houses from a railway carriage in the BBC TV film, *Where We Live Now*, 1979

36. Interview with Mrs Sitch, 1986
37. Roy Lacey, *Cowpasture: The Everyday Life of an English Allotment*, David and Charles, 1980
38. Harry Allen, *Village Allotments*, painted at Two Dales 1937, Harry Allen catalogue, Graves Art Gallery, Sheffield, 1986
39. Miriam MacGregor, *On Allotments*, The Whittington Press, 1985
40. Edward Burra Exhibition Catalogue, Hayward Gallery, 1980
41. Mark Francis, *The Park and the Garden in the City*, Centre for Design Research, University of California, 1986
42. Thomas Sharp, *Town and Countryside: Some Aspects of Urban and Rural Development*, Oxford University Press, 1932
43. Richard Hoggart, *The Uses of Literacy*, Penguin, 1958

Chapter eleven

1. Thorpe report, paras. 29, 30
2. Howard Newby, *The Deferential Worker*, Penguin, 1977; John Benson, *The Penny Capitalists*, Gill and MacMillan, 1983
3. Newlyn R. Smith, *Land for the Small Man*, King's Crown Press, New York, 1946
4. John Benson *op. cit.*
5. Howard Newby *op. cit.*
6. John Benson *op. cit.*
7. Thorpe *op. cit.*, para. 289; interviews and communications 1986–7
8. Interviews and communication 1986–7
9. Interview with Sutton Bridge District Secretary, NUAW, 1987
10. Report of the Committee of Enquiry into Statutory Smallholdings, Final Report cmnd 3303 HMSO, 1967
11. Thorpe *op. cit.*, paras. 295, 296; interview 1987
12. Interviews with Parish Clerks of Upwell, Parsons Drove, Outwell, Wisbech; and with Archie Broughton and Mr Preston of Sutton Bridge
13. Fred Gresswell, *Bright Boots: An Autobiography and Anthology*, 1956, quoted in John Benson *op. cit.*
14. Interview 1987
15. Visit 1987

16. M. Chamberlain, *Fenwomen*, Virago, 1975; A. Garvie, 'The Fen Tigers', *New Society* 48, pp. 429–30; J. Burgess, 'Filming the Fens', in J. Gold and J. Burgess, *Valued Environments*, Allen and Unwin, 1982

17. M. Chamberlain *op. cit.*, Howard Newby *op. cit.*

18. Linda MacDowell and Doreen Massey, 'A Woman's Place?', in Doreen Massey and John Allen, *Geography Matters*, Open University, 1984

19. Interviews with Parish Clerks, *op. cit.*

20. Thorpe *op. cit.*, figures 13, 14

21. Newlyn R. Smith *op. cit.*; Thorpe *op. cit.*; interview with Mrs Grundon, Parish Clerk, Flitton, and allotment-holders of the parish, 1986–7

22. Interviews with Mrs Grundon *op. cit.*

23. Interview with Tommy Taylor 1987

24. Joanna Little and Paul Cloke, 'Class Distribution and Locality in Rural Areas: an example of Goucestershire', *Geoforum* in press

25. Interviews with parish Clerks of Tysoe, Brailes, Stourton, Long Compton, Idlicote, Tidmington and Little Wolford

26. Interview with Mrs Pogmore, Parish Clerk, Brailes

27. Interviews with Parish Clerk of Two Dales; and Clerks of Aspatria, Great Clifton, Broughton in Allderdale; and Great Lumley, Kimblesworth , Sacriston, near Chester le Street

28. Fiona Shave, 'Allotments in 1976', unpublished dissertation, Oxford Polytechnic, 1977

29. Howard Newby *op. cit.*

30. Thorpe *op. cit.*, para. 34

31. Elizabeth Galloway, *Design for Leisure Gardening*, University of Birmingham, 1977

32. Fay *op. cit.*

33. Elizabeth Galloway, *From Allotments to Leisure Gardens*, University of Birmingham, 1976

34. *ibid.*

35. *ibid.*

36. Department of the Environment statistics. These may obscure the actual degree of change, as they indicate no private plots by 1958, and even if those leased by the city are omitted, there were plots owned by Bournville Trust and others at that time, as noted in Elizabeth Galloway 1976 *op. cit.*

37. Elizabeth Galloway 1976 *op. cit.*

38. Birmingham City Development Plan, 1960

39. Elizabeth Galloway 1976 *op. cit.*

40. *ibid.*

41. Department of the Environment statistics and Elizabeth Galloway *op. cit.*

42. Helen Marshall, 'Leisure Gardens in Birmingham', unpublished dissertation, Southampton University, 1978

43. Visit and interview with Clive Birch, 1987

44. Data of the Birmingham and District Allotments Council, 1987

45. Birmingham and District Allotments Council *op. cit.*

46. Bill Williamson, *Class, Culture and Community: A Biographical Study of Social Class in Mining*, Routledge and Kegan Paul, 1982

47. Bill Williamson *op. cit.*

48. S.M. Gaskell, 'Model Industrial Village in South Yorkshire and North Derbyshire and the Early Town Planning Movement', *Town Planning Review* 50, No. 4, pp. 437–58; R.J. Waller, *The Dukeries transformed the social and political development of a twentieth century coalfield*, Oxford History Monographs, 1983

49. A.R. Townsend and C.C. Taylor, 'Regional Culture and Identity in Industrialised Societies: the Case of North-East England', *Regional Studies* 9, pp. 379–93, 1975; G. Payne and W. Williamson, 'Communal Leeks', *New Society* 14, No. 364, pp. 445, 1969

50. Frank Atkinson, *Life and Tradition in Northumberland and Durham*, J.M. Dent and Sons, 1977

51. Bishop Auckland Rural District Council, Bye-laws enacted under the Public Health Acts, Section 12, 1902

52. Peter A. White, *Portrait of County Durham*, Robert Hale, 1967

53. Interviews with Tommy Taylor and Tom Kilner, 1987; 'Kilner and Summerfield', *The Pigeon Racing Gazette* 38, Pt. 2, 1982

54. Interviews and visits with Walter Scott and friends, Hordon Colliery, 1987

55. Poem by Keith Armstrong 1985

56. Sunderland Borough Council, Report on Allotments, 1980

57. Ian Sutherland, 'Flying the Doos', *New Socialist*, October 1984

58. Peter Hammond, 'The Importance of Allotment Gardening in

the Community' (with particular reference to County Durham), unpublished dissertation, Co-operative College, Loughborough, 1985

59. Ronnie Jones, interviewed by Colin Ward for the BBC TV film, *New Town, Home Town*, 1979

60. Interview with Walter Scott, *op. cit.*

61. Interview with Ron MacParlen, 1987

62. Interview with Harry Bone and his wife, 1987

63. Bill Williamson *op. cit.*

64. Peter White *op. cit.*

65. Paul Richardson, 'Leek Theft Wipes out Champion', *Garden News*, 10 January 1987; Joe Jones and Harry Bone were both later the subject of a BBC TV documentary, *The Mighty Leek*, Forty Minutes, 9 April 1987

66. Norman Dennis *et al.*, *Coal is Our Life*, Eyre and Spottiswoode, 1956

67. Ian Sutherland *op. cit.*

68. Interview with City Allotments Officer, 1987

69. C.N. Clarke, *Farewell Squalor*, Easington Rural District Council, 1946

70. Dennis Hardy and Colin Ward, *Arcadia for All: The Legacy of a Makeshift Landscape*, Mansell, 1984

71. Visit and interviews 1987

72. Interviews 1987

73. Thorpe *op. cit.*, paras. 478–81

74. Interviews 1987

75. Newcastle City Council, Report on Vacant Land in the City, 1986

76. Dave Thomas, 'Ramshackles', Darlington Arts Centre, December 1986

77. Interview with Terry Powell, Ystraad, 1986

78. Department of the Environment Allotment Statistics

79. Peter Hammond *op. cit.*

80. Interviews and visits 1987

81. Interview 1987

82. Communications 1987

83. Interview with Secretary to Little Moor Allotments Association, 1987

84. Interviews Great Lumley, Kimblesworth, and Sacriston, near Chester le Street, *op. cit.*

85. Sunderland Borough Council *op. cit.*

86. South Tyneside Borough Council, *Allotments in South Tees-side*, 1986

87. Department of the Environment *op. cit.*

88. Tony Rolfe, 'An Investigation into the Potential of the Urban Allotment as a Viable Recreation Resource', unpublished dissertation, Middlesex Polytechnic, 1986

89. Thorpe *op. cit.*, chapter 10

90. Patrick Wright, *On Living in an Old Country*, Verso, 1985

91. Tony Rolfe *op. cit.*

92. *ibid.*

93. Interview 1986

94. Communication from London Borough of Tower Hamlets, 1986

95. Interview with Glasgow Housing Department, 1987

96. Visit 1986

97. Peter Riley, *Economic Growth*, Friends of the Earth, 1979

98. Gillian Tindall, *The Fields Beneath*, Granada, 1980; comment in *Landscape Design*, Part 116, pp. 6–7, 1976

99. *London Government Act*, HMSO, 1963

100. Communication from Chris Shirley-Smith, co-ordinating Community Development Worker, London Borough of Camden

101. Jon Fuller, 'The Provision of Model Allotment Garden Sites in the Inner London Borough of Hackney', London Association of Recreational Gardeners Symposium 1984 and 1986; interview and visits 1986

102. Interview and communications, Bill Gladwell and Sheila Beskine, 1986–7; Four Corner Films *op. cit.*

103. Newham Allotments Federation, *Annual Report*; communication from Bill Gladwell *op. cit.*

Chapter twelve

1. Amartya Sen, *Food Battles: Conflicts in the Access to Food*, Coromandel Lecture, New Delhi, 1982; Amartya Sen, 'The Right Not to be Hungry', *Contemporary Philosophy*, Vol. 2, 1982

2. The Allotment Authorities are Parish Councils, District Councils, Metropolitan and Outer London Boroughs. Other councils *can* but are not obliged to provide sites, e.g. Inner London Boroughs, the Urban Development Corporations – Statutory

Protection does not apply to their sites. See Allotments Act 1950, Section 9

3. John Thackray Bunce in *Birmingham Weekly Post*, 6 May 1899
4. 'The Allotment System', *The Penny Magazine*, No. 14, 1845
5. John Clarke and Chas Crichter, *The Devil Makes Work*, Macmillan, 1985
6. Allotments Act 1908
7. *ibid.*, Section 25
8. Thorpe report, paras. 290, 291
9. Irene Evans, *Land for the People*, Scottish Socialist Society, 1985
10. *Hansard*, House of Lords, 369, No. 47, 17 March 1976; *Hansard*, House of Lords, 3 December 1984 and 10 July 1985
11. Agricultural Land (Utilisation) Act 1931
12. Joan Mary Fry, *Friends Lend A Hand*, Friends Book Centre, 1947
13. South Tyneside Borough Council, *Allotments*, 1986
14. Bob Wallis, 'Food from Leisure Gardens', *Municipal and Public Services Journal*, 3 September 1976
15. *City Farm News*, National Federation of City Farms, Bristol; interviews at Kentish Town City Farm, 1986
16. Thorpe *op. cit.*, para. 69; *The Recreational Gardener*, No. 34, 1986
17. Allotments Act 1925, Section 4
18. Allotments Act 1950
19. Interview with Glasgow City Council Allotments Officer, 1987
20. Robin Best and J.T. Ward, The Garden Controversy, Studies in Rural Land Use, Report No. 2, Wye College, University of London, 1956
21. Thorpe *op. cit.*, paras. 569–83
22. Interviews with Parish Clerks in Cumbria, Bedfordshire, Warwickshire, Essex, County Durham and Cambridgeshire, 1986–7
23. Peter Riley, *Economic Growth*, Friends of the Earth, 1979
24. Interview 1987
25. Peter Riley *op. cit.*
26. As an Inner London Borough, Hackney is not *obliged* to provide allotments. See London Government Act 1963
27. Jon Fuller 'The Provision of Model Allotment Sites in the

London Borough of Hackney', London Association of Recreational Gardeners Symposium, 1984

28. *Hansard, op. cit.*, 1985, 1986
29. *The Times*, 7 January 1975
30. *Recreational Gardener*, No. 3, July 1974
31. *Garden*, September 1981
32. *Recreational Gardener*, No. 3, July 1974
33. Interview with Munton and Fyson PLC, 1987
34. Peter Riley, personal communication, 1986
35. Peter Riley 1975 *op. cit.*
36. Allotments Act 1922
37. *Town and Country Planning Association Journal*, September 1935
38. Peter Watson, 'Growing Pains', *Vole*, No. 2, December 1977
39. Communication 1987
40. Interview with Tom Hume, 1986
41. Allotments Act 1925, Section 8, restated in Town and Country Planning Act 1959, Section 23
42. Before 1965, the Ministry of Agriculture
43. Local Government, Planning and Land Act, Standing Committee, 12 February 1980
44. Allotments Act 1908, Section 32.2
45. *Recreational Gardener*, No. 18, May 1979
46. *ibid.*, No. 34, February 1986
47. Town and Country Planning Act 1971, Section 244
48. *Recreational Gardener*, No. 27, January 1983
49. *ibid.*, No. 34, February 1986
50. Inspector's decision, 17 December 1985, Department of the Environment
51. *ibid.*
52. *The Surveyor*, 28 March 1975
53. Allotments Act 1922, Section 12
54. Department of the Environment statistics
55. Thorpe *op. cit.*, chapters 3 and 4
56. Department of the Environment *op. cit.*
57. *ibid.*
58. Thorpe *op. cit.*, para. 191 and table 15
59. Department of the Environment *op. cit.*
60. Thorpe *op. cit.*
61. Borough Plan Report of Studies, Enfield Borough Council, 1979

62. Department of the Environment *op. cit.*
63. *ibid.*
64. J.F. Garner, *The Law of Allotments*, 4th ed., Shaw and Sons, 1984
65. Department of the Environment *op. cit.*
66. British Rail communication, 1987
67. Communication from British Coal, northeast area, 1987; and with National Union of Mineworkers, Yorkshire and South Wales Regions, 1986; communication from Allotments Officer, Stanley, County Durham, 1986
68. *Communication* British Waterways Board, 1987
69. Allotment Extension Act 1884; Charities Act 1960
70. Allotment Act 1908
71. Commons Act 1876, Section 19
72. *Garden*, summer 1979
73. Charities Act 1960
74. Charity Commission submissions to the Thorpe report, 1968; communication 1987
75. Communication from Church Commissioners, 1987
76. Thorpe report, para 92, 546–59; *Recreational Gardener*, No. 32, November 1984; *Gardener*, November 1974; I.G. Male, *Urban Allotment Gardens*, postgraduate thesis, Leeds Polytechnic, 1979; studies by Harlow and Braintree District Councils and Sunderland Borough Council, 1980–6
77. London Borough of Enfield 1987
78. Braintree and Sunderland *op. cit.*
79. Communication 1987
80. Interview with Ron MacParlen, 1987
81. *Recreational Gardener*, No. 2, April 1974
82. *ibid.*
83. *Guardian*, 11 April 1980
84. *Recreational Gardener*, No. 21, February 1980
85. Four Corner Films, *On Allotments*, 1976; interviews and communications with Bill Gladwell and Sheila Beskine, 1986–7
86. Jo Parfitt, 'London's Allotments', *Illustrated London News*, March 1976
87. Interview with Dr Schwitzer, 1986; P.A. Smith, 'Cultivating the inner city', unpublished dissertation, Oxford Polytechnic, 1978
88. L. Evans, E. Galloway, H. Thorpe, *The Rationalization of Urban Allotment Systems*, Birmingham University, 1977

89. Interview with Cardiff Allotments Officer, Mal Jones, 1986
90. The Birmingham rationalization study considered the drainage, soil and pollution levels of every site in the city; the condition of sheds, the level of cultivation and of facilities (Evans *et al.*, 1977). Sunderland was particularly concerned to provide separate sites for livestock, and the council evaluated the appearance of each site, and analysed where people who were on the waiting list lived, so that new sites could be located closest to them (Sunderland Borough Council 1980)
91. Interview with Terry Melville, Allotments Officer, Rhondda District Council, 1986
92. Interview with Terry Rendal, 1986–; newsletters of Maldon Horticultural Society and Proofs of Evidence presented to the Public Inquiry for the Maldon Local Plan 1986
93. Tony Rolfe, 'An Investigation into the Potential of the Urban Allotment as a Viable Recreation Resource', unpublished dissertation, Middlesex Polytechnic, 1986
94. Communications and interviews with Bill Gladwell 1986–7, and Annual Report to the Newham Allotments Federation, 1987
95. Inspector's report on the South Docklands Beckton Local Plan Report on Objections November 1986
96. Anonymous interview 1986
97. *Recreational Gardener*, November 1974 and May 1981
98. Allotments Act 1950, Section 10
99. Irene Evans *op. cit.*

Chapter thirteen

1. L. Gordon and E. Klopov, *Man After Work*, Progress Publishers, Moscow, 1975, quoted in R.E. Pahl, *Divisions of Labour*, Basil Blackwell, 1984
2. Irene Evans, letter to *New Statesman*, 27 September 1985
3. John Berger, *Pig Earth*, Writers and Readers, 1979
4. Denis Cosgrove, *Symbolic Landscape and Social Formation*, Croom Helm, 1984
5. Jeff Bishop and Paul Hoggett, *Organizing Around Enthusiasms: Mutual Aid in Leisure*, Comedia Publishing Group, 1986
6. National Economic Development Council, *Directions for Change: Land Use in the 1990s*, NEDC, 1987

7. Town & Country Planning Association, *Comments on Department of the Environment Draft Circular 'Development Involving Agricultural Land'*, TCPA, 10 April 1987

8. Robin Grove-White addressing the Annual General Meeting of the Open Spaces Society, 8 July 1986

9. Don Forrest, interviewed on the opening of the Culpeper Community Garden, Cloudesley Road, London N1, 16 May 1987

10. Peter Turner at Bishop's Park allotments, Fulham, 1987

11. John Brinkerhoff Jackson, *Discovering the Vernacular Landscape*, Yale Univesity Press, 1984